CENTERING BORDERS IN LATIN AMERICAN AND SOUTH ASIAN CONTEXTS

This book presents inter-disciplinary research on contemporary borders with contributions from scholars and cultural practitioners located in different contexts in the Americas and South Asia. There has been significant sociological work on borders; however there is a relative dearth of humanities research on contemporary border realities, particularly in South Asia.

This volume introduces new frameworks of critical insights and knowledge on border narratives and cultural productions. It addresses and goes beyond the impact of the partition in South Asia to train a unique comparative and aesthetic lens on borders and borderlands in relation to Latin America and the U.S.A. through oral narratives, photographs, 'objects', films, theatre, journals, and songs. It maps border perspectives and their reception in a framework of cultural politics. It revolves around themes such as violence and modes of survival; women's narratives of migration, trafficking and incarceration; abduction of children; vulnerability as experience; rationalities of mass killings; and proliferation of countercultures to map border perspectives in a framework of cultural politics.

First of its kind, the volume will be useful to scholars and researchers of comparative literary and cultural studies, South Asian studies, Latin American studies, border studies, arts and aesthetics, visual studies, sociology, comparative politics, international relations, and peace and conflict resolution studies.

Debaroti Chakraborty is Assistant Professor in the Department of Performing Arts, Presidency University, India.

Debra A. Castillo is Stephen H. Weiss Presidential Fellow, Emerson Hinchliff Professor of Hispanic Studies, and Professor of Comparative Literature at Cornell University, U.S.A., where she directs the Migration Studies minor.

Kavita Panjabi is former Professor of Comparative Literature and Founder of the Centre for Studies in Latin American Literatures & Cultures at Jadavpur University, Kolkata, India.

CENTERING BORDERS IN LATIN AMERICAN AND SOUTH ASIAN CONTEXTS

Aesthetics and Politics of Cultural Production

Edited by Debaroti Chakraborty, Debra A. Castillo and Kavita Panjabi

Routledge
Taylor & Francis Group
LONDON AND NEW YORK

First published 2023
by Routledge
4 Park Square, Milton Park, Abingdon, Oxon OX14 4RN

and by Routledge
605 Third Avenue, New York, NY 10158

Routledge is an imprint of the Taylor & Francis Group, an informa business

British Library Cataloguing-in-Publication Data
A catalogue record for this book is available from the British Library

Library of Congress Cataloging-in-Publication Data
A catalog record has been requested for this book

ISBN: 978-0-367-40482-6 (hbk)
ISBN: 978-1-032-29017-1 (pbk)
ISBN: 978-0-429-35642-1 (ebk)

DOI: 10.4324/9780429356421

Typeset in Sabon
by Newgen Publishing UK

CONTENTS

FIGURES

CONTRIBUTORS

Sucheta Bhattacharya is Professor in the Department of Comparative Literature, Jadavpur University, Kolkata, India. Her specialization is 19th-century literature of India and Britain. She has developed interest in Border studies since early 2000. She also teaches Translation studies and is passionate about both translation in practice and its theoretical foundation.

Parthasarathi Bhaumik is Associate Professor of Comparative Literature at Jadavpur University, Kolkata, India. He has worked with the British Library, UK, as a Chevening Fellow, and built a database on 'Nationalism, Independence, and Partition in South Asia (1900–1950)'. His latest published work is *Bengalis in Burma: A Colonial Encounter (1886–1948)* [Routledge]. He is presently visiting Associate Professor at the Tokyo University of Foreign Studies.

Moushumi Bhowmik is a singer, writer, and archivist based in Kolkata, who lives and works between India, Bangladesh, and the UK. She runs the website entitled 'The Travelling Archive: Field Recordings and Field Notes from Bengal', and has recently completed her art practice-led doctoral research on listening to old wax cylinder recordings of the Dutch scholar Arnold Bake, from Bengal, at the School of Cultural Texts and Records, Jadavpur University. She writes in both Bangla and English, travels and performs in many countries, lectures, and teaches as well, while also collaborating with artistes across many disciplines, at home and abroad. Her main areas of interest are home, displacement, and listening to history and time.

Debra A. Castillo is Stephen H. Weiss Presidential Fellow, Emerson Hinchliff Professor of Hispanic Studies, and Professor of Comparative Literature at Cornell University, U.S.A., where she directs the Migration Studies minor. She is past President of the international Latin American Studies Association. She specializes in contemporary narrative and performance from the Spanish-speaking world (including the United States), gender studies, comparative border studies, and cultural theory. Her most recent books include *South of the Future: Speculative Biotechnologies and Care Markets in South Asia and Latin America* (with Anindita Banerjee) and *The Scholar as Human* (with Anna Sims Bartel).

Melissa Castillo Planas is Associate Professor of English at Lehman College in the Bronx, NY, U.S.A., specializing in Latinx Literature and Culture. She is the author of the poetry collection *Coatlicue Eats the Apple*, editor of the anthology, *¡Manteca!: An Anthology of Afro-Latin@ Poets*, co-editor of *La Verdad: An International Dialogue on Hip Hop Latinidades*, and co-author of the novel, *Pure Bronx*. Her most recent scholarly book project, in Global Race and Media series (March 2020), *A Mexican State of Mind: New York City and the New Borderlands of Culture*, examines the creative worlds and cultural productions of Mexican migrants in New York City. Her second book of poetry, *Chingona Rules*, was released in 2021.

Debaroti Chakraborty is Assistant Professor in the Department of Performing Arts, Presidency University, India. Her doctoral research focuses on women's narratives from borders in the context of India and Latin America. As a researcher-artist she has been making cross-cultural and intercultural performances based on lived experiences, narratives, and oral history with collaborators and communities in India, in the United States, in U.S.–Canada border, and U.S.–Mexico border. As a an invited lecturer, she teaches Latin American Literatures in other universities and academic centres. She also writes as a performance critic with *The Telegraph*.

Sawon Chakraborty is a PhD candidate in the Department of Comparative Literature at Jadavpur University, India. His research is concerned with the relation between the modernity of Bengal and the partition of India. He pursued his M. Phil degree from the same department and did his graduation and master's from the Department of Bengali, Jadavpur University. He was awarded the SYLFF fellowship at master's level in 2016 and M. Phil level in 2018.

Rimple Mehta is Lecturer at the School of Social Sciences, Western Sydney University, Australia. She has previously worked at the School of Social Work, Tata Institute for Social Sciences, Mumbai and School of Women's Studies, Jadavpur University, Kolkata. She has written on gender, borders, trafficking, feminist methodology, and the criminalization of mobility. Her monograph titled 'Women, Mobility and Incarceration: Love and Recasting of Self across the Bangladesh-India Border' was published by Routledge in 2018 and focuses on the experiences of Bangladeshi women in prisons in India.

Jimmy A. Noriega is Associate Professor of Theatre at the College of Wooster, U.S.A and President of the American Society for Theatre Research. He is the co-editor of *Theatre and Cartographies of Power: Repositioning the Latina/o Americas* (2018) and 50 Key Figures in Queer US Theatre (2022). His research focuses on Latinx and Latin American theatre and performance. He has directed over 50 productions in English and Spanish, including invited performances at theatres and festivals in over a dozen countries.

Kavita Panjabi is former Professor of Comparative Literature and Founder of the Centre for Studies in Latin American Literatures & Cultures at Jadavpur University, Kolkata, India. She has been active in the South Asian women's movement and the Pakistan India People's Forum for Peace and Democracy for three decades, and writes driven by a lively interest in people's perspectives and oral histories. Her book *Unclaimed Harvest: An Oral History of the Tebhaga Women's Movement* is a result of such research in West Bengal and Bangladesh; and *Old Maps and New: Legacies of the Partition* is a cross-border diary across India and Pakistan. She has edited anthologies on Sufism and Bhakti in South Asia, and on Feminist Culture & Politics, and an earlier volume on borders with Debra Castillo entitled *Cartographies of Affect: Across Borders in South Asia and the Americas*.

Minni Sawhney is Hispanic Studies Professor at the Department of Germanic and Romance Studies, University of Delhi, India. She has researched in El Colegio de Mexico for her doctorate on Mexican nationalism in Carlos Fuentes in 1995 and later at UNAM in 2004 for a project on the foreigner in contemporary Mexican literature. Since the last ten years she has been publishing on Mexican–U.S. Border literature, the narco novel, and the narco corrido.

Debasish Sen Sharma is a postgraduate in English and Film Studies from Jadavpur University, India. He has been working as an independent film maker and a theatre practitioner since the last 30 years. He has directed two feature films, five documentaries, and produced multiple contents for television and web media. He is also engaged with theatre as an actor, playwright, and a director and has collaborated in many national and international projects. He is the Founder-Director of Chaepani, a forum of ideas and expressions through art forms. As a visiting lecturer, he teaches Film Studies in different universities in India and abroad.

ACKNOWLEDGEMENTS

This volume is a result of collaborative research in Border Studies across Cornell University and Jadavpur University that has been housed in the Centre for Studies in Latin American Literatures and Cultures (CSLALC), Department of Comparative Literature, Jadavpur University, Kolkata, since 2009. We gratefully acknowledge the support of both universities and all the students, research scholars, faculty and resource persons associated with this research at the CSLALC.

Debaroti Chakraborty
Debra A. Castillo
Kavita Panjabi

INTRODUCTION

Debaroti Chakraborty, Debra A. Castillo, and Kavita Panjabi

This book explores diverse cultural productions, narratives, and artistic expressions to understand how the presence of borders in people's daily lives as well as in larger political contexts shape consciousness and emotional/affective being. The complex layers of lived experiences, shaped by borders, lie embedded or are often articulated through artistic, cultural, or emotional expressions which have the capacity of activating an alternative history of borders. An understanding of these cultural resources unfolds realities that are silenced by or are in conflict with the state-sponsored politics of visibility, audibility, and representation. This volume of essays foregrounds how cultural productions stemming from experiences of borders carry the potential to facilitate a cognitive shift from perspectives of the border to border perspectives. It offers a comparative cross-cultural reading of diverse resources to enable a perspective that centres borders as a lens for understanding experiences, memories, and affective responses. It draws upon cultural resources of the borderlands and explores a variety of genres – oral narratives, photographs, 'objects', films, journals, songs, modes of humour, and others – to weave a tentative, but textured tapestry, and to map out a new framework of border perspectives. The prioritization of cultural resources in the context of experiences of borders evokes, on one hand, 'new ways of seeing' while on the other it paves the way towards a crucial debate about the aesthetics and politics of representation at the borders. The border narratives explored in this collection evokes an understanding of the aesthetic structuring of resistance, of assimilation of identities, of survival across borders, of confrontations of political and private domains, and of valourizations of the fluidity and transferability of borders. The essays in the volume come together to activate a nuanced prism relating to the experiences of borders; it is a prism that is indicative of the constitution of a new aesthetic lens to (*a*) look at the changing significations of contemporary borders that find representation in the newly invented forms/metaphors/themes/images informed by subjectivities of borders; and (*b*) understand how lived

DOI: 10.4324/9780429356421-1

experiences shape personal lives and consciousness which contribute to processes of history making.

How does this aesthetic lens enable access to new grounds and fresh perspectives in the engagement with border politics? Does it also point to new grounds for ethical engagement? These questions point at a discussion around the ongoing transnational threads in the context of borders and how they relate to the past – in trajectories of continuities and disruptions.

In *Border Writing: The Multidimensional Text*, Emily Hicks proposed that border does not correspond to an abstract universal framed by 'post-modern', 'post-contemporary', 'post-colonial', 'postindustrial' (etc.) cultures nor do they add up to *a* 'sub-culture' or *a* 'counter-culture' that is subservient to a single dominant culture. Instead, border experiences – as reconstructed and re-enacted – emerge as potent sites of metaphors for the modern condition: in-between-ness, liminality, hybridity, bifurcated consciousness. Cultural and artistic expressions from the borders and of the borders, central to this exploration, evoke an interesting paradox: how to think about experiences rooted in the material, everyday life of the borders and their relationship to history through forms of representation that are presumably mediated and crafted?

As an outcome of the modern nation-state, borders evoke a conceptual, metaphorical, as well as material site of analysis for understanding the structures of contemporary culture, economic systems, identity, and ethnicity. Contemporary borders are not only determined by geopolitical situations but manifest themselves in complex overlaps of race, ethnicity, religion, class, and nationality. Trevor Noah, a South African comedian and writer working in the United States, says in one of his recent shows:

> Mixed race people are categorized as black in America. The only catch is nobody tells you this. You have to be liked and successful first. Before that they say you are mixed. You achieve success and you get upgraded to black. All the famous mixed people do it. Singers. Like Alisha Keys...mixed...but they say 'black' singer. Sportsmen. Like Tiger Woods...mixed...but they say 'black' golfer. Most famous mixed person on the planet by far...Barrack Obama. Mixed...half and half, straight down the middle. But then they say America's first 'black' President...which is interesting because when he was running they called him the mixed candidates!
>
> (Noah, 'Being Black in America', YouTube)

Humour – as an artistic form – feeds on nuances of cultural borders on one hand, and on the other it helps to observe and articulate the rampant tensions in a performative idiom sanctioned by public consensus. Borders, in the materiality of their existence as well as in the conceptual domain, are perceived as nuanced spaces of experience rather than just as strict political divides.

The larger social, geopolitical, and historical premises of contemporary borders are shaped by multiple structures – of technologies of globalization and transnationalism, of economic systems, and of identity. Contemporary policies of governance prioritize ritualistic surveillance and rigid militarization of geopolitical borders as necessary conditions of security even as these borders become more and more porous to the passage of commodities and bodies as commodities. The global map is marked by states and societies that are separated by the political divides of barbed wire fences and border security personnel, yet these border societies are simultaneously – and organically – bound by geographical contiguities such as rivers, agricultural fields and cultural continuities that defy the logic of political divides. Contemporary transnational discourses as well as international political diplomatic systems address borders and borderlands both as ambiguous spaces that can be inhabited and as realms within which abrasive histories, multiple identities, and violent exclusions are played out. The aesthetic displays of border fencing, checkpoints, and deportations symbolically enact the inviolability of the state even as the porosity of borders sanction exploitative networks that facilitate 'illicit' flows of migrant labourers, trafficked women and children, goods, criminals, and arms. These paradoxes create endless possibilities of cultural identity, territoriality, belonging, and dispossession. 'Border' as an idea thus sanctions permeability, porosity, assimilation along with its sense of division, and resilience.

The modern nation-state implicates the so-called 'margins', like borderlands and enclaves, for the imagination of the modern nation-state. Thereby, violence on the borderlands becomes a tool of governmentality by the modern nation-state. The relative locations of the margin and the centre and the power dynamics between them are changeable as well as transferable. Thus, the presence of the borders impacts human lives and consciousness not only in situations of border crossings or living at the borders/borderlands but also in the ways in which identities, *difference*, choices, group formations, and representations are over-determined. While, on the one hand, the border is a site of violent separation, policing, and surveillance, on the other hand, identities are constantly negotiated in, on, and through borders. Thus, in the domain of lived experiences, borders emerge as nuanced and ambiguous physical, political, and conceptual realities in relation to geopolitical location, cultural identity, state policies, and governmentality. The lived experiences of those who inhabit/encounter borders emerge as reliable ground at several levels for the study of how these experiences take on alternative physical and metaphorical significances which puncture the improvable/non-improvable, curable/non-curable, legal/illegal, non-disposable/disposable, and other such binary categories of inclusion and exclusion charted out by the modern state.

Over the last few decades, there has been an emergence of a solid body of academic scholarship and cultural resources that critique the partition of India (1947) that manifested as a political and territorial separation of groups and societies. Partition, as a historical event, has deeply influenced communal and ethnic patterns, generational dynamics, and individual life stories as well as the sense of home, memory, and identity.

It is of profound importance to question why partition continues to remain as the determining reference point even today. In conversations with a mixed class of undergraduate students who have not been affected by the partition or do not carry inherited memory of the partition, one of us – Debaroti – realized how practices of the everyday and identity formation are shaped by intergenerational 'affect'. One of the favourite exercises with students is to create an 'I-image' – to talk about how 'I' understand myself in relation to my name, religion, class, caste, languages 'I' speak, where 'I' live, what 'I' like to see, hear, say, do, wear, eat, etc. Every time a chaos of multiple identities, voices, choices, sense of home, or the lack of it emerges from a class of 20 people, who are of the same age and who live in a similar geographical space. While thinking of what we 'choose' from our individual family histories to identify ourselves with and how we define autonomy, we arrive at an acutely hybrid condition of cultural history, linguistic inheritance, geographical location, political affinity, and other personal/political choices. Inevitably, the making of these contemporary (postcolonial?) identities are shaped by migration, displacement, inter-cultural, inter-religious, inter-caste, inter-regional relationships in a subcontinent marked by a history of porous borders. The logic of strict borders (like the partition of India) in the subcontinent of South Asia fails to represent individual identities, which, in essence, speak of the rich cultural matrix of South Asia rather than of the tight-jacketed notion of the modern nation-state.

However, while the political logic of partition has faced sharp critique when analysed against stories of human lives devastated by it, the politicization of religion continues to shape communal divides, ethnic identities, minority politics, and to propagate a hegemonic notion of the 'other'. Even as we make efforts to engage with lived experiences and consciousness that explore the contemporary issues of borders as distinct from the logic of partition, the notion and effects of borders and policy-making emerge as being inextricably linked with that of partition. The contemporary political and social strategies of 'managing' borders thus lay claim to the logic of partition when it comes to making political amendments, negotiations, and renewals.

Partition and border, as linguistic signs, evoke two different concepts – while both denote a division of geographical landscape, border can also mean an edge, a limit, a space that can be occupied. Partition refers to a strict division of resources whereas, as Sophia A. Mcclennen posits it, 'borders, as a result, more readily lend themselves to poetic conceptualizations of liminality, border gnosis, and contact zones' (Mcclennen 170). So, while drawing upon the historical impact and context of partition, it is important to emerge out of the long shadow of partition and prioritize alternative ways of understanding the contemporary nature of borders.

Indian Parliamentary debates often evade questions relating to the failure of democracy in principle and in practice in the everydayness of existence in the border state. The stories of human lives reveal that it is not enough to speak the language of rights and duties, of crime and punishment, of votes and numbers, of allies and opposition; they call for attention to the fact that democracy is, first and foremost, an inter-relational philosophy that shapes the quality of human life and society. Current situations at the borders – the forms of violence, and the ways in which violations in daily life transform the aesthetics of life – all of these need to be understood in relation to the past. The inevitable affect in the context of partition was one of having to grapple with a fracture or rupture, depicted by terms like 'displacement', 'dislocation', 'trauma', 'disaster', and 'division'. The factors leading to each of these situations, mentioned before, are now being shaped by complex and changing notions of home, citizenship, belongingness, and cultural identity in this contemporary globalized world. So, there is a felt need to understand, and bring into discourse, the newer experiences of rupture that, on one hand, have connections to the history of borders while are also mapped by the changing contours of national borders and boundaries, on the other.

India has raised a fence along approximately 70 percent of India's 4,023 km border with Bangladesh. The remaining length of the border largely runs across the delta's shifting rivers, unfenced but patrolled. And while there is a 150-yard 'no-man's-land' on either side of the border, many houses can still be found that have a front door in one country and a backyard in the other.

This border was first drawn between East Pakistan and India during the partition in 1947. In 1971, when the people of East Pakistan launched and won the muktijuddha or the Liberation War against West Pakistan, they renamed their land Bangladesh in a tribute to the Bangla language and culture that formed the bedrock of their identity; this was despite the fact that they constituted a Muslim majority population, the ground on which they had been clubbed with Pakistan across the entire expanse of a Hindu majority India. This historical choice of the people of Bangladesh is often cited to prove that linguistic and cultural identity can often surpass religious identity.

Illegal migration, that has been one of the most sensitive issues between India and Bangladesh, started with the partition in 1947, and continues right into the present day, largely from Bangladesh into India but in the reverse direction too, albeit far less in number. There is no consensus whatsoever on the number of illegal Bangladeshi immigrants in India – they range from an estimate of a few thousands every year to 15 million in all. This large-scale influx of Bangladeshis into India is due to various 'push' factors such as political upheavals, religious persecution, demographic pressures, environmental crises, and 'pull' factors such as employment opportunities, medical care, availability of land, and education (Datta13). On the other hand, there seem to be approximately 500,000 illegal Indian immigrants in Bangladesh, who are largely employed in jobs, and send money back home through indigenous hundi transfer systems (Financial Express).

Human rights violations are rampant in the context of human trafficking across the Indo-Bangladesh border, and this includes both sex trafficking and forced labour trafficking, but one of the problems is that Indian laws do not yet explicitly recognize and punish all forms of forced labour trafficking. It is estimated that approximately 50,000 Bangladeshi girls are trafficked to or through India every year and around 500,000 Bangladeshi women and children aged 12 to 30 years have been illegally sent to India in the last decade (Times of India). At least 50 girls and women are lured and sold across the border every day in Bangladesh, with false offers of employment or marriage without dowry, by local touts, family members, neighbours, or even 'fake husbands'. Middlemen are usually in a nexus with law enforcement agencies on both sides.

According to some experts India has the largest problem of human trafficking, especially of minors. About 300,000 Bangladeshi minors work in the Indian red light districts of Kolkata and other cities. On the other hand, about 13,000 Bangladeshi boys and girls, some as young as five, have been trafficked in the last 5 years to destinations such as India, Pakistan, Dubai, and The United Arab Emirates with India becoming a transit point for the traffickers (Hartjen and Priyadarsini). Existing laws pertain to bonded labour or prostitution, but the scope of trafficking is much wider and there are no provisions in law as yet for the prevention of trafficking, or the protection and rehabilitation of victims. While girls are often rescued under the sex trafficking laws, and rehabilitated or repatriated, trafficked boys usually end up facing criminalization:

> Caught between a rock and a hard place are the unfortunate young adolescents who are unlucky enough to fall foul of the local police or border security forces within Indian territory or while crossing the border. Booked as criminals under the same laws that punish illegal adult migrants to India, they are incarcerated in shelter homes, and in the absence of bilateral agreements on their repatriation and/or rehabilitation, remain there indefinitely, unwanted by one country, and unclaimed by the other.
>
> (Basu)

In 2016, a draft was of the Trafficking of Persons (Prevention, Protection, and Rehabilitation) Bill that was referred to as India's first ever anti human trafficking law. Significantly, the Bill aims 'to treat survivors of trafficking as victims in need of assistance and to make rehabilitation a right for those who are rescued', but it has been inordinately delayed. In the meanwhile, the Covid pandemic has aggravated matters especially in relation to the trafficking of children:

> Children make up almost a third of all human trafficking victims worldwide, with the situation being more disturbing in India for children. According to the NCRB 2018 data, 51% of all trafficking victims were children, of which more than 80% were girls. The COVID 19 pandemic has further led to an increase in a number of children who are more susceptible to trafficking. The recently orphaned children in India, due to the Covid-19 pandemic, also run the increased risk of trafficking in the garb of adoption, employment or livelihood and shelter.
>
> (Bhaskar)

In July 2021, the Bill has been put into the public domain yet again for debate[1] and it is hoped that finally there will be laws to address the dire violations and abuse of children and others in fields of forced labour too.

There still remains the question of voluntary migration across the borders of unequal states in search of livelihoods, and as Datta succinctly puts it, 'Border control and migration projects both require further discussion to unlock the polarities in the debate between right to mobility and countering the human trafficking crime' (Datta 22).

Migration across the border is not new. In the sixties and seventies, poor families from Jessore and Satkhira begged their way to domestic jobs and bars and brothels in big cities – Calcutta, Bombay, etc. and were also taken as far away as Saudi Arabia. Bar work, which became widely available after 1990, often entailed sex work but not always. There were 'contract marriages' whereby men married women for the purpose of trafficking them to Mumbai. This posed a threat to the very fabric of society. Migration of unskilled women's labour to the Middle East is another area of concern. It happens under severely exploitative conditions as it is illegal. As the existing ban does not prevent women from migrating nor protect their rights, there are demands for lifting the ban. There is a need for recognition of women's migration as a fact and as a right (Blanchet iv).

Patrolling against all illicit activity on the Bangladesh border, India has the world's largest border guarding force, the Border Security Force (BSF). According to the National Academy of Pre-recruitment Training, 'The BSF has grown exponentially from a few battalions in 1965, to 186 battalions with a sanctioned strength of 257,363 personnel including an expanding air wing, marine wing, artillery regiments, and commando units'. Investigative reports have made recommendations against the immunity the BSF enjoys

(Datta). The number of Bangladeshis killed or injured every year by the BSF is aggravated by the number of Bangla speaking borderlanders now being pushed into Bangladesh as illegal immigrants under the purview of the National Register of Citizens. This has led to increasing human rights violations on the border, and to growing concern in Bangladesh. Odhikar, a Bangladeshi Human Rights organization, reports in Forum Asia:

> According to information gathered by Odhikar, from 2009 to 2019, a total of 455 Bangladeshi citizens were killed by the Indian Border Security Force. Furthermore, 657 Bangladeshis were injured and 518 Bangladeshis were allegedly abducted by BSF during this period. In 2019 alone, 41 Bangladeshis were reportedly killed by the BSF.... Apart from this, the Government of India has already started pushing Bangla-speaking Indian nationals into Bangladesh, who have recently been excluded from the National Register of Citizens (NRC) [and] made to identify illegal immigrants in India, which is a matter of grave concern. [Parenthesis mine].

While the NRC has been understood in terms of the targeting of Bangladeshis, the enactment of the controversial Citizenship (Amendment) Act (CAA) in December 2019 has further heightened the political tension on both sides of the border. This law provides a fast track to citizenship for non-Muslims from Bangladesh, Pakistan, and Afghanistan who faced religious persecution and entered India before 31 December 2014 (Dasgupta). It has been met with widespread protest in India too as a majoritarian Hindu move discriminating against Muslim populations in South Asia.

On the other hand, the Rohingya refugee crisis too has become a bone of contention between India and Bangladesh, none of whom have signed the 1951 Refugee Convention that spells out refugee rights and makes it a responsibility of the camp country to protect them. The Rohingyas have been fleeing persecution in Myanmar for several years, but the military crackdown in 2017–2018 led to a massive exodus. Citing internal pressures and security concerns, such as the appropriation of a vulnerable Rohingya population by jihadi groups at the border, India refused to take direct responsibility for the devastated refugees, but offered to extend support to Bangladesh:

> Refusing to bow under international pressure over Rohingya crisis, India made it clear that it would not compromise with the security concerns of the country. However, the government decided to extend help to Bangladesh in providing all amenities to the fleeing Rohingyas, who are being relocated in camps there. India also asked Myanmar to end persecution of Rohingyas.
>
> (Datta)

By March 2021, after the latest spate of exodus, Bangladesh was estimated to have up to 5 lakh Rohingya refugees. It set up a massive refugee camp in Cox's Bazar, where the UN High Commissioner for Refugees (UNHCR) has issued ID cards to Rohingya refugees in an attempt to minimize their human rights abuse. Bangladesh too is now facing pressure from within to ease the Rohingya refugee situation. It recently moved thousands of Rohingya refugees to a new and remote island called Bhasan Char in the Bay of Bengal. Bangladesh is reluctant to take back Rohingya survivors who leave the country's shores for refuge in other countries like Malaysia; on the other hand, India has been cautious about accepting Rohingya refugees due to its own domestic compulsions (Datta). This leaves the Rohingya refugees, one of the most traumatized populations in the world today, literally nowhere.

Though the histories of borders in South Asia are distinctively different from those in Latin America, the border functions in similar patterns in these contexts in the way human lives are organized around it. The partition of India gave rise to a history of separation of land, of people, of lives and loyalties, of the communal 'othering' of Hindus by Pakistan, and of Muslims by India. While the Pakistani and Bangladeshi fear of dominance by the economically stronger India continues unabated, the Indian 'fear' of Bangladeshi Muslims infiltrating India for better economic prospects has been blown into monumental proportion. Yet Indians and Pakistanis on the western front of India and Indians and Bangladeshis across its eastern borders remain connected, across these manufactured divides of state and religion, through contiguities of language and culture. The U.S.–Mexico border too is steeped in a history of territorial acquisition, of the economic dominance of Mexico by the United States, and of the U.S. 'fear' of infiltration by the ethnic, linguistic, and cultural other. The Mexican American War (1836–1848) enabled the United States to acquire vast tracts of land, intensifying the uneven economic relations across borders on one hand and creating complicated racial divides on the other. Debra Castillo and María Socorro Tabuenca Cordoba, in the book *Border Women: Writing from La Frontera*, posit the ambivalence of the northern Mexican border – from one side it serves as definitive barrier and from the other as an inconsequential (immaterial, metaphorical) line. The equivocal nature of the border becomes pronounced in the individual's interaction with the border as an abstract space or as a divisive line during border crossings. The lived experiences of the border, that evoke registers of absurdity and uneven-ness, give birth to powerful contemporary theories that attempt to explain modern socio-cultural phenomena in the context of borders. Cristina Rivera Garza, the winner of a 2020 MacArthur 'genius' award, writes movingly about her own family history on both sides of the border in her *Autobiografía del algodón*, in which she describes the interlocked history of her family in northern Mexico and Texas, as labour migration, immigration, deportation, and more immigration lead to her, a Mexican citizen, being offered an academic position in Houston, a city her father helped build.

So there has been a network of theoretical postulations on borders, including Rolando. J. Romero's comment that 'Very few places have been subjected to as much verbal abuse as at the border between the United States and Mexico' (Romero 36) and Etienne Balibar's understanding that borders do not work in the same way, and people bring different baggage with them when they cross (Castillo and Tabuenca 1–2).For instance, the U.S.–Mexico border produces a set of general categories like the *pollo* (the undocumented border crosser), the *migra* (the U.S. immigration officer), *the coyote* (the person who brings the pollo across the border), and the *turista* (the North American visitor to Mexico).

Ongoing violence in Central America (several countries in the region have sadly been in the list of the ten most violent countries in the world for years) and the increasing prevalence of ecological disasters propelled by human-caused climate change have only exacerbated the problem. The end of the second decade of the 21st century was marked by successive waves of immigration and increasingly harsh U.S. official response. The unaccompanied minor influx of 2013–2014 (a 90% increase over previous years), prompted the Obama administration to limit the grounds for asylum and to fast-track removal proceedings, a process movingly documented in Valeria Luiselli's 2017 *Tell me how it ends: An essay in 40 questions* and her 2019 novel, *Lost Children Archive.*

Since 2018, Central Americans have been banding together in large caravans to mitigate the dangers in the long route through Mexico to the United States, which has been plagued by criminal violence. President Trump responded with a suite of punitive measures, including increased enforcement to prevent people from crossing the border to ask for asylum, leading to large migrant camps in Mexican border cities like Tijuana; his 'zero tolerance policy' that led to the infamous family separation in 2018 that took thousands of parents and children, some of them mere infants, into separate custody with no plans for reuniting them – and indeed, no solid trail of paperwork that would allow reunification. Trump also instated the so-called 'Migrant Protection Protocols' or 'remain in Mexico' policy that required asylum seekers to return to Mexico while their cases were proceeding in court (this policy was ended by Biden in January 2021, and his decision upheld by the Supreme Court). Together with increasingly stringent restrictions on who can ask for asylum and on what grounds, Trump famously – and in contravention of international law – effectively instated a death to asylum policy. It is worth noting that in the current climate, domestic abuse, gang violence, and climate disasters are not legal grounds for requesting asylum. Along with these restrictions, Trump convinced the three most dangerous countries in Central America, to sign 'safe third country' agreements, so that migrants would legally have to ask for asylum there, rather than in the United States (Mexico resisted pressure to also sign such an agreement). Among the very few 'caravaneros' to succeed in his asylum claim under the Trump regulations is Douglas Oviedo, a Honduran activist and youth pastor whose story was first documented on the website 'Humanizando la deportation'. Oviedo later wrote a longer story of the collective experience in his 2020 testimonial play, *Caravaneros*.

Immigration remains a hotly debated issue in the United States, with Joe Biden and Kamala Harris quietly retaining many of Trump's restrictions, while speaking compassionately about the need for immigration reform and a path to citizenship for long-term immigrants already in the United States. New caravans were forming in Spring 2021, but in June 2021, Harris, in her first international visit, gave her infamous 'do not come' speech, alongside Guatemalan president Alejandro Giammattei.

The latter half of the 20th century, from around the 1980s, the India–Bangladesh border witnessed incoherent economic reforms veering towards neoliberalism on one hand and intensifying economic deprivation of the poor sections on the other; this period was also marked by transforming cross-border dynamics that brought issues of de-territorialization, illegal passage of human beings and commodities, and the influx of refugees to the centre of political systems (Keller 15–19). The recent re-configurations in economic and political systems had a remarkable impact on the history and nature of borders. In the essay 'India in the 1980s and 1990s: A Triumph of Reforms', Arvind Panagariya cites a seminal work of Economic historian J. Bradford DeLong which claims that the sources of India's recent acceleration in economic growth may be traced back to the early or mid-1980s, before the exchange crisis of 1991 and the shift of the government of Narasimha Rao and Manmohan Singh towards neoliberal economic reforms (Panagariya 3). Singh, in his historic 1991 budget speech, drew a close connection between his proposals and the policies initiated by India's first Prime Minister Jawaharlal Nehru and carried forward by his grandson Rajiv Gandhi. The neoliberal policies charted out in 1991 brought about expansion of service sectors and catapulted a liberalized investment and trade regime. The political enactment of border strategies, collaborated by liberalizing economic reforms, had a telling effect on the way borders began to control human lives and traffic. This also marks a shift in the understanding of contemporary border relations in South Asia as distinct from that of partition and its effects. Likewise, the Southern Common Market, or MERCOSUR, was established by treaty among Argentina, Brazil, Paraguay, and Uruguay in 1991, later adding other members from the western hemisphere. In a similar neoliberal move, the North American Free Trade Agreement, or NAFTA, was put into effect on 1 January 1994, seeking to deepen economic ties among the United States, Mexico, and Canada. In response, The Zapatista Army of National Liberation (EZLN), an indigenous group in Mexico, staged an armed uprising in the southern Mexican state of Chiapas to protest NAFTA and the Mexican government's endorsement of neoliberalism at the expense of the poor majority among its own citizen. Thus, contemporary borders need to be situated within the relations of power and economy that map the world today, to understand the forms of politicization. The cross-readings of South Asian and Latin American border narratives within a comparative framework may enable richer and more varied understandings of the echoes and resonances between border cultures.

This collection develops a prism to cull insights about border realities from a wide range of cultural resources including oral narratives, cinema, documentaries, objects and media, and performance. As a multi-generic and multi-textual volume, it posits the persistent challenge of locating a cohesive premise that can deal with the structural and aesthetic complexity of diverse cultural productions. However, this volume seeks to foreground the potential of the embedded polyphony in diverse cultural productions that represent border lives and realities.

The multiple ways in which an event/situation at the borders impact lives often prompt varied forms of human behaviour and responses and shape the aesthetics of lives as well as the narration of those events. An experience of the present may be filtered through a memory of the past as well as a consciousness of the present. Now how these experiences are articulated in a cultural/artistic expression also relates to the question of mediation, of an ethical, political, and aesthetic choice. This volume encourages readers to look at these diverse materials through a new aesthetic lens that can enable an understanding of the modes of revisiting the past, of relating situations of the present with the past, of exploring how the past is performed in artistic/creative expressions.

The aesthetics of creatively transforming experiences lies not just in stating or recording events but in elaborating them, in interpreting them, in revisiting them, and in re-enacting them. These processes of conscious or intuitive mediation could be referred to as poetic structuring of truth. One can make meaning of how events/experiences are filtered through memory, human behaviour, language, images, objects, and performance through a close attention to these processes of articulation. Memory, in the process of cultural productions, is thus understood not just as a repository of information but rather as a realm characterized by an ongoing process of reconstruction and elaboration of meaning (Portelli). Forgetting is an essential function of memory while cultural productions may bring back either what is forgotten because it has no meaning to the present consciousness or a traumatic memory, which is not bearable or cannot be articulated in the present state of consciousness. So even the slippages and silences in memory, as surfaced in artistic forms, can evoke meaning in terms of the impact of an event in the inner consciousness of one situated within a specific history. For instance, a seemingly unrelated incident in the present may trigger a memory of the past, which had remained deeply embedded in the collective psyche and has the capacity to influence one's interpretation and narration of a present-day experience. The intent of creative expressions thus often goes beyond the immediate, the historical, the factual in re-staging how past events or experiences as well as contemporary conditions of living shape consciousness and modes of relating to the world around. A reading of cultural resources, thus, allows an alternative entry point – an understanding of the layers of interiority and how the imprints of interiority of consciousness informed by experiences of the border are processed and creatively represented. An understanding of the multi-toned quality of diverse cultural productions may help point at the complex nature of truth as processed in an individual's experiences at the border.

'Truth(s?)', as experienced and articulated, is/are shaped by ways of living, specific histories, experiences, and sensory perceptions. They are embedded and embodied in the processes of artistic productions such that they burst the boundaries of materiality and empirical truth. The close readings of the diverse material also presuppose the ethics of reading varied aesthetic modes of representation. The ethics of reading brings to the core questions of what is central in an artistic reproduction, of the politics of understanding the 'truth' of cultural productions. Each aesthetic form uses its own language to make meaning of a particular experience/story/theme. So the ethics of approaching each artistic form is to underline the potential of and to observe the processes of that particular form in the artistic structuring of an event as perceived, absorbed, and recalled. This marks a shift in the understanding of 'truth' – of articulations that are accepted as valid based on not only what is narrated, but why and how something is narrated in a particular way rather than on its factual accuracy – comprises the ethics of approaching diverse cultural resources.

Artistic expressions help foreground that realm of consciousness where events are received, experienced, and aesthetically processed in ways that are capable of mobilizing future possibilities. This politics of reading cultural productions also emphasize a prioritization of poetic 'truth' which is different from factual 'truth'. It involves an understanding of the processes through which material events are processed in an individual's layers of consciousness, of how facts are transformed into value, of how these expressions have the potential to shape culture and history in ways that factual truth may not (Panjabi 19). The indeterminate zone between fact and poetic truth is foregrounded in the re-enactment of experiences such that the truth lies embedded in how they are told, in which specific circumstances they are told and in understanding why one chooses to express them in the particular creative form – how does a particular form enable the representation of personal experiences, feeling of nostalgia, loss, fear, longing, in-between-ness modes of making meaning and history that cannot be accessed through other forms.

Maruška Svašek employs the terms transit, transition, and transformation to understand the emotional significance embedded in objects in the processes of cultural and material production in an interconnected world. The framework of transit, transition, and transformation makes connection between two types of 'movement' – first mobility through time and space and secondly 'emotional dynamics'. The first type of movement, she explains, has spatial dimensions that are intrinsic to 'being-in-and-thus-moving-through-the-world' while the second type signifies a traffic between geographical space, social dimension, and affect. She writes:

> Ideas of emotivity also differ widely from one society to the next and in some societies a concept of emotion as would most commonly be understood by the term 'emotions' in English, is entirely absent (Lutz, 1988, Wierzbicka, 2004). In other words, emotional processes are at least culturally constituted, informed by situated social practices.
>
> (Svašek 8)

Emotional dynamics, as analysed above, seeks a renewed approach that pushes the boundaries of emotions understood either as physical processes or as cultural constructions. They appeal as an important component of subjectivity, subject–object relationships, and aesthetics responses that lie at the core of cultural productions. The aesthetics of cultural productions, explored in this volume, focuses on how experiences situated in border cultures and realities can have a strong emotional imprint and a representative and performative dimension. Here re-enactment as a form in various modes brings attention to 'embodied experience' shaped primarily by two kinds of engagement. On one hand it builds upon aspects of emotional experiences, subjectivity, and sensory perceptions that relate to the intuitive and impulsive tendencies, while on the other it relies on the craft of interpretation and representation guided by aesthetic choice and the intellect.

The representative forms stemming from borders prioritize the potential intensity of human experiences at the borders; they foreground 'affect' that is shaped by experiential and relational encounters between people in conditions of ambiguous and multiple realities of borders. However, a focus on aesthetics in this context does not seek to eulogize borders as spaces of assimilation of cultures and practices, to separate articulations from realities in the appreciation of artistic processes or to draw attention to borders as sites of metaphors in contemporary discourses. Rather, it explores subjectivity as a prism to analyse how borders affect people's lives, practices, and their relation to history. It is important to bring home the validity of affect in understanding an alternative history of borders since it relates to the impact of events in the intimate, private, and public life and in recognizing 'in-between-ness' as a state of being, i.e. a state of consciousness rather than a transitional passage in the context of present-day borders and migration.

This collection brings to the fore inter-disciplinary research on borders with contributions from scholars and cultural practitioners from different contexts including Cornell University, Lehman College, Jadavpur University, Presidency University, Delhi University, and the College of Wooster. The contributors comprise academicians, artist-researchers, theatre makers, a filmmaker, and a musicologist who delve into discussions on different kinds of cultural productions: testimonies, oral narratives, films and documentaries, sociological reports, the new media networks, contemporary literature, art, song, and modes of humour, legendary narratives that cut across fields of art, anthropology, sociology, cultural studies, and performance studies that build on recent debates in border discourses. The authors explore transnational experiences through the prism of cultural resources from South Asia and Latin America that are diverse and yet strongly interconnected.

The first section of the book, 'Oral Narratives: Experiencing Violence, Forging Modes of Survival', includes essays by Rimple Mehta and Debaroti Chakraborty, which discuss oral narratives by women who have to cross borders between India and Bangladesh as part of their everyday life, who have been living in correctional homes for years, penalized for their 'crossings' or who live in the borderlands. Both studies explore 'listening' to the experiences of borders which evoke modes of rethinking the divide. They also allow us to access the historicity of private lives in the context of borders. Simultaneously, the narratives critically question the modes of negotiations in border encounters and the segregation between private and public domains of women. Mehta's essay explores the experiences of violence of Bangladeshi women, apprehended under section 14 of the Foreigners Act 1946, in Correctional Homes in Kolkata. The narratives of the Bangladeshi women suggest that perpetrators and sites of violence change but the Indo-Bangladesh border remains central to their experiences of violence. The trajectory of violence in the lives of women engaging in transborder mobility can be plotted along a continuum where the border is shown up to be the catalysing moment and site of violence in a series of violent experiences. Debaroti's essay studies *Beyond Boundaries*: testimonies of women who have been trafficked and engaged in labour migration across India and Bangladesh borders by Therese Blanchet, and Hondagneu Sotelo's *'I'm Here, but I'm There: The Meanings of Latina Transnational Motherhood'* to foreground how border women retrieve meaning out of a need or choice of crossing over or living at the borders. The violations in daily lives at the borders significantly transform lives, they change the aesthetics of life, of how women relate to the nature and to their immediate surroundings. These evoke alternative modes of making meaning that are not addressed in any of the mainstream discourses. The oral narratives of women draw attention to subjectivity, to how the sense of self is curtailed by an increasing militarization of the borders.

The second section, 'Photography: The Ethics of "Evidence" and Erasure/Elision', with contributions from Debra A. Castillo and Kavita Panjabi studies how media, objects, and other forms of visual representation have the capacity to interact with specific sets of conditions at the borders such that they can be produced and reproduced to politicize border tensions, to re-enact violence, and to acquire multiple meanings and identities that are not essential to the material nature of the objects. Castillo's essay explores Nadia Villafuerte's works with a particular focus on the novel *Por el lado salvaje* to understand the conflicting ethical and moral contexts as well as notion of care for a menaced/menacing/burdened child in exploitative border realities. The author explains how Villafuerte's focus on child/adolescent figures reminds us of how often the melodramatic stories we tell ourselves secure a specific imaginary context for making ethical statements, for emitting judgments that have life and death. It posits how the general modes of recognition relating the innocence of the child to the future of the nation become twisted and strange in the border context, where the migrant child's innocence is suspect, and hence presages the wrong kind of future, becoming, in essence, a threat to liberal security and the concept of national self. While Castillo's work studies the depiction of the 'child figure' in narrative, Panjabi's essay addresses the function of the photographic image in the representation of a young Bangladeshi girl subject to cross-border violence. She cites the produced 'evidence' of Felani, crossing back illicitly into her country, shot at by Indian forces while still high on the wire, refused water, and then left to hang till she bled to death – as also a young man caught on the U.S.–Mexico barbed wire was. Visual media functions as the predominant mode of establishing 'self-evident' knowledge of border violence; this gives it the power to inflect the futures of our violent bordered realities. The essay raises certain questions central to the function of the photographs that were circulated in the media – how do photographs that provide evidence of violence paradoxically catalyse its disappearance from public memory in India? What is the function of the 'truth claim' that such 'evidence' makes – why is it antithetical to responsible action? Both the essays in this section address the questions of what an alternative 'ethics of seeing' would involve, and what kind of renewed engagement with lived realities – and ourselves – such an alternative ethics would demand.

The third section, titled 'Cinematic Representations: Vulnerability as Experience and Metaphor', comprises essays by Melissa Castillo Planas and Sucheta Bhattacharya that study how visual reproductions of memories, fear, longing, aspirations, and experiences can illuminate the complex forms of subjectivity and feelings that can emerge from geographical mobility and transformation in life worlds and objects. Castillo Planas examines the portrayal of shipping containers in a diverse set of cultural texts to bring to the fore the gendered peculiarities of social death on the Atlantic Borderlands. She writes

> As the unearthing of the African burial ground in lower Manhattan in 1991 demonstrates, the financial center of New York is literally built on the bodies of black labour. Since the 1990s, it has been built on the backs of Mexican migrant labor.

Her work builds on the foundational theories of Paul Gilroy, Gloria Anzaldúa, and other writers of the Black Atlantic/Borderlands to bring together black and brown bodies in a longer history of containment with relation to labour. While her essay discusses the vulnerabilities of black and brown bodies situated in the geopolitical space of Atlantic borderlands, Bhattacharya's work examines how children are often seen as pure and uncorrupted and therefore as sites, both psychological and physical, where the trauma and lessons of border experiences can be seen clearly written. This essay explores the symbolic significance of placing the child at the centre of cross-border cinematic narratives in India and Latin America. The child as an observer or a victim of a border, whether geopolitical, economic, or cultural, has often been represented in popular culture, particularly in cinema. Bhattacharya writes that most often the child enters the state of an adult by its experience of crossing the border, the geopolitical border often turning into a signifier for an experiential border on the other side of which lies disillusioned adulthood. The makers rely on the trope of the child to talk about the aspirations of a yet-to-be-achieved adulthood or may be to eulogize a state of innocence which would inevitably be lost. The crossing over, therefore, metaphorically depicts a journey towards the loss of a certain kind of innocence but also the gain of an inescapable experience of the border. Bhattacharya explores how certain characteristic markers are carefully embedded in the cinematic narrative of the child, who embarks on a journey of crossing over, that help deny subjectivity to this child. The state of 'child-hood' like that of 'colour-hood' feed into the ways in which bodies are rendered disposable based on labour, race, ethnicity, and age. The visual representations, explored in this section, deal with vulnerable identities caught in transit, transition, and transformation. The study reveals how border ambiguities (like that of adulthood) are strategically written into matters of 'affect' embodied by an object or a child in narratives of a particular kind of passage or crossing over.

The fourth section, 'Audio-/Visual Languages of Perception: Humour and Satire – Subversion as Resistance', brings together chapters by Parthasarathi Bhaumik and Sawon Chakraborty that explore how social interactions, under conditions of displacement, of divisiveness, of denial, of de-territorialization, across borders make grounds for the production of creative modes of negotiation, assimilation, and resistance based on human relationships. Bhaumik's essay engages with the issue of masking violence and displacement with humour during and after the partition of Bengal in 1947. It studies the historical tradition of humour emerging out of social interactions across the border as comprising modes of coping with geographical, political, and cultural barriers, and of stabilizing and institutionalizing identity. Such cross-border humour, he argues, helps to detach the notion of identity central to it from the acute sense of loss and at the same time to highlight the absurdity of the historical imposition of the geographical and political border. Chakraborty's chapter explores how Chhitmahal dwellers (living in the enclaves of Bangladesh in India) draw upon the metaphors of *Hijra* and scarecrows as sites for the formation of self and resistance. The cultural objects and folk songs, specific to the geopolitical region, are appropriated by the dwellers as sites of identity formation. The strange paradox of how a 'denial of nationality' has shaped their identities and subjectivities surfaces in these modes of representation. All the essays in this segment explore the 'embeddedness' of knowledge in the creative processes of resistance, assimilation, and survival as Adorno suggests – understood by immersion, identification, and subsequent distancing in the politics of representation.

The fifth section, 'Songs: Transformations of Identity across Borders', brings together essays by Moushumi Bhowmik and Minni Sawhney who listen to orally transmitted songs as repositories of identities and memories, and as embodied modes of cultural and historical continuum which defy the political logic of borders. Bhowmik listens to those songs of the sailors and stokers and oilmen, from Sylhet and Noakhali and Comilla that the Dutch scholar of music and Sanskrit, Arnold Bake (1899–1963) had recorded in 1934. She places them alongside other songs from the region, recorded after Bake's time, especially songs which have made other journeys in the bodies of other 'sailors', some willingly travelling to other lands, some displaced from home and hence forced into journeys in search of home. This chapter places multiple time, space, and cultures into a perspective of borders to understand the deep resonances that exist in the oral cultures. Multiple meanings, parallels, and stories surface through the many crossings that the songs have made and continue to make, especially in the context of the broken land of Bengal, marked by the seemingly endless process of border-making. The songs inhabit the body of the singer/performers as much as they are embedded in the culture when they make crossings across borders. Sawhney studies the corridos (folk ballads) and life of Jenni Rivera, a Chicana singer of wetback immigrant parents who exemplifies the struggle of Mexican Americans in California. Borders of gender, class, and race are played out in the politics of reception and production of Rivera's music, which allegedly has been excoriated for being apologetic about the drug trade. The essay shows how the criticism directed against her is elitist as it recognizes art only if it is mainstream, conventional, and highbrow. The author explores Rivera's corridos to show how she inscribed a strong Mexican-ness in an industry where she did not have the conventional symbolic capital to become famous.

The last section, 'Performance: Challenging Rationalities of Mass Killings', presents essays by theatre makers Jimmy Noriega, Debasish Sen Sharma, and Debaroti Chakraborty with an introduction to Sen Sharma and Chakraborty's piece by Kavita Panjabi. These works document and analyse the process of co-creating a performance on borders, by artists in India, Latin America, and the United States. Both the essays study how a mode of immersion in a creative process on one hand renders historical incidents of massacre, violation, and mass killings communicable and on the other, emerges, though sometimes in the form of a visceral response, as a sharp tool of critiquing statist discourses. The artist-essayists drive home the role of art and cultural production in creating an alternative space for social justice. Noriega discusses how the production, *Women of Ciudad Juárez* by Christina Michaus, uses theatre as a space to reflect on, examine and talk about the scandal of high femicide rates in Ciudad Juárez, a border town in Mexico. The author shows how theatre enables the surfacing of multiple voices of women, who have been victims of assault on their bodies and psyche, to show how their gruesome realities have been reduced to a contest of numbers and gross display of injustice by statist regimes as well as mainstream feminist discourses. The process of developing the theatre thereby emerges as a mode of resistance and makes an intervention into the existing narratives and evidence reports of femicide which largely disregard the perspectives and subjectivities of the women who have victims at the borders. The essay, written in two parts, by Kavita Panjabi, Debasish Sen Sharma, and Debaroti Chakraborty, explores the political and aesthetic processes through which Rabindranath Tagore's short story *Kabuliwalah* (1892) and Zaheda Hina's fictitious letter *Kumkum Theek Theek Hain* (2008) was adapted on stage as a multi-media production titled *Dear Earth…Hope You Are Keeping Well!* The play, hinged on these two literary texts, journeys across deeply embedded borders – of narrow nationalisms in South Asia, of cultural xenophobia, of religious fundamentalism, of terrorism through bridges of shared history and cultural traditions of the subcontinent. It then looks at the challenges of making of a performance based on personal feelings and responses of the co-creators to forge a language of sharing beyond borders. The performance critiques the futility of the narrow political divides that we erect in the name of security, in the name of territory, in the name of governance and comments on how these borders translate into psychological borders that lead to mass displacements and homelessness today across South Asia. Both the chapters in this section talk about how performance as an embodied representative form, heightens the veracity and intensity of border experiences through its quality of liveness and potential of direct communication.

In 2019, official documents from the U.S. consulate in Kolkata emphasized their attention to 'cultural diplomacy' as a political strategy to address differences across borders. The irony of this official language is that it was formulated around the same time when governmental policies in the United States and India sought to bolster majoritarian politics by harping on borders across divides of race, ethnicity in the United States, and religion and class in India. For instance, the U.S. President Donald Trump set in motion his plan to build an 'impenetrable, physical, tall, powerful, beautiful, southern border wall' between the United States and Mexico (The Washington Post, 31 August 2016), while Amit Shah, the Home Minister of BJP, the ruling party in India, asserted '...whoever wants to protest can protest but the CAA will not be taken back' (The Hindu, 21 January 2020) in favour of the discriminatory Citizenship Amendment Act 2019 that allows Indian citizenship to Hindu, Sikh, Buddhist, Jain, Christian minorities who fled from neighbouring Muslim majority countries of Pakistan, Bangladesh, Afghanistan before December 2014 due to religious persecution or in fear of religious persecution but excludes Muslims from the purview of this Act. In the thick of such statist discourses and the debates surrounding them, this collection encourages a deep and analytical engagement with the humanities at large that offers a prism into the alternative histories of how human lives are shaped by the borders and how the stories from the borders make claims to a different kind of truth and social justice. A sensitive reading of these narratives helps to glean alternative perspectives of borders, missing in other kinds of discourses that, in turn, have the potential to mobilize resistance and influence policy-making strategies related to human rights.

Note

1 https://wcd.nic.in/acts/public-notice-and-draft-trafficking-persons-prevention-care-and-rehabilitation-bill-2021.

References

Banerjee, P., and Roy, P. *Crossing Boundaries – Cross Border Mobility of Boys between Bangladesh and India – An Explorative Study*. Kolkata: Sanjog, 2011.

"Bangladesh-India Economic Relations." *The Financial Express*. 15 August 2009.

Basu, Ratnabali. Review of the Research Named *Crossing Boundaries*. Mixed Pickle/Groupe Developpement, SARO, 2012.

"'Being Black in America' – Trevor Noah – (African American)." *YouTube*, uploaded by Trevor Noah, 26 July 2019, www.youtube.com/watch?v=sXje3oJ8T8o.

Bhaskar, Shivani. "Trafficking in Persons (Prevention, Care & Rehabilitation) Bill 2021: A Boon for Child-Rights?" *The Logical Indian*. 8 August 2021, https://thelogicalindian.com/humanrights/trafficking-in-persons-child-rights-30120.Blanchet, Therese et al. *Beyond Boundaries: A Critical Look at Women Labour Migration and the Trafficking Within*. Dhaka: USAID, 2012.

Castillo, Debra, and Tabuenca Maria-Socorro Cordoba. *Border Women: Writing from La Frontera*. London: University of Minnesota Press, 2002.

Datta, Prabhash K. "India versus Bangladesh over New Rohingya Crisis Ahead of PM Modi's Dhaka Tour." *India Today*. March 1 2021, www.indiatoday.in/news-analysis/story/india-versus-bangladesh-over-new-rohingya-crisis-ahead-of-pm-modi-s-dhaka-tour-1774221-2021-03-01.

Datta, Sayontoni. *Adolescence at the Border: A Study on Cross-border Trafficking and Safety along the Indo-Bangladesh Border*. Kolkata: Justice & Care, 2018.

Hartjen, Clayton A., and S. Priyadarsini. *The Global Victimization of Children: Problems and Solutions*. London: Springer, 2012.

Hicks, Emily. *Border Writing: The Multidimensional Text*. Minneapolis: University of Minnesota Press, 1991.

Johnson, David, and Michaelsen Scott. *Border Theory: The Limits of Cultural Politics*. Minneapolis: University of Minnesota Press, 1997.

Keller, Renata. "U.S.-Mexican Relations from Independence to the Present." *Oxford Research Encyclopedia of American History*, March 2016. http://oxfordindex.oup.com/view/10.1093/acrefore/9780199329175.013.269 (Accessed on February 26, 2017).

Luiselli, Valeria. *Lost Children Archive: A Novel*. Reprint, New York: Vintage, 2020.

Luiselli, Valeria. *Tell Me How It Ends: An Essay in 40 Questions*. Trans. Jon Lee Anderson. New York: Fourth Estate, 2017.

Oviedo, Douglas. *Caravaneros*. Davis: Humanizando la deportation, 2020.

Panagariya, Arvind. "India in the 1980s and 1990s: A Triumph of Reforms" in *Indian Monetary Fund Working Paper*. Delhi: IMF, 2004.

Panjabi, Kavita. "Transcultural Politics and Aesthetics: Testimonial Literature" in *Literary Studies in India: Genology*. Kolkata: DSA. Comparative Literature: 1–26, 2002.

Portelli, Alessandro. "*A Dialogical Logical Relationship. An Approach to Oral History.*" www.swaraj.org/shikshantar/expressions_portelli.pdf (accessed 23 December 2016).

Rivera Garza, Cristina. *Autobiografía del algodón*. Mexico: Literatura Random House, 2020.

Romero, Rolando. "Border of Fear, Border of Desire." *Borderlines: Studies in American Culture*, vol. 1, no. 1, September 1993, pp. 36–70.Rustom, Bharucha. *Theatre and the World: Performance and the Politics of Culture*. New York: Routledge, 1993.

Svašek, Maruška. *Moving Subjects, Moving Objects: Transnationalism, Cultural Production and Emotions*. New York: Berghagn Books, 2012.

"Well-Oiled Network Gets 50,000 Bangladeshi Girls Trafficked." *The Times of India*. 10 January 2018, https://timesofindia.indiatimes.com/india/well-oiled-network-gets-50000-bangladeshi-girls-trafficked-into-india-every-year/articleshow/62436540.cms.

Further Reading

Anzaldúa, Gloria. *Borderlands – La Frontera: The New Mestiza (English and Spanish Edition) by Gloria Anzaldúa (1987-08-06)*. San Francisco: Aunt Lute Books, 2021.

Biemann, Ursula. "Performing the Border." *Rethinking Marxism*, vol. 14, no. 1, 2002, pp. 29–47. *Taylor and Francis*, doi:10.1080/089356902101242044.

Carrol, Amy Sara. "'Accidental Allegories' Meet 'The Performative Documentary': Boystown, Señorita Extraviada, and the Border-Brothel→ Maquiladora Paradigm." *Signs: Journal of Women in Culture and Society, University of Chicago Press Journal*, vol. 31, no. 2, 2006, pp. 357–396. doi:10.1086/497278.

Castillo, Debra, and Kavita Panjabi. *Cartographies of Affect: Across Borders in South Asia & The Americas*. 1st ed., Kolkata: Worldview Publications, 2011.

Chishti, Muzaffar, and Faye Hipsman. "Dramatic Surge in the Arrival of Unaccompanied Children Has Deep Roots and No Simple Solutions." *Migrationpolicy.Org*, 2 March 2017, www.migrationpolicy.org/article/dramatic-surge-arrival-unaccompanied-children-has-deep-roots-and-no-simple-solutions.

Dasgupta, Rajashri. "With SC Set to Hear Petition, Killings at Bangladesh Border Back in Focus" *The Wire*, 5 March 2020.

"Felani Murdered Nine Years Ago: Odhikar's Statement on the Killings of and Human Rights Violations on Bangladeshi Nationals along the Border by Indian Border Security Force." 2020. *Forum Asia*, 6 January. www.forum-asia.org/?p=30762.

Franco, Jean. *Cruel Modernity*. Durham and London: Duke University Press Books, 2013.

Johnson, David, and Michaelsen Scott. *Border Theory: The Limits of Cultural Politics*. Minneapolis: University of Minnesota Press, 1997.

Mufti, A.R. "Towards a Lyric History of India." *Boundary 2*, vol. 31, no. 2, 2004, pp. 245–274, doi:10.1215/01903659-31-2-245.

Muggah, Robbert, and Carvalho De IlonaSzabo. "Latin America Is the World's Most Dangerous Region. But There Are Signs It Is Turning a Corner." *World Economic Forum*, 7 February 2020, www.weforum.org/agenda/2018/03/latin-america-is-the-worlds-most-dangerous-region-but-there-are-signs-its-turning-a-corner.

Nandy, Ashis. *The Intimate Enemy: Loss and Recovery of Self Under Colonialism*. Delhi: Oxford University Press, 1983.

National Academy of Pre-Recruitment Training: https://napt.in/bsf.

Panjabi, Kavita. *Unclaimed Harvest: An Oral History of Women in the Tebhaga Movement*. New Delhi: Zubaan Books, 2016.

Schendel, Willem Van. "Stateless in South Asia: The Making of the India-Bangladesh Enclaves." *The Journal of Asian Studies*, vol. 61, no. 1, 2002, pp. 115–147.

Smith, Claudia Sadowski. *Border Fictions: Globalization, Empire, and Writing at the Boundaries of the United States*. Charlottesville and London: University of Virginia Press, 2008.

Sklodowska, Elzbieta. "The Poetics of Remembering, the Politics of Forgetting: Rereading I Rigoberta Menchu" in *The Rigoberta Menchu Controversy*. Ed Arturo Arias. Minneapolis: University of Minnesota Press: 251–269, 2001.

Welchman, John. C. *Re-thinking Borders*. London: Macmillan Press Ltd, 1996.

Part I

ORAL NARRATIVES

Experiencing Violence, Forging Modes of Survival

1

MOBILITY ACROSS BORDERS, CONTINUUMS OF VIOLENCE AND RESISTANCE[1]

Rimple Mehta

> Felani Khatun, a fifteen-year-old girl was shot at the dawn of 7 January 2011, while she was climbing over the barbed wire fence at the border in the vicinity of Choudhuryhat (in Coochbehar district, India) and Phulbari (in Kurigram district, Bangladesh). Her father was taking her back to Bangladesh to get her married. Felani's father crossed over the barbed wire fence but Felani's clothes got stuck in the same and she shrieked. Hearing her scream, the BSF fired at her. Her body was hanging upside down from the fence and was handed over to the Border Guards Bangladesh (BGB), the Bangladeshi security force only after thirty hours
>
> (Ramachandran)

> Khukuli Khatun, an eighteen-year-old student was the only girl studying in class X, in her village Hatkhola of Chapra Block in Nadia District of West Bengal. All other girls, of her age in her village, had dropped out from formal education. On 20 November 2008 she had an argument with a BSF jawan M. Silva Kumar of the 42nd Battalion and she was shot at point blank range by the jawan. The bullet tore her stomach and came out through her back. According to Khukuli's dying statement the jawan was in an inebriated state and had tried to molest her which led to a scuffle and resulted in him shooting at her in the stomach. On hearing the gunshot, her family members and other villagers had rushed for her rescue. The killer and two of his fellow *jawans* (soldiers) threatened the mob that they would fire again, if anyone dared to rescue injured Khukuli. Subsequently the killer and his accomplices escaped on their bicycles, the guns still pointed at the mob.
>
> (Jonaki)

It has been more than two decades since the Human Rights Watch published the 'Trigger Happy?' report which brought to light that India's border security had killed 1000 people both Indians and Bangladeshis between

DOI: 10.4324/9780429356421-3

2001 and 2010, suggesting the frequency of deadly shooting every four days (Human Rights Watch, *Trigger Happy?*). The brutality by the Border Security Forces (BSF) on border crossers has continued and it is alleged that the Indian border forces have killed at least 334 Bangladeshis since 2011 and 51 of those in 2020 itself (Human Rights Watch, *India: Investigate*).

Khukuli and Felani are therefore illustrative of several other cases that go unreported and unnoticed. These are not simply cases of conflict between BSF and the local community or border crossers. These are symbolic of anxieties of sovereignty-threatened states that have consigned its security in the hands of uniformed armed men. Khukuli challenged the violence perpetuated and condoned within the patriarchal structure and was killed in the process. Felani dared to trespass the border between the two nations and her dead body hung over the barbed wire, symbolically representing the victory of sovereignty over its alleged transgression.[2] The case of Felani was posited in a way that it seemed that the 'protectors' of the border were trying to prevent instances of illicit entry of people or goods into the sovereign state, suggesting that they were only doing their duty. Violence is therefore justified in the interest of the sovereignty of the state. Instances of violence – whether it is Felani or Khukuli – need to be seen in the context of the challenges they pose to the nexus of state and patriarchy. Their perceived challenge to these structures put them in vulnerable situations to the extent that it cost them their lives.

Women's bodies are symbolically projected to represent the boundaries of the nation as well as reproducers of the nation (see Ramaswamy). Women are seen as markers of the territorial space of the nation as well as the property of nation, therefore in need of defence and protection from the 'patriotic sons' (Mostov). The task of 'protecting' the women of the nation is delegated to the patriotic sons who may justify the invasion of feminine spaces of another nation if it threatens their sovereignty in any manner. This relationship between women and the nation is underlined by the danger of exclusion and the pressures to conform to national cultures and values. They are seen as the bearers of cultural values by virtue of being the markers, bearers, and reproducers of the nation. Therefore, mobility of women across borders is often a much contested issue, because they are perceived as not only transgressing the political nation, which they seemingly embody and represent, but also social norms and codes of conduct. Through their mobility, women challenge the notion of rootedness. They challenge the androcentric notion of settlement, guided and established by the male breadwinner, by going back and forth the border and by pursuing their aspirations and desires through this mobility.

The trajectory of violence in the lives of women engaging in cross-border mobility can be plotted along a continuum where the border becomes one moment and site of violence in a series of violent experiences. The family, community, and state contribute to violence at varying degrees at different times in the lives of women. In this context, this chapter will discuss the experiences of violence in the lives of Bangladeshi women in prisons in Kolkata, India. It will focus on the violence experienced by these women on a continuum; before crossing the border, while crossing the border to come to India, during their stay in India and while returning to Bangladesh; coupled with emotions of fear, anxiety, and shame and how they navigate through all this. Through this focus, this chapter seeks to show how in our survival as citizens we become complicit in the survival of violence in their lives. Further, through the narratives of the Bangladeshi women in prisons in Kolkata, it will suggest an alternative to the violence of survival.

Conceptualizing Violence

This chapter looks at violence in two ways, first, as violence which is inherent in the androcentric statist ideology of exclusion and second, as violence which is manifested through the normative practises of the family, state, and community. These two understandings are not mutually exclusive and are closely tied to each other. The modern state is a gendered state with power and security as its cornerstones (Mohsin). Gender inequality is inherent in the militarist security ideology and practises of a militarized state and society. Banerjee and Basu Ray Chaudhury observe, the border is a 'site where this contest over inclusion and exclusion is played out every day' and, in turn, 'becomes a zone of endemic violence where masculinity is privileged' (xvii). Moreover, the state is based on an exclusionary model where the border separates the citizens from the foreigners. The border, therefore, becomes a symbolic axis between us/them, insider/outsider, here/there, and citizen/foreigner. It is also representative of a power relation that is intrinsically patriarchal. For its survival, it is important for the modern state to maintain boundaries of 'us' and 'them' and constitute processes of 'othering' through hegemonic practises of exclusion. Border control becomes central to this ideology. Pickering and Cochrane point out, 'border control is understood to comprise highly selective and complex performances of state power staged at multiple locations through technologies of selection, detention, deterrence, expulsion, and pre-emption, involving a range of state and non-state actors' (29). Hegemonic practices of 'othering' coupled with technologies of border control create situations of vulnerability for the most marginalized groups. The citizens become complicit in the violence which ensues as a result of this border control, for it is in the name of their protection that these systems of control are initiated. Dhar succinctly explains this idea:

> A more complicated understanding of the binaries Us/Them would entail an appreciation of the complicity of Us, even if implicit, in structures of violence closest to home. Maybe, not overt acts of violence. But complicity in the somewhat covert flow of violence, the

> silent, almost surreptitious survival of violence, violence sustained in the 'rule of order', violence sustained in everyday life, which in other words, is the everyday life of violence – violence in family, home, workplace, school – violence in the individual, in peers, in groups – in communities, in institutions – in the state, judiciary, army – violence in our very survival.
>
> (64)

Violence, since it is inherent in and perceived as necessary for our very survival, attains a certain kind of legitimacy and hence is considered normal and necessary. Several institutions work together for the survival of the 'us' against 'them'. To ensure this, the family and community work as close aides of the state. The family, the community, the market, and the state constitute a pervasive and interactive system for legitimizing violence (Mathur 53). Consequently, violence is weaved in the everyday life of the 'us' and 'them'. Kannabiran aptly points out,

> It is within the realm of the normal, the routine, that violence against women is deeply embedded, and it is because the greatest part of violence against women is the violence of normal times that it carries with it the guarantee of impunity irrespective of penal, punitive or constitutional safeguards. Sudden conflagrations of violence, seemingly inexplicable upsurges, must then be understood in the context of this steady, ever present violence of normal times.
>
> (3)

This nuanced understanding of violence explains the brutal killings of Felani and Khukuli. As mentioned earlier, these killings need to be seen through anxieties of the state and the way cultures of violence are woven through the everyday practises, which are extremely gendered. The experiences of women and men who engage in extra-legal cross-border movements are significantly different (Pickering 1).

Experiences of violence faced by women at the borders are significantly marked by sexual violence. Their body is perceived as overtly sexualized and easily available. Kannabiran points out that, 'Sexual terrorism is always part of larger political projects that hinge on the absolute appropriation of women's bodies' (4). Therefore, violence for them becomes both a stimulus and a deterrent to mobility. Experiences of violence within the family and community necessitate their movement from one place to another to look for a safer environment. Violence in various forms at the border constitutes a moment in this continuum of violence that they are constantly trying to escape. Their survival from violence becomes linked to the citizen's survival and the latter's complicity in the survival of violence.

Violence inflicted on women may not be directly at the border as a physical, geographical site but is induced by its exclusionary and inherently violent nature. Border crossing neither begins nor ends with the extra-legal crossing of a territorial border (Pickering). A border is not merely a political or geographical space but ramifies itself into a normative socio-cultural space. What kind of subjectivities does this multi-headed hydra known as the border create? How does it further marginalize women and create situations of vulnerability? In turn, how do women subvert these situations of vulnerability and create safe spaces for themselves? These are some of the questions through which this chapter will navigate.

Narratives of Violence

Bangladeshi women in Correctional Homes in Kolkata, participants of my doctoral research,[3] crossed the border and came to India, either to escape multiple situations of vulnerability, were in search of a livelihood or had aspirations of a better life. Under various circumstances they were arrested by the police in India under section 14 the Foreigners Act 1946 for entering the country without valid documents. Section 14 (c) states that a person arrested under this Act could be sentenced for imprisonment from two to eight years and is also liable to pay a fine. The Bangladeshi women, who were in the average age group of 18 to 22 years, were generally imprisoned for two years along with a fine amount.

For most of these women, initially, crossing the border, was a matter of moving from a vulnerable and violent situation in the hope of finding a better/safer space for themselves. Child labour, early or child marriage, and intersecting forms of socio-cultural and economic disadvantage marked their childhood experiences and later shaped their decisions of mobility. Rina, who was 21 years old had divorced her husband because he was addicted to drugs, and moreover, she had not consented to the marriage. She said,

> My parents married me off when I was really young...I didn't want to get married...but didn't have the courage to say this in front of my mother...this is why I am still upset with my parents...I try to stay aloof from everyone. So I decided to come to India for sometime...also because I needed money to raise my child.

The majority of the women stated that their relationship with their husband had been severed because he either deserted them and remarried or was violent, or they themselves chose to walk out of their marriages as their family members had forced them to marry. Circumstances of domestic violence, severing of relationships, and the subsequent deepening of economic crisis necessitated a certain mobility for the Bangladeshi women. Any hope of a better life was promptly embraced. This hope often came in the form of traffickers who promised jobs in another city in Bangladesh or India. Women who started working in a garments' factory in Dhaka or other cities in Bangladesh reckoned a certain Pia as their co-worker and confidante who put forth the possibility of going to India. The *spectre* of Pia seemed to be present in a number of narratives of the Bangladeshi women who had been trafficked. Pia seemed to be the principal organizer of the journey that they would make to India. Thereafter, a few of her associates guided the women to various destinations in India. It was much later that the women realized they had been sold to brothel owners. The garments' factories in Bangladesh, which are often seen as the way to empowerment of women proved to be the source site of violence. Siddiqi points out that by entering the public space of work, as per the acceptable social norms of behaviour, they had already exposed themselves to the dangers of sexual vulnerability and thereby put themselves at the risk of losing the 'honour' embodied in their reputation (L16). Safina, a 21-year-old unmarried woman said,

> I went to Dhaka and started working in the garments business, I earned some money...sent some of it home and spent some as well...there were a lot of problems at home and I tried to sort them out...I got into a lot of trouble...this friend of mine, I know her well, I was very fond of her, she told me Safina it is very difficult here, come with me...I asked her where, she said somewhere else where we would be paid a lot of money... I asked what kind of work I would have to do and she said never mind the work, just come with me...she asked me if I trusted her and I said alright, and then I got everything ready and came to the border with her and she brought me here and made me wait at the Sealdah station and made some money arrangements with this man who was there... and then there was this man who asked me my name...I told him my name...and he told me that I'm in a lot of trouble...I asked him what it was...and he told me that I had been sold off...I asked him how he found out...he said that he was one of them, said that he didn't want my life to be ruined...I escaped after I heard him say those things... they started looking for me...I arrived at a police station, I surrendered myself.

At the time of this journey some of the women realized the ploy that the traffickers were using and tried to escape.[4] Nargis, a 22-year-old widow, who had been in a shelter home in Kolkata for two years and then in a correctional home for two years said,

> I knew there was something wrong...when I was sitting in the train with this dalal (agent) he was being very nice to me...He offered me an apple...I could sense that there was something behind his apparent good behaviour so I told him I want to go back...He then

> told me that once someone gets on this path they do not return...I tremble even when I think of him now...*Didi* (elder sister) why did he say that one cannot return...is it true?

Unlike Nargis, many women who managed to escape the clutches of the traffickers found themselves to be further victimized by the Border Security Forces. Twenty-year-old Reshmi said,

> The BSF caught me...kept me in their camp for a night...they kicked me in my stomach. I fell unconscious after that. I had to be admitted to the hospital. It's been two years and three months...some parts of my body still ache because of the rape and beating from the BSF... they wronged me, raped me and tortured me.

Though the perpetrators of violence were changing, violence itself continued to have a looming presence in the lives of the women. The narratives of Safina, Nargis, and Reshmi indicate the centrality of the border in their experiences of violence.

On their arrival in Kolkata, most of them were either arrested from the railway station itself or found themselves in confined rooms of a brothel. A number of Bangladeshi women approached or were approached by NGO workers at the railway stations; and often they were caught by the police at the station crying because they did not know where to go from there. There were only few who reached their destination to work as a domestic worker and were later arrested from various locations. In the instance that they found themselves in a brothel, they took a few days to come to terms with this reality, and then a number of them succumbed to the exploitation, while they also actively thought of ways to subvert it. Instances of abuse by the brothel owner, police, and the customers were a routine affair. Khushi, 17-year-old girl was first trafficked within Bangladesh for organ trade and then after a few years to Pune, India for sex trade, said,

> The police raped me...they raped me in the room in which I was staying in the brothel...this was a year after I arrived at the brothel... we used to be locked up in the rooms and were not allowed to go out...I cried and asked aunty (brothel owner) why she did this with all the girls...and then I got beaten up very badly.

Though over a period of time they learnt to bargain for themselves in the brothel and resist the physical and sexual abuse, they still did not have access to the money that they earned. They would call up their family members telling them that they were working in a garments' factory in Dhaka. They knew that if their family members found out that they were working in a brothel, they would have to face humiliation and insult. However, they always worried about the psychological and physical violence they would have to face if their family found out that they were working in a brothel. Contact with the family was difficult, if not terminated once they were arrested and later imprisoned.

Some of the women, like Shamoli Khatoon, who refused to succumb to the exploitation, were arrested from the brothel itself while some others were arrested when they were trying to escape from the brothel. Shamoli said,

> They sold me for 60,000...they took me to a brothel...the women there told me that they will not give me any money but I could stay there...they wanted to keep me to make me do *kharap kaaj* (immoral work)...I begged them and told them that I will not do any *kharap kaaj*...in the evening around 5 they got me arrested.

Violence in different forms was to follow both in the prison and in the courtroom. Bangladeshi women were often scorned in the prison for leaving their country and coming to India only to add to the prison population. They were perceived as sexually aggressive and violent in comparison to the Indian woman who 'did not pose many administrative challenges'. The Bangladeshi women were unable to meet their family members because they feared arrest and did not come to meet them in the prison. Moreover, as mentioned earlier, their family members were not aware that they were in a prison and that too in India. This apart, there were multiple hierarchies between the women in prison. The Bangladeshi women occupied the lowest level in this hierarchy. They would often perform chores for the Indian women who would then provide them with some benefits in the form of clothes, extra food, or some cosmetics. Besides, there were women who were labelled as '*pagol*'[5] and were at the receiving end of violent behaviour both from the warders and from the other prisoners. They often had few friends and did not get adequate medical attention. With each passing day their sense of isolation and alienation seemed to get more acute. One of the participants told me about a woman who would often get 'hysterical' in the cell and all the others would be scared of her and move to one side. Some would try to wrestle with her 'to get her back to her senses'. Women who were labelled as '*pagol*' often faced a lot of moral policing from the other prisoners. For instance, I quote an observation from my field notes:

> When Nargis came out of the cell she did not have an orna (stole). Just then all the girls started shouting '*aye aye tor orna ta kothay*' (hey, where is your stole). Nargis ran out of the cell covering her chest with her arms and said that it was hanging outside to dry. She went to the clothesline outside the cell and put the orna around herself.
>
> (18 May 2011)

Bangladeshi women would engage in moral policing towards each other so that they could uphold the image of a 'good' Bangladeshi woman in India. While they thought that it was important to question the prison administration, they thought it to be equally important to project the image of a 'moral' Bangladeshi woman to preserve the *maan-shonmaan* (honour) of their *desh*. Despite all their efforts, the prison administration often hurled a number of abuses on them. I quote again, an instance from my field notes:

> 'These Bangladeshis are like beggars. They only know how to fight and abuse each other. These are very dangerous women,' said the warder to the male guard responsible for the women's ward and the latter started laughing. The latter took a look at the jackfruit tree and asked the warder if they cook and eat that. The warder said no they didn't because who would pluck them from the tree. The male guard replied, 'Why don't you tell these Bangladeshis girls to do it. I am sure they are adept at climbing tree. Anyways they are so uncivilised.'
>
> (18 May 2011)

Such perceptions often added to the struggles of the women who tried to reconcile with the complete absence of contact with the outside world. But the male guards of the prison, responsible for chaperoning the women prisoners to the hospital or interview room, often made use of the walks to have flirtatious conversations with them. The relationship between the male guards and the women prisoners was a complex one where the women depended on them for some material benefits or news from outside but also were at the receiving end of their rebuke.

As the day of release drew closer, the anxiety of the women increased exponentially. First, they were anxious about the process through which they would be sent back and second, the time that this process would involve. Their anxiety over the date of deportation increased with each passing day. More often than not, the date when their sentence finished, and the date of deportation were not the same. They would have to wait in prison, sometimes for months on end, till the day all the paper work was completed and the prison staff received orders to hand them over to police escorts to be handed over to the BSF at the border, and then to the Bangladesh Border Guards on the other side of the border.[6] This delay is what made the relationship between the state and these women a particularly tenuous one. It is this institutional form of violence, so well-choreographed with the exclusionist idea of the state, which the women found most difficult to grapple with. The Bangladeshi women, without legal documents, were not allowed 'to step foot on Indian soil' outside the prison. The prison staff therefore could not release them from prison till they received their orders of deportation. The orders for deportation involved a number of agencies; one of them, of course, was the Deputy High Commission of Bangladesh in Kolkata. The delay in orders for deportation often took place because of the tussle between the Deputy High Commission of Bangladesh's denial of these women as citizens of their country and the insistence of the Indian state that their identity was Bangladeshi. This often happened because the women gave incorrect names and addresses at the time of their case registration. They did this because they feared that if their family members were contacted, they (the family) would find out that they were in prison or that prior to being in prison they were involved in commercial sex.[7] Some of them had not told their families that they had come to India. In the process of trying to protect their own 'honour' and that of their families, they often gave an incorrect address without realizing the impact it would have on their release and the process of being sent back. It is not to suggest that the responsibility for delay in being sent back was with the women. One cannot deny the politics between the two countries with regard to migration/illegal migration, which has peppered their relations from 1947.

In the period in between their release and deportation, these prisoners are referred to as *jaankhalash*, implying released prisoners. The women said that *jaankhalash* meant that they were living in prison like a 'free public'; but ironically, *jaankhalash* means 'the end of life'. It could signify that their life as a prisoner had ended. At another level, it could imply that so far, by virtue of being in prison, they had the definitive status of being a Bangladeshi, but the moment they finish serving their sentence, their identity becomes ambiguous. They are neither Bangladeshi nor Indian. This throws light on the liminal existence that they had while they lived in prison as a *jaankhalash*, while their identity as a Bangladeshi was getting established so that they could be sent back.[8]

There was a great deal of antagonism that prevailed in the prison because of many reasons including the constant competition for space and resources. But there were times when the women came together for a common cause. More often than not, the common cause among the Bangladeshi women was with respect to the delay in their release after they had finished serving their prison term. They would come together in large numbers to protest this delay, which they viewed as a laxity and unwillingness to work on the part of the prison staff. Some of the women who had entered the prison prior to 2009 said that there was a time when more than 500 women used to stay in a space created for about 100 of them, many among these were *jaankhalash*. It was only after an instance when they jumped the walls of their ward and threatened to harm the prison staff with stones and bricks that immediate steps were taken that hastened their deportation. They often went on hunger strikes demanding their release once they had served their respective prison terms. The Bangladeshi women had observed that a show of aggression on their part could bring about a change in the situation. This probably gave them an incentive to continue their acts of resistance in order to finally achieve the 'freedom' for which they had initially decided to leave their 'homes'.

Prior to returning home there was another hurdle they had to cross with regard to 'protecting' their *maan-shonmaan*, i.e. the Border Security Force. There were several rumours, stories, and information about BSF raping and torturing the Bangladeshi women before they were finally asked to run to the other side of the border to Bangladesh. Due to a lack of a formal process of handover, the Bangladeshi prisoners are often taken to the border in the middle of the night and asked to run across to the other side in Bangladesh. The women heard some of these stories from the prison staff or police who had accompanied the released Bangladeshi women to the border or through communication with women who had been released and had returned to India only to be imprisoned again. They had heard that the BSF often raped women before releasing them at the border to go back to Bangladesh. In the initial conversations the women would often be extremely anxious about being raped on their way back as this would imply losing whatever little 'honour' they had remaining with them. However, their narratives with regard to rape by the BSF shifted over time. Gradually, they began laughing and joking about it saying how a few minutes of sex would ultimately lead them to the much desired freedom. This can be analysed at two levels – first, that with time their trust in the researcher became stronger and they felt safe to say what they felt without the fear of being judged and second, they had begun to understand the inevitability of the process of going back which involved an unpleasant or exploitative experience with the BSF. These narratives need to be seen in the context of systemic oppression faced by the Bangladeshi women in prison.

Resistance and Love of Survival

Women's security in India and Bangladesh is jeopardized, threatened, and their lives and dignity are at great risk, on a daily basis from the likelihood of sexual assault to domestic violence in public and private spaces. This threat diminishes women's capacity and ability to exercise their fundamental freedoms. Their vulnerability tends to increase in a place that is not very familiar to them. In such places it becomes important to preserve one's own integrity as well as reinvent oneself to take charge of the new conditions of survival.

An important shift in the research process was a shift in their narratives from 'violence' to 'love'. As a feminist researcher, I went to the prison to understand their experiences of violence through their narratives, but they preferred to talk about their experiences of love in the prison. They challenged the researcher's intentions to hear their stories of violence and established through their narratives that it was a certain idea of love and being in love in prison that helped them go through their everyday life. They tried to silence their memories of violence and did not want to think about it anymore. Thus, despite fractured relationships with their husbands and violent marriages, the women prisoners still longed for relationships. Love and intimacy in the prison was one of the ways in which these young women fulfilled roles they believed were destined for women, reassuring themselves of their identity as women, and simultaneously expressing their desires in a voice they had suppressed in circumstances of forced and unhappy, violent marriages (Mehta, *So Many Ways*). The women were in love with men and/or women in prison. They devised ingenious ways to meet their 'lovers', particularly if they were in the men's ward. Interview room in the prison, waiting room at the courts, police van which carried them to the court, celebration of some festivals became spaces and occasions which the women would use to exchange glances or a few words with the person they desired. Often letters were also exchanged between the prisoners. Looks and smiles were sometimes all that two prisoners exchanged during their entire 'relationship'. But the women expressed that having a love interest gave them a sense of security, that someone in the same enclosed space as they cared for them or thought about them. It is important to specify here that this shift in narrative, from violence to love, happened soon after there was a change in the space where the interviews took place. The interviews and my meeting with the Bangladeshi women used to take place in a large damp school room decorated with wall hangings made by the prisoners. The school room was no longer in use and the school teacher retired a few months after I started visiting the correctional home. Thereafter, the warder asked me to talk to the women under a mango tree. The mango tree and its expanse, the comfort that it provided on a hot summer afternoon, the unpredictability of its contours excited the women and gave them a sense of purpose as they waited for a mango to fall (Mehta, *The Mango Tree*). The space of the mango tree and their stories of love weaved into each other. The romance of the mango tree caught on fast with the love that they claimed to have for another fellow prisoner/s. The concrete space of the mango tree and the abstract concept of love provided them with a reason to survive, to mark out a language of survival which was not based on violence but a certain sort of hope. A discussion about resistance should not lose focus of the materiality of the violence and injustice these women faced in their day-to-day lives (Mehta, *So Many Ways*). Their narratives suggest that perpetrators and sites of violence change but violence persists in their life in a continuum, with the Indo-Bangladesh border as central to their experiences of violence. This discussion should not, in any way, be misconstrued as an exercise in romanticizing the experiences of these women or belittling the depth of the love they feel. It needs to be seen as a way of resistance and survival. A way in which they suggest that their spirit is indomitable.

Conclusion

In this chapter, we have seen how violence survives in the life of the Bangladeshi women prisoners along a continuum. The survival of violence gets linked with the survival of the traffickers, the brothel owners, warders, prison administration, as well as the BSF. Each of these stakeholders violates the bodies of the Bangladeshi women not only physically and/or emotionally but also by their existence in the system against undocumented cross-border mobility. As already pointed out, along with them, the citizens also become complicit in this survival of violence. Brutal killings of Felani and Khukuli are not single-handed offences committed by some errant BSF personnel. It is a manifestation of a system, which breeds on violence for its survival. It is a culmination of the continuum of violence that the women throw light on through their narratives. It is through these brutal killings that the violence of the everyday life, so neatly woven into institutions and practises, comes to the forefront to jolt the individual conscience.

This chapter does not seek to suggest that there is a seamless flow of violence in the lives of these women, which then seamlessly transpires into narratives of love. While I see border as a moment in a series of violent experiences, I understand that different forms of violence situate women's experiences differently. But my intention is not to hierarchize that violence and experience. The Bangladeshi women prisoners' experiences of violence need to be seen in the context of their challenge to the norms instituted for women by the family, state, and community. These norms may be historically located in the social, legal, and political relations and structures in India and Bangladesh. Contemporary legal and political debates around the Citizenship Amendment Act 2019 (CAA) in India also impact the realities of the Bangladeshi women. The limited focus of the CAA in terms of who may lay claim to citizenship in India may have further amplified their vulnerabilities and created newer contexts of violence. Further research needs to be done with the Bangladeshi women in prisons in India, especially in the present political context in India.

The narratives of the Bangladeshi women enable us to access the specific ways in which they interacted with the various social and institutional borders and boundaries that they were confronted with. Their perceived deviations from normative modes of behaviour put them in situations of extreme vulnerability as it was perceived to challenge the nexus of the patriarchal state, family, and community, premised on the control of women's mobility and through it their sexuality. Through all these experiences of marginality and violence, the women showed grit and determination to survive, to take control of their lives, and to move on. The shift in their narratives from violence to love involved a series of negotiations to exercise an agency, both with the instruments of the state and with me, the researcher. Through this shift, the women suggest an alternative to the violence of survival by adopting love as their premise for survival. While their experience is embedded in the violence of survival, through their voice they propose a love of survival as a mode of survival.

Notes

1 Parts of this chapter have been published previously, and edited and revised from Rimple Mehta, 2018, Women, Mobility and Incarceration, Abingdon: Routledge, and Rimple Mehta, 2017, Mobility across Borders and Continuums of Violence: Experiences of Bangladeshi Women in Correctional Homes in Kolkata: The Bernard and Audre Rapoport Center for Human Rights and Justice, University of Texas, School of Law. Working Paper Series, Issue 2. Available at http://blogs.utexas.edu/rapoportcenterwps/.

2 According to the Memorandum of Understanding and related treaties signed between India and Bangladesh, if citizens of the two countries illegally cross the border, it would be considered trespass and as per law those persons should be handed over to the civilian authority. However, it has been repeatedly noticed that India has been violating treaties, shooting at anyone seen near the border or anyone trying to cross the border, which is a clear violation of international law and human rights. – See more at: http://odhikar.org/violations-in-the-border-area/#sthash.4GRsyqwr.dpuf.

3 The fieldwork for this research was done between 2010 and 2011.

4 It is difficult to fathom why an associate of Safina's trafficker would facilitate her escape. This may have been due to the differences between the chain of traffickers.

5 *Pagol* literally translates as 'mad', implying mentally ill.

6 The Ministry of External Affairs, India, has mandated the respective Foreign Nationals and Non Resident Indians (FN/NRI) Departments in different states, permission to carry out the process of sending the Bangladeshis back to their country. The prison authorities in West Bengal are meant to send the list of Bangladeshis in their custody to the FN/NRI Department in West Bengal that, in turn, is to send the list to the Deputy High Commission of Bangladesh in Kolkata. The latter is to send the list of names to the respective police stations in Bangladesh. The police are entrusted with the responsibility of verifying the names and sending the list back to the Deputy High Commission of Bangladesh, who, in turn, is supposed to send it to the FN/NRI Department. The latter sends orders to the prison authorities to repatriate the Bangladeshi prisoners following the due processes.

7 There seemed to be a dichotomy in wanting to hear from their families and the shame and fear of contact with their families. There is a push and pull factor here between psychological yearning and lived reality. Also, they were not sure how the prison staff or the police doing the verification in their village would represent their lives in India. If they themselves contacted their families, they could have control over how their experiences were represented.

8 Evidence from stakeholders suggests that over the last few years there have been efforts to adopt a more formalized approach for deportation through regular meetings between the border security forces in India and Bangladesh and transfers through designated Immigration Check Posts (ICP). However, there needs to be further research to understand to what extent such processes have replaced the practice of pushbacks and their effectiveness in ensuring the safety and security of the individuals. This is particularly important as there is data which suggests that between 1985 and 2017, around 2528 Bangladeshis were 'pushed back' after having been declared foreigners. See *The Economic Times*, Dhaka to take back migrants, 30 May 2018, available at https://economictimes.indiatimes.com/news/politics-and-nation/policy-change-dhaka-to-take-back-migrants/articleshow/64380489.cms (accessed 23 September 2019).

References

Banerjee, Paula, and Anasua Basu Ray Chaudhury. *Women in Indian Borderlands*. Sage Publications India Pvt Ltd, 2011.

Dhar, Anup Kumar. "Survival of Violence: Violence of Survival." *Identity, Culture and Politics* vol. 5, no.1 & 2, 2004, pp. 60–85.

Human Rights Watch. *India: Investigate Alleged Border Force Killings*, 2021, www.hrw.org/news/2021/02/09/india-investigate-alleged-border-force-killings.

Human Rights Watch. *'Trigger Happy': Excessive Use of Force by Indian Troops at the Bangladesh Border*, 2010, www.hrw.org/report/2010/12/09/trigger-happy/excessive-use-force-indian-troops-bangladesh-border

India: Act No. 31 of 1946, Foreigners Act, 1946, http://mha1.nic.in/pdfs/The%20Foreigners%20Act,%201946.pdf

Jonaki. "The Murder of Khukuli Khatun & Thereafter…" vol. 2, no. 1, Sanlaap, 2009.

Kannabiran, Kalpana, editor. *The Violence of Normal Times: Essays on Women's Lived Realities*. Women Unlimited, 2005.

Mathur, Kanchan. *Countering Gender Violence*. Sage, 2004.

Mehta, Rimple. "So Many Ways to Love You/Self: Negotiating Love in a Prison." *International Feminist Journal of Politics* vol. 16, no. 2, 2014, pp. 181–198.

Mehta, Rimple. "The Mango Tree: Exploring the Prison Space for Research" *Reflexivity in Criminological Research: Experiences with the Powerful and the Powerless*, edited by Karen Lumsden and Aaron Winter, Palgrave Macmillan, 2014, pp. 47–57.

Mohsin, Amena. "Gendered Nation, Gendered Peace." *Indian Journal of Gender Studies* vol. 11 no. 1, 2004, pp. 43–64.

Mostov, J. "Our Women"/"Their Women": Symbolic Boundaries, Territorial Markers, and Violence in the Balkans. *Peace and Change* vol. 20, 1995, pp. 515–529.

Pickering, Sharon. *Women, Border and Violence: Current Issues in Asylum, Forced Migration and Trafficking*. Springer, 2011.

Pickering, Sharon, and Brandy Cochrane. "Irregular Border-Crossing Deaths and Gender: Where, How and Why Women Die Crossing Borders." *Theoretical Criminology* vol. 17, no. 1, 2012, pp. 27–48.

Ramachandran, Sujata. "Devouring the Maps: Diasporas, Discourses, Discrimination, and Banglo-Indians." *South Asian Review* vol. 32, no. 3, 2011, pp. 199–220.

Ramaswamy, Sumathi. "Maps and Mother Goddesses in Modern India." *Imago Mundi* vol. 53, 2001, pp. 97–114.

Siddiqi, Dina M. "Miracle Worker or Woman Machine? Tracking (Trans)national Realities in Bangladeshi Factories." *Economic and Political Weekly* vol. 35, no. 12, May 2000, pp. L11–L17.

Further Reading

Mittal, Tusha. "Blood on the Border." *Tehelka Magazine* vol. 8 no. 41, 2011, p. 15. http://archive.tehelka.com/storymain50.asp?filename=Ne151011BLOOD.asp, accessed on 26 September 2015.

2

DEFYING THE NATION

Women's Narratives of U.S.–Mexico and India–Bangladesh 'Border' Crossings

Debaroti Chakraborty

Towards a Methodology of Understanding 'Bordered Subjectivity'

This chapter stemmed from my doctoral research broadly based on how women transform their private experiences of motherhood, of relationship with people, home and nature, of intergenerational exchanges shaped by their encounters with geopolitical borders, into modes of empowerment and resistance. These encounters, at several levels, lead to the creation of a new subjectivity that is intrinsically linked with experiences of borders. My central engagement, on one hand, is with the nature of a new gendered subjectivity that plays a crucial role in shaping an alternative history of contemporary borders and on the other to engage with why the concept of 'border' becomes significant in analyzing the way contemporary global forces map lives. The materiality of a frontier or a dividing line evokes several other registers – metaphorical, spatial, psychological, phenomenological, as well as psycho-sexual. All of these categories are related to lived experiences across zones of contact where bodies, identities, and relationships are constantly negotiated, erased, assimilated, or created. How do we address these fluid spaces that shape consciousness in ways beyond the set of implications posited by a partition or the border – a geopolitical line that strictly divides resources? Sophia A. McClennen posits 'borders, as a result, more readily lend themselves to poetic conceptualizations of liminality, border gnosis, and contact zones' (Castillo and Panjabi, 17). The concept of borders thus sanctions permeability, porosity, assimilation along with its sense of division and resilience. Thus, drawing upon narratives of trauma and violence of the 1947 partition of India, when we try to understand borders in relation to contemporary experiences of women, the narratives of migration and displacement, of exploitation of bodies and labour in transnational and transregional flows of capital, become poignant sites of analysis. This

DOI: 10.4324/9780429356421-4

exploration posited a challenge – I was faced with a paucity of cultural resources that represent lived realities of contemporary borders, so I tried to read sociological reports and oral narratives on contemporary borders with the tools of literature. This methodology of reading sociological testimonies offered me new insights into how daily lives are organized across the borders which at an empirical level documents experiences of victimhood, histories of migrant women, and the workings of sponsorship systems, uneven economy. The narratives of the everyday, of women's shifting roles in crossing the 'borders', of negotiating with questions of identity, give birth to a new symbolic order/meaning. Some of the narratives of women who have crossed the U.S.–Mexico or the India–Bangladesh border started to unfold deeper resonances for me in terms of how they re-arrange aesthetic lives across the border, how they negotiate as well as re-orient family configurations and gender roles. This chapter foregrounds a deep-seated contradiction of how on one hand the modern nation-state affirms its so-called margins or borderlands to impose tools of violence as modes of governance and on the other hand, the women's personal narratives of border crossing, human connections, survival, and sustenance spell out modes of resilience, and the ambiguous nature of borders as opposed to the strict partitioning of the world across impermeable geopolitical borders.

In 1997, the Government of Bangladesh re-imposed the illegality of women's cross-border labour migration excepting only 'highly skilled professionals'. The state thereby reserves the power to differentiate and determine 'skill' and what constitutes legitimate labour. Though the ban was partly lifted following protests, it was still functional for domestic workers. However, these measures, adopted since 1981, have not stopped women from migrating. While the militarization as well as the aesthetic displays of surveillance across the borders kept on increasing, the border continued to be more and more porous to women's labour and bodies. This strange paradox, which also prompts acts of defying the presence of 'border' compels one to probe into the nature of the border. The presence of the border is necessary for the state to impose its categories through demarcations of territory, identity, and security. Ironically, the border woman, who is at the centre of my study, claims agency through her subjective modes of negotiations at the border. These negotiations pertain to physically crossing the border in search of work, to carry goods, to opt for a better life, to claim identity, to actively participate in the cross-border transactions. Such border crossings are often accompanied by multiple challenges such as modes of illegalities, stereotypes of moral degradation, mourning, and yet, a simultaneous urge to build new social mores, to undercut the material presence of the border and thereby the psychological barriers of racial and gender hierarchies. In the cross-border trajectories, the tropes of memory, isolation, nostalgia, and assimilation, as found in the narratives of displacement, lose prominence making way for mobility, resistance, and agency. Now, when we turn towards the narratives of women who cross the border – forcibly, for labour migration or are trafficked and those who live on the borderlands, we witness specific modes of negotiation. Their stories depict a sense of constant movement across geographical space, identity, and social relationships while simultaneously evoking a sense of home in their trajectories of mobility.

The lives of the border women, in contemporary times, are shaped by the relationship between the material border as a strict divide, the iconicity of the borders, and the lack of obviousness of the borders in lived realities. Each of these lives is bound by stereotypes of disposability normatively imposed by the nation-state that situate them very differently from the lives of middle-/upper-class women who were displaced from their homeland (in Bangladesh) since the mid-twentieth century, in exchange of a new territorial and national identity. For the latter, memory, experience of displacement, and home shared a nuanced relationship with claim over territory and geopolitical borders. However, women who are moving back and forth through the geopolitical borders cope with the vulnerability of their lives with an acceptance and appropriation of modalities enacted by the borders. They do not rely on the prism of memory or of metaphors, but create an alternative narrative of borders through telling stories of their personal experiences of border crossings, need for mobility, and experiences of daily lives on borderlands.

Affect, Experience, and Truth: Close Readings of Oral Narratives

Some narratives of women living on the Indo-Bangladesh borderlands have been collected by Paula Banerjee and Anusua Basu Roy Chaudhury in their book *Women in Indian Borderlands*, and Therese Blanchet's *Beyond Boundaries* documents the narratives of women who have migrated or have been trafficked into India from Bangladesh. I will read these in relation to Hondagneu-Sotelo's essay *'I'm here, but I'm there': the Meanings of Latina Transnational Motherhood* focusing on the fragments of interviews of Mexican women who migrate to the United States to work as nannies. A close text reading of the oral narratives prioritizes the interiority of the narrators, to study how 'bifurcated consciousness' is linked to and also shapes the experiences of contemporary borders. The presence of the geopolitical borders between India and Bangladesh and the United States and Mexico, in all their arbitrariness, ambiguity, and porosity, constantly evoke multiple narratives of border crossings. The oral narratives often treated as relevant sociological reports explore how uneven economy across borders influences labour migration, illegal border crossings, and trafficking, but certain ambiguous realms of experiences remain unexplored in reading of these testimonies. Social organizations count upon these personal stories of women to aid their processes of psychological therapy of victims of border violence or to understand the vulnerability of women at the borders.

However, they turn a blind eye towards the significance of these subjective experiences in understanding resistance and modes of negotiation that, in turn, influence formation of identities. My exploration of women's contemporary narratives of lives on the borderlands and of border crossings revealed an unexpected lack of cultural resources except for some sociological documents and NGO reports. This prompted me to use the methodological tools of close text reading to analyze the available testimonies of women to glean insights that do not usually come to the fore through other kinds of methodologies.

If we follow Piyara's story from Therese Blanchet's collection, after sharing her experiences of sexual violence and betrayal by an intermediary, Joynob, who happened to be from her home of origin, she complains:

> Joynob is still after me. She wants my money because she knows I am earning well. A few months ago, she offered to accompany me to get an abortion. I don't know what she fed me but I felt very sick in my head afterwards. She hit me many times. When I told others that she had fed me some harmful medicine, she said I was mad.
> (Blanchet 115)

After she has been socialized into brothel culture, she does not object to sex work anymore but wants to be paid. This becomes her mode of having control over her labour. Interestingly, in her narrative the violence of Joynob starts to take predominance over other forms of violence. If read through the lens of Piyara's subjectivity, while on one hand the response might emerge from a sense of submission to her condition of being trafficked, on the other hand it becomes her means of refusing the state of victimhood inhered in trafficking. In her narrative, she keeps bringing up the betrayal and exploitation that she has faced from Joynob. There is a palpable effort to communicate the loss of trust as an overwhelming pain that she still feels in the face of complete devalorization of her body and existence.

Sita says in her story 'When I had my first menstruation, she took me to Bombay and sold me there to a *malkeen*'. Their memories of crossing the border and entering into sex work radically transform their experience of sexuality. Sita continues:

> Under our *malkeen*, there were 65 girls and I was the youngest. I could not speak Hindi. One day, the police raided our place. In court, I spoke Bangla and said I had come out of my own accord. I was quite tall and I looked older. I was returned to my *malkeen*.
> (Blanchet 119)

Her negotiations with the political border inadvertently also made her aware of linguistic borders that made themselves felt when she was in Mumbai.

While narrating her experience in the court, she says that she affirmed her agency convincingly in Bangla. This mode of claiming linguistic agency becomes important to her notion of holding on identity while crossing borders. After being trafficked to Mumbai, when Sita returned to Kolkata, according to her it feels like home. While it almost remains impossible to be socialized into native homes, the migrant women find their own notions of home on the other side of the border through the passage of language, culture, songs, and even food.

Shyama's story reveals an unusual perspective as she says that when she was sent to the brothel in India for sex work, she had attained 'marriageable age' and so she could cope up with the work. Why does Shyama qualify the age at which girls are usually married off in her village as the appropriate age to be able to cope with sex work? What is the impact that the border has on the body of a girl who is made to cross it at the age of 15, absorbed into sex work, and medicated with contraceptive pills so that she does not become pregnant? How does this experience inform her understanding and negotiations with the idea of marriage? Shyama narrates:

> I started work at an age when girls are married, so I could cope. But my little sister was too young. I did not like this. Sometimes she cried, I felt very sad but there was nothing I could do. We were 60 girls in one building. Quite a few were Nepali. Under one *malkeen*, there were 10 girls. Most days, I did 6 to 7 men, sometimes I did more. Clients were Pakistani, Saudi, Kuwaiti and Indian. At first, I did not like it, and then it was O.K. If a girl refused to work, she was beaten.... My mother was in this line, I was the eldest of the family and I felt responsible for my brothers and sisters. I had to help my mother.
>
> (Blanchet 116)

Shyama's story transcends the culture of silence and guilt, since she is speaking from within a highly controlled brothel. The way she has organized her life, her every day, and her sense of duty towards her family becomes a mode of refusal to consider her state of victimhood in trafficking. She claims agency over her work, particularly, when she candidly mentions that her mother is also in the same profession. She draws parallels between her ability to cope with sex work and the hardship and responsibility that a girl at her age has to take when she is married. The conflation of the experience of trafficking with that of the 'hardships' of marriage, on one hand trivializes her state of victimhood in trafficking and on the other questions the social consensus around the early marriage of a girl child in her village. A remarkable compassion as well as contradiction can be noticed in the way she feels bad for her younger sister. Though she says that her little sister is 'too young' to be absorbed into sex work, her sister was 13, only, two years younger to

Shyama, when she had entered the profession. So, in a way she slips into the role of a protective mother when she talks about her sister. What knowledge is specific to this female body that has a different experience of sexuality, of marriage, of deprivation of biological motherhood in the context of crossing the border? This is how a gendered body enters an alternative history that questions the official discourse of nation, of the gender roles, of the social stereotypes sanctioned by the nation-state.

Mala's story unravels two other very important aspects that find resonances in the other narratives. She narrates:

> Sitadi always visits our village with her Kabuli husband. That is why people do not suspect her profession and she could convince my parents. She changed my name to Menuka. It is the name of a goddess. Now I am that goddess.
>
> (Blanchet 125)

Each of these women has a story to tell, a story of violence, a story of insertion into another culture, a story of socializing, a story of a name. Noticeably not only are identities made ambiguous but the process of naming has an unspoken narrative of its own. Most of the women who have crossed over the border from Bangladesh and entered sex work have taken up names like that of Sita, Shyama, and Menuka. All of these names carry specific iconic/religious connotations related to codes of honour, chastity, virtuosity, and divinity in traditional Hindu mythology. According to mythology, Sita, the central female protagonist in the epic *Ramayana*, is described as the daughter of the earth. She symbolizes the ideal chaste wife. Shyama, meaning the dark-complexioned, is one of the many forms of the Hindu mother-goddess Kali who represents nature in its most elemental state. Menuka, in traditional Hindu mythology, is considered to be the most beautiful *apasara* (dancer of heaven), who was sent to the earth to break sage Visvamitra's penance. Menuka thus symbolizes celestial beauty. The women, through different modes of transaction across borders, rupture each of these traditional socially acceptable notions of chastity, motherhood, beauty, and fertility as they claim the symbolic names of the respective icons. This act of drawing upon cultural archetypes to name themselves represents a mode of dealing with the sense degradation and loss of dignity in incidents of border crossing. Through this subjective choice of taking on specific names, these women appropriate as well as add newer interpretations to the existing social archetypes of womanhood associated with traditional mythology. Interestingly, the religious icons are also rendered fluid and porous in legitimizing different kinds of gendered identity in cross-border transactions. Their experiences of the border are aesthetically structured in a manner such that the testimonies are referred to as 'stories'. The indeterminate zone between fact and 'poetic' truth is foregrounded in the telling of 'stories' such that the truth of the narratives lies embedded in how they are told, in which specific circumstances they are told, and in understanding why one chooses to tell them in the particular way that they narrated.

Another common trope of these 'stories' of migration is the presence of a 'guardian' figure who sanctions the movement of a girl from her native village to the other side of the border. The narratives of labour migration or that of trafficking essentially involve the presence of a guardian figure from within the known community, a *mashi* (an aunt-like figure in Bengali), an uncle, a close relative, or a neighbour. This is rooted to a traditional symbolic order that sanctions the migration of women beyond the boundaries of their 'domestic' worlds if they are accompanied by their husbands/guardians. The women, while crossing borders, appropriate this dominant symbolic order that defines the honour of their families. Even during the period of nation-construction in India in the 19th century, this symbolic order was used to define the principle of *sahadharmini* – an ideal companion to the man who is synonymous to the nation. Strangely, the same symbolic order is appropriated by women when traffickers in the garb of husbands/guardians facilitate the process of border crossing. A woman given in marriage easily obtains the moral sanction of the community and the nation-state at large, which, in turn, allows the migration of the woman. The cultural consensus around these codes of morality makes the borders porous thereby creates a narrative of mobility across the borders as well as allows migrant women to return and socialize in their native villages. Sita escapes the suspect of her community since she returns with a 'kabuli' husband. Sita appropriates the moral sanction surrounding marriage to cross over so many borders within border: border of sexual chastity, the cultural border within a community, the border of the traditional configuration of a marriage, and, finally, the border dividing nation-states. Sita forges modes of her sustenance as well as means to return to her native village by 'taking on' a husband. It is interesting to understand the gap that lies between human desire to be accepted, to socialize, to return to one's home, and the social norms that dictate practices and behavior. Sita moves across the border with a 'kabuli' husband, and her village community also accepts her return without probing into her marriage. This story reveals the futility of these social codes of moral surveillance.

The narratives of border crossings, of fear and violence, of the abrasive formations of nation-state shape our understandings of ourselves and our communities, leading us to create borders within borders. These narratives are situated within the broader problematic of partitioned self. The nation-state and the territorial implications of its borders often push the subject towards a partitioned self. The self under oppression seeks to articulate its subjectivity – a bordered subjectivity that is collective as well as personal, that is a result of the convulsions of history but has to find home beyond that moment in history. Undoubtedly, my theoretical discussion on the metaphorical border hinges upon Gloria Anzaldúa's much commented and cited work Borderlands/*La Frontera*. Metaphors like the 'migrant' (Hall), 'nomad' (Bradotti), 'frontier' (Grosberg), 'hybrid' (Bhabha), 'circuit' (Rouse), 'fringe' (Burgin), 'margin' (Hutcheon) evoke an alternative cognitive map in the contemporary discourse of border studies. The nature of the U.S.–Mexico border is a nuanced one wherein the northern Mexican border serves from the one side as a definitive barrier and from the other as an inconsequential (immaterial, metaphorical) line. Gloria Anzaldúa celebrates the 'hybrid progeny' and consciousness that results at the confluence of races, due to a constant 'crossing over' (Anzaldúa 99). It is this consciousness that is articulated through a class-specific, gender-specific, and colour-specific subjectivity of border women. The constant 'crossing over' is thus a socio-cultural phenomenon that underlies the porous nature of 'borders'. She writes:

> Cradled in one culture, sandwiched between two cultures, straddling all three cultures and their value system, la *Mestiza* undergoes a struggle of flesh, a struggle of borders, and an inner war.
> (Anzaldúa 100)

Anzaldúa's articulation holds deep significance while analyzing the growing phenomenon of transnational motherhood across the U.S.–Mexico border. Anzaldúa bordered consciousness finds resonance in the very title of Hondagneu-Sotelo's essay '*I'm here, but I'm there': the Meanings of Latina Transnational Motherhood*. The women's narratives from India–Bangladesh border that foreground the changing meanings of family constructions gave me an entry point into a further complicated issue of transnational motherhood with similar implications in the context of Latina immigrant women who work as nannies or housekeepers in Los Angeles while their children are left in their places of origin. These immigrant women from Mexico and Central America construct alternative models and meanings of motherhood that contradict the white, middle-class ideological model of privatized, isolationist motherhood in the United States. These transnational mothers, spanning national borders, forge new terrains in developing alternative strategies of mothering that are implicitly gendered, racial and class based. Borders here become even more nuanced with the category of race intersecting with the wide spectrum of class and economic divides that inform subjectivity. Within a broad historical paradigm, the women who migrate or are trafficked into sex work across the Indo-Bangladesh border are refused the claim over biological motherhood by statist hegemony, while Latina women who are forced to 'leave back' their biological children to cross national borders for employment in the United States are constructing an alternative paradigm of motherhood in the United States. In this context, I emphasize the creation of a new subjectivity, an autonomous identity by re-defining motherhood across a different spatial and cultural coordinate.

Transnationalist proponents argue that the international circulation of people, goods, and ideas create new transnational cultures, identities, and community spheres. Even the ashrams (shelter homes) that sprouted up in post-partition India for accommodating women who chose to have their kids rather than be rehabilitated into their 'original' families, became new community spheres for mixing of ideas and sharing of stories. These fluid spaces are firstly organized along principles of gender and they emerge as semi-autonomous spaces in their own right. One common characteristic that builds into these spaces is indeterminacy of settlement, places of uncertainty that nevertheless transcend national borders.

As Evelyn Nakano Glenn puts it, 'Mothering is not just gendered but also racialized' (Hondagneu-Sotelo and Avila 551). More than often, the ideal of solo mothering at home is prescribed and perpetrated by the rapid industrialization and urbanization programs as well as by transforming family configurations. Transnational mothers, in a way, challenge both cultural models of white, middle-class motherhood as well as Latina motherhood. While the white, middle-class mothers subscribe to the model of solo privatized mothering, the Latina women often integrate their children into the workplace. In both cases, however, mothers are with their children. Transnational mothers are in contrast separated from their children by time, space, and culture. They are engaged in occupation that is segregated not only by race, class but also by nationality/citizenship. Hondagneu-Sotelo and Ernestine Avila interview a few women, who are transnational mothers, to understand how they reformulate their own notions of mothering to address the spatial and temporal gulfs. I will explore fragments of interviews of 26 women who work as house cleaners and as live-out or live-in nanny-housekeeper in the Riverside County of Los Angeles.

Transnational motherhood comes with a rejection of the ideal of the biological mothers raising their own children. When interviewed, most live-in nannies who leave their children 'back home', in order to earn, make a distinction in saying that their stance is not abandonment of their children, even if they do not return. On a material level of analysis there is a gendered demand of this job in the United States that requires an immigrant to be free of family obligations in order to acquire work as a live-in nanny. A Salvadoran woman says that she plays her role as a mother by sending in money for her sons back home. Her physical absence is not, according to her, to be counted as her emotional absence. Thus, she is distributing herself psychologically across the national borders by re-positioning her sense of motherhood. Another woman, working as a live-in nanny in the United States sums up this stance when she said 'I'm here, but I'm there' to her two daughters in El Salvador, over the phone. Another curious instance is that of a woman who has got all her legal papers in the United States, has been living there for the last 19 years but says that she doesn't want her children to come there and work for low wages. This shows that even legal papers sanctioned by the state do not ensure a permanent sense of settlement for many of these immigrant women. The displacement and the sense of economic deprivation get psychologically ingrained in a manner that force them to weave newer modes of resistance while inhabiting the same geographical space. Moreover, at times, the class status of the transnational mothers in their country of origin, stemming from her role in the professional field and her status as the employer of another care-giver back home plays into her sense of divided self. Her bordered subjectivity is determined by the parameters that she adheres to as an employer, a mother, and a working professional. Contradictions spell out in the respondents' interview when they say that labour migration is not a form of 'abandonment' of their children. Carolina as well as Emelia call it a 'sacrifice'. They are thus trying to formulate a new model of motherhood by replacing the image of the 'ideal mother' as a care-giver with that of a breadwinner. When Carolina, a Guatemalan woman was interviewed, she indicated other nuanced barriers. She talks of her apprehension at touching the young girl whom she tended. The apprehension comes from a historical 'othering' ensuing from racial discrimination while the need of the self to love someone informs the bordered subjectivity. This ambiguity remains at the core of such intersection of race and borders. The indeterminacy sinks in further when the impermanence of the job looms large. Though it's a job in which the nanny is required to replace the mother as a care-giver, the contract is finite. The uncertainty of the relationship leaves the space fluid thus rupturing the emotional traffic as well. Contemporary global configurations give rise to transnational motherhood that continues the colonial legacy of incorporating women of colour into the United States through unequal and coercive relations across national borders and systems of labour which do not recognize family rights. Ursula Biemann writes 'The border is a highly gendered region. Economic power relations along the lines of gender difference are spelled out in sexual terms' (Biemann, 29–47). Studies on transnational motherhood is a more recent development, which brings to the fore the coercive state laws that disrupt family ties and do not address the individual's question of choice and agency.

Amy Sara Carroll suggests that the Border functions as a Mobius strip for rethinking questions of the (re)production of space, postmodernism, deterritorialization, and re-territorialization. Thus, the U.S.–Mexico borders can be looked upon as a system with multiple and slippery meanings in which the borderland become a space for identity production. Additionally, the borderlands exemplify the gap between the border's iconicity and the everyday allegorical practices of bordering. Traditionally, the border territory is conflated with the female body and the 'woman' is portrayed as the borderlands' victim. Amidst these metaphorical theorization of borders, an attempt to study the women's narratives is to validate the presence of 'bordered subjectivity' of women in these narratives which is in struggle with the capitalist/neo-liberalist ideology of commodification and to develop an adequate theoretical lens to study these narratives. While the 'border' becomes a central category of analysis, it is important to unpack the several registers of the border. The way in which the northern Mexican border functions makes it extremely paradoxical: from the one side it serves as a definitive barrier and from the other as an inconsequential (immaterial, metaphorical) line that is constructed and dismantled through cultural discourse.

The new meanings and arrangements of motherhood created by transnational Latina immigrants eke out a new idiom that does not resemble that of their home country or of the destination. The cultural institutions of industrialization and urbanization as well as cultural ideologies and symbols like that of Catholicism and Virgin Madonna have idealized solo mothering and cast employment as oppositional to motherhood. Traditional models of motherhood and femininity in Mexico and Central America are prescribed through cultural archetypes like that of Virgin de Guadalupe on one hand and negative femininity through that of La Malinche and La Llorona on the other.[1] Latina women, unlike middle-class white women, need to work for pay and they forge out income earning strategies that also help them negotiate with the notions of 'idealized' mothering. So, they engage themselves in sewing jobs or other kinds of jobs that they can do from home while looking after children or they incorporate their children into their workplaces while doing agricultural work, domestic work, and others. However, in both cases the mother is in close proximity with the child. The arrangement of transnational motherhood predicated upon segregation not just of gender but of race, class, and nationality/citizenship sharply contrasts these traditional models and separates the mother from her children across huge gaps of time and geographical space. It is important to understand how these women reconfigure their notions of motherhood mediated by the experience of being a nanny that involves the act of mothering in some of their employers' home across borders. The women who migrate as transnational mothers transgress certain traditional models of family and motherhood. First, working as a domestic help or a live-in or live-out nanny do not always pay enough money to raise a 'family wage', but the woman's dignity plummets down the social hierarchy in the places of 'origin'. Secondly, the work entails a temporal and spatial segregation from community, home, children, and family. Thus, the structures of the social and the personal such as family and motherhood, imposed by the nation-state, are appropriated and re-inflected in modes of resistance by women who are trafficked or who cross borders for labour migration in the context of the Indo-Bangladesh as well as U.S.–Mexico borders.

A Salvadoran woman, working as nanny in the United States says:

> I've been here 19 years, I've got my legal papers and everything. But I would have to be crazy to bring my children here. All of them

> have studied for a career, so why would I bring them here? To bus tables and earn minimum wage? So they won't have enough money for bus fare and food?
>
> (Hondagneu-Sotelo and Avila 558)

Paradoxical meanings surface from these testimonies. The women initially come for a finite period of time but they end up staying for long periods to earn money. The trope of gradually bringing along children is ubiquitous in many narratives since it relates to the efforts of re-rooting oneself and finding a home in the new country. But, in some cases, as in the case here, the experience of racial and class-based discrimination and exploitation is so strong that one would rather have her children build their careers in their places of 'origin' rather than travel to the United States even if it is legitimized. Contrary to this, she replaces her indignity of working as a nanny in the United States, by her ability to send money for a proper education of her children. Motherhood, thereby, in many narratives is re-defined through the responsibility of breadwinning rather than that of physical care-giving. Maria Elena, who has left behind her 13-year-old son with his father in Mexico to work as a transnational mother echoes a different sentiment. She says:

> You cannot give love through money. I came here but we are not apart. We talk (through telephone), I know (through telephone conversations) when my son is fine. I can tell when he is sad by the way he speaks.
>
> (Hondagneu-Sotelo and Avila 564)

She tries to bridge the polarity that is created between an ideal mother who gives her child care and one who stays away from her child for employment. While some transnational mothers emphasize the worth of their earnings to rear their children back home, some like Elena foreground the primacy of emotional traffic that a mother shares with her children despite the physical separation. Both are modes of resisting the cultural stigma that devalorizes certain forms of motherhood.

Transnational Central American and Mexican mothers rely on a system of shared mothering for their children back home because the concept of collective, shared mothering prevails in Latina culture as opposed to individualistic mothering. They articulate a reliance on biological ties, particularly on their own mothers rather than the child's father's mother. This sense of trust can be understood through the subjective bond that a woman shares with her mother in relation to giving care to one's own child. A woman remarks 'As Hispanas we do not believe in bringing someone else in to care for our children' (Hondagneu-Sotelo and Avila 560). The assertion is rooted in her belief in a cultural value system. A paradox appears in the way they resist the mothering of a paid care-giver for their own children while they themselves earn as transnational mothers.

Another important aspect of subjectivity of a transnational mother reveals itself when one points at the difference in dignity with which she treats her child's care-giver back at home and the way she is treated by her employer. A Honduran woman, a former biology teacher, who had left her four sons with a paid care-giver shares the following experience.

> We are very different back there...we treat them (domestic workers) with a lot of affection and respect, and when they are taking care of our kids, even more so. The Americana, she is very egotistical. When the nanny loves her children, she gets jealous. Not us. We are appreciative when someone loves our children, and bathes, dresses and feeds them as though they were their own.
>
> (Hondagneu-Sotelo and Avila 561)

The bordered subjectivity of this woman is implicated not just by class but by race. She thinks of her relationship with her child's care-giver as matters of affect and emotion while, on the contrary, she expresses disappointment about the indignity with which she is treated by her employer. So, the denial of emotional ties and respect affects her more than the uneven economy and deprivation across the cultural borders.

Another nuanced experience entails the nanny's bonding with the employer's children and the sudden disruptions of it due to issues of mistrust or termination of contract. An ambiguity of experience lies in the profession of care-giving where labour is also related to affection and acts of bonding. Can this labour be segregated from the emotion invested in the act of care-giving? Carolina mentions that she tried to treat her employer's children with the same affection that she had for her own children. She says:

> I love these children, but now I stop myself from becoming too close. Before, when my children weren't here (United States) I would give all my love to the children I cared for. That was my recompensation (for not being with my children). When the job ended it hurt so much. I can't let that happen again.
>
> (Hondagneu-Sotelo and Avila 565)

The emotional ties with the employer's kids often turn into disruptive experiences of mothering. Though the terms of the job are contractual, it is associated with indignity along with economic exploitation. The subjectivity shaped by the nature of the job cannot be quantitatively measured or analyzed in terms of labour. The de-humanized treatment often meted out by the employers is predicated upon a dissociation of body/labour from the mind/affect. So a study of these narratives of transnational mothers becomes important in understanding how relationships are arranged across borders while Latina women are being incorporated into the United States through coercive labour systems without a recognition of their emotional ties or family rights.

'Bordered Subjectivity' in the Context of Border Theorizations

I would like to draw upon the premise of 'intersectionality' developed by Cora Kaplan and push it further to look at the intersections of border and gender. Kaplan discusses how subjective identity is shaped by the intersections of class and gender and must be analyzed through a lens that recognizes this overlap. An attempt to study these women's narratives would be to validate the presence of 'bordered subjectivity' of women in these narratives which is in struggle with the capitalist/neo-liberalist ideology of commodification. While 'border' becomes a central category of analysis, it is important to unpack the several registers of border. The way in which the northern Mexican border functions makes it extremely paradoxical: from the one side it serves as a definitive barrier and from the other as an inconsequential (immaterial, metaphorical) line that is constructed and dismantled through cultural discourse. Interestingly, the articulation of bordered subjectivity of women had to be discerned from their multiple testimonies and interviews. The absence of women's border writings from the India–Bangladesh as well as U.S.–Mexico borders prompts us turn towards testimonies as sites that validate the innumerable registers of border – intimate-space in 'memory', the space in the 'body', the space in 'psyche', which in turn challenge notions of state territoriality and patriarchal ideologies. In the book *Border Women*, Castillo and Cordoba refers to Norma Cantú's articulation in her introduction to 'Canícula' where she writes 'life in la frontera is raw truth, and stories of such life, fictitious as they may be, are even truer than true' (Castillo and Cordoba 108). Thus, as she moves towards fiction, she feels a compelling need to establish a certain claim on the essential truth of her work: 'I was calling the work fictional autobiography, until a friend suggested that they really are ethnographic and so if it must fit a genre, I guess it is fictional autobio-ethnography' (Castillo and Cordoba 108). In such a work, the claim to veracity is related to an articulation or rather structuring of subjective truth that is informed by the metaphorical as well as material presence of the border. Rosina Conde has declared that even before taking cognizance of the geographical border, the first border she was made aware of was the border of gender. As discussed in *La Frontera*, in an interview Rosario Sanmiguel said that she does not remember of living in a world without borders:

> The border is a very violent space. It strikes at you from every angle. The fact is that the US is right next to us and the Migra is constantly

> watching our coming and going. The border is the way in which we dwell and walk through all its spaces. We all swarm through the air and intertwine: rich and poor, Mexicans and Chicanos, cholos and preppies, men and women, heterosexuals and homosexuals, First World and Third World. The border is violent but fascinating. When you discover every nook and cranny, you cannot stay away from it.
>
> (Castillo and Cordoba 8)

Such an articulation of the border seeks to re-orient the daily lives across borders through a new set of conceptualization of lived spaces – the streets, the home, the air, the earth, and the body. In this context, Parweena Bibi's testimony collected in the book *Women in the Borderlands* holds rich symbolic meaning in terms of how the presence of the border confers a different 'everyday'. She stays in village named Hatkhola in the border district of Nadia and has to cross the border daily, to visit a relative, to go to the market, to tend the field, or to send her children to school. She says:

> To go out to the other side, we have to keep our IDs with the border (security) people. When our children go to school they have to keep their IDs. When my husband goes to tend to the fields, he has to submit the ID. When I take him some lunch, I have to keep my ID with them. When people come to visit us from the other side they have to keep their ID with them. If we go to the market, the hospital or any other place it's the same. At 6 p.m. they close the gates, and lift for the day ends for us.
>
> (Bhaduri 183)

This practice becomes a ritual of their everyday lives in a manner that it is normalized as a daily practice. The sense of identity, related to social behavior, is confined to a piece of paper. But what implications of 'home' does it bear for the psyche which has to constantly submit to state vigilance for going in or out of one's own home? How are relationships across borders transformed when one has to submit an ID card for visiting neighbours? The connotation of an ID card in itself is simultaneously appropriated to meet the parameters that would license mobility in the everyday. The borderland dwellers use the ID card to carry on with the regular activities of their lives, to meet neighbours and family on the other side while they refuse to accept the ID card as a marker of their identity. The negotiations and appropriations at the personal level, despite these ritualistic practices of surveillance serve to unfold the porosity of the border.

> We cannot cultivate the more lucrative items like papaya, which fetches a good price. No, everything has to be just three feet tall, so

> we have 'path' and paddy. During harvest, we have to specify the number of sacks of harvest we will be collecting and have to enter them in their register. Now, just tell me, is it possible to be absolutely accurate? Sometimes we may enter a certain number and then have a sack or two extra, but that will just be confiscated by them.
> (Bhaduri 183)

When asked what the border means to her as a woman who lives on the borderland, Parweena unexpectedly related it with her inability to grow a tree beyond three feet height since it will obstruct the surveillance system of the border guards. Her experience of the presence of the border relates to the way it curtails her subjective relationship with nature. Amidst discourses on strict militarization of the border and normative punishment meted out to violators, Parweena Bibi's story punctures the national narratives and technology of the border thus bringing a new kind of subjectivity to the fore. Her articulation foregrounds that the way in which the presence of the border curtails her subjective relationship with nature takes predominance in her chambers of affect over other forms of violence and repression cast by geopolitical borders.

Radha Rani Das, a 45-year-old Hindu woman, migrated from Khulna, Daulatpur in Bangladesh. One of her daughters, her brother, and her mother live in Bangladesh. Her husband died of an ailment and she lives in Basirhat, a border town in West Bengal. She narrates how her experience of crossing over the border also resulted in partitioning herself; she could never find 'home' on any of the sides of the border.

> We had both Muslim and Hindu neighbours. But Muslims were the majority in numbers and that's why I had to come away... Say, they tortured my daughter. I know that if any girl looks nice they are abducted, there were two goons after my daughter. They are Muslims we are Hindus. If they harass a girl then all our pride and respect is gone. Isn't it? Unable to bear the torture we came away here. They said that in that country you have everything. What luck! Now I have to work to survive. In that country, no woman, no (house) wife ever went to work outside. In this country I am working. I run my household myself I am working in another's house and surviving. I don't have any respect. I am surviving. After crossing the border, we were put up at someone's place for the night. It was the broker who had arranged to put us up. Next day we came here to Bashirhat. It was the first time that we had come to this country. Before coming, I did not think a lot about India, but people there (in Bangladesh) used to say that it was good in India. I could live in peace with my children. People used to recommend that I go to India, so that I could live in relative safety and security with my children. That is why we came

> away. After coming here I found it was true. Now it's all the same, as I won't get the same people I had left behind back home any more. Here no one harasses us. We are free here. No one tries to take advantage of us. I can depend on my neighbours if any need help. But no political leader has done anything for us.
>
> However, I always miss Bangladesh. Sometimes I cry for it. But I cannot return to it. How will I go back home?
>
> (Bhaduri 200)

The incoherence in narration is a telling device to understand the spilt in one's consciousness. While on one hand she embodies the societal codes of honour and the loss of it, the constructed fear of the 'other' religion, on the other she reiterates that she misses Bangladesh and wants to go back 'home'. Displacement created such a deep rupture in her that she is unable to come to terms with what denotes 'home'. On one hand she says that now she is free, she feels socially more secured while on the other she says it has amounted to a loss of respect for her. Despite the relative sense of safety, her craving for the people she left behind underlines how human relationships are built as well as lived beyond the geopolitical 'borders'.

Parweena Bibi spoke about how many women from her village migrate to Mumbai for a better life. She says:

> We don't know how they are, and what life they are leading. We are looking forward to hearing their news. For here there is no future. Also, Mohameddans we hear find it difficult to find jobs in other places.
>
> (Bhaduri 184)

While her apprehensions are ingrained with the perspective of a woman who experiences border at a more psychological and symbolic level, Halima Begum, who migrated to Mumbai for labour, talks about how she has two households: one in Mumbai and another in Jessore. It is interesting to note that many women like Halima earn in Mumbai but buy land and property in Bangladesh. It reveals how they reap the economy of labour migration/trafficking to accumulate land, i.e. settlement in Bangladesh. Many migrant women, who work as bar girls in Mumbai, often 'take' men as husbands to work at home and are paid by the women. This process of 'contract marriages' ascribe a code of chastity on the woman who can then carry on with her work in a more secured surrounding. Sharing a wife's income on a 50–50 basis was considered a fair arrangement by these men while the women readily referred to such partners as 'husbands' for their own security. Such an arrangement brings a strong counterpoint to the question of women's labour at the domestic front within the patriarchal ideology. Interestingly, contract marriages appropriate the moral code conferred on a family arrangement by the nation-state to facilitate illegal migration. This organizational arrangement changes the meaning of marriage just like transnational motherhood in the context of U.S.–Mexico border changes that of motherhood. The definition of motherhood and the meanings of labour and relationships are organized in myriad ways across the border which have a telling effect on the subjectivity of women inhabiting these in-between spaces.

An insightful perspective evolves from Srabanti Karmakar's testimony who is from the village of Haridaspur and who is a constable of the Border Security Force (BSF). Srabanti speaks expansively about her childhood and how she had seen one of her uncles in uniform. The fact that she can also be in the uniform had always inspired her to pursue the dream. She continues:

> My father likes to read newspapers and discuss politics, so since childhood I knew about Pakistan's harmful intentions. Then I came to know about Taliban, that every day there is some blast, some infiltration. Every day one of our jawans is killed on some place in the border or the other. Regarding Bangladesh its' a little different. See wherever there is no fencing they try to take stuff out, so we have to be extremely attentive during our vigils. And where there is fencing we have to be more careful alert, because if any part of the fence is cut or damaged then we have to pay for it. A months' weapon is taken away from us, we have to work 28 days extra over the period which we sign for in the contract.
>
> I am really doing something worthwhile; no woman from my family has worked before. Its' peaceful here, though my village is even better; but I like this work. All the sirs, all the people in the force are really nice, and meet us with a lot of respect. We do miss home, but we all have become like a big family. In fact when we go home on holidays now, we wait eagerly to get back here and exchange all the news. We women constables miss each other when we go away. However, we are told not to be too friendly with the local people here. We are not encouraged to mix with the local people here. The moment we become friendly with them, they will take advantage and ask us to help them move goods across the border. The Bangladeshis can take things from here precisely because they are helped by people here, so we are not encouraged to interact with the people here much. We keep aloof and maintain our distance. So you see, our work is tough and it's really something for the country. I am so proud of doing this work and of doing something for my country. Honestly, I never thought I would be up to it and reach this place and achieve this. The people in my village today look up

> to me. My mother now says how was I to know that you would become such a big person?
>
> (Bhaduri 187)

The narrative of her life sounds like an inspirational success story of a woman from a village, who has dared to break societal restrictions and has achieved her dream. But the rhetoric of the nation-state and the way in which it creates the stereotype of a strong woman, who is like a man and thus is fit to be incorporated into the duty of the state, resonates strongly in her narrative. The modern nation-state uses a strategy of ruling in which by giving one the assumption of being a free autonomous subject, the state has a stronger control over the subject. Srabanti takes a lot of pride in asserting that she is not married and has never thought of marriage. Marriage and family ties are posited as oppositional to the image of this woman in the BSF and the subject adheres to it in ignorance of the erasure of her desire. She uses the violent rhetoric of the nation-state when she speaks of the hatred towards Pakistanis. Her bordered experience comes to the surface whenever her articulations about the hardships faced on duty is punctured by the pride that her community takes in her achievement. This slippage informs her entire narrative as she aesthetically structures it almost as a journey through hurdles towards success.

By emphasizing the presence of hybridity, characterized by contradictions and incoherence in narrations, this work explores whether partitioning across borders in the era of globalization, pushes its subjects towards a partitioned self, thus making the geopolitical divide just one of the many borders that a subject copes with. The creative ways in which daily lives are organized across borders, like, for instance, through a re-articulation of motherhood, marriage, relationships with the earth and nature, suggest the relative permeability of the border. A close reading of the narratives of women through the lens of subjectivity prompted me to recognize how the homophone 'defying the nation' as opposed to 'deifying' the nation finds validity in the acts and articulations of the border women. As discussed, the women forge subjective modes of resistance and negotiation for survival and for claiming identity in their encounters with borders in the context of crossing or living on the borderlands. In the course of their negotiations, they rupture the patriarchal hegemony embedded in nationalist ideologies by appropriating the models of 'ideal' family, 'ideal' motherhood, and chastity and morality determined by the nation-state.

Note

1 Virgen de Guadalupe, also a representation of Virgin Mary, is the cultural icon of Mexico. The image of the Virgin of Guadalupe is of a woman with brown skin, one that and reconciles Mexico's history and blends its Spanish and Aztec heritage.

According to history, La Malinche was a Nahua woman from the Mexican Gulf Coast who was the interpreter and mistress of Spanish Conquistador Hernan Cortes. In Mexican culture, she is perceived as the ambiguous image of the mother who as well the traitor La Llorona (The weeping woman) is the ghost of a woman who lost her children and now cries while searching for her children in the river. Traditionally, she is the image of deviated motherhood.

References

Anzaldúa, Gloria. 1987. *La Frontera.* San Francisco: Aunt Lute Books.

Bhaduri, Aditi. 2011. "Voices of Women in the Borderlands." In *Women in Indian Borderlands.* Eds. Paula Banerjee and Anusua Basu Ray Chaudhury. New Delhi: Sage Publications: 179–202.

Biemann, Ursula. 2002. "Performing the Border." *Rethinking Marxism, 14,* 1: 29–47 https://dms213fall2015.files.wordpress.com/2015/09/performingtheborder.pdf (Accessed 22 March 2017).

Blanchet, Therese. 2002. *Beyond Boundaries: A Critical Look at Women Labour Migration and the Trafficking Within.* Dhaka: USAID.

Castillo, Debra and Kavita Panjabi (Eds.) 2011. *Cartographies of Affect: Across Borders in South Asia and the Americas* Kolkata: Worldview Press.

Castillo, Debra A. and Maria Socorro Tabuenca Cordoba. 2002. *Border Women: Writing from La Frontera.* London: University of Minesota Press.

Hondagneu-Sotelo, Pierrette and Ernestine Avila. 1997. "I'm Here but I'm There: The Meanings of Latina Transnational Motherhood." *Gender and Society, 11,* 5: 548–571.

Kaplan, Cora. 1997. "Pandora's Box: Subjectivity, Class and Sexuality in Socialist Feminist Criticism." In *Feminisms: An Anthology of Literary Theory and Criticism.* Eds. Robyn R. Warhol and Diane Price Herndl. New Jersey: Rutgers University Press.

Further Reading

Banerjee, Paula. 1998. "Refugee Repatriation: A Politics of Gender." *Refugee Watch,* Issue No. 1, January www.mcrg.ac.in/rw%20files/Rw1.doc#ref (Accessed December 2016).

Banerjee, Paula. 1998. "Refugee Women: The Forgotten Majority." *Refugee Watch,* Issue No. 4, December www.mcrg.ac.in/rw%20files/RW4.DOC (Accessed 15 September 2016).

Banerjee, Paula. 2002. "Dislocating Women and making the Nation." *Refugee Watch,* Issue no. 17, December www.mcrg.ac.in/rw%20files/Rw17.doc (Accessed December 2016).

Butalia, Urvashi. 2000. *The Other Side of Silence.* Durham: Duke University Press.

Carroll, Amy. S. 2006. "Accidental Allegories Meet the Performative Documentary: *Boystown, Senorita Extraviada,* and the Border-Brothel Maquiladora Paradigm." *University of Chicago Press Journal, 31,* 2: 357–396.

McClennen, Sophia. 2011. "Life in the Red Zones; Or the Geographies of Neoleberalism" In *Cartographies of Affect: Across Borders in South Asia and the Americas*. Eds. Debra Castillo and Kavita Panjabi. Kolkata: Worldview Press: 165–191.

Mohanty, Chandra Talpade. 1984. "Under Western Eyes: Feminist Scholarship and Colonial Discourses." *Boundary 2*, *12*, *3* and *13*, 1, Spring–Autumn: 338–358.

Mufti, Aamir R. 2004. "Towards a Lyric History of India." *Boundary*. 2, May: 245–274.

Schendel, Willem Van. 2001. "Working Through Partition: Making a Living in the Bengal Borderlands." *IRSH*, *46*, 3: 393–421.

Part II

PHOTOGRAPHY

The Ethics of 'Evidence' and Erasure/Elision

3

ABDUCTION/OBLIVION

Villafuerte's *Por el lado salvaje*

Debra A. Castillo

Early in Nadia Villafuerte's[1] novel, *Por el lado salvaje* (On the wild side), one of the author's central point-of-view characters, Lía – the middle school age daughter of a poor Afro-Mexican maid from the southern border town of Paredón, Chiapas – finds a dictionary in the house of her friend, Margit. She reads: 'Abducción: acción de atar a alguien y llevarlo a algún sitio. Bombay, Beirut, Tel Aviv, Cairo, Kyoto…' 'Abduction: the action of tying someone up and taking them elsewhere' (loc 77). In this quick, almost throw-away line, Villafuerte hints at the tensions that will be prevalent throughout this text and that set up the pitiless aesthetic of the novel we have just begun to read. The foreshadowing implicit in the choice of the word 'abduction', followed by a non-standard definition, prepares us for a titillating tale of force and trauma, of child trafficking in exotic locales that provide a touch of travelogue spice. And yet, in the course of the novel, while Lía is often coerced, she never conceives of herself as an abducted child despite the horrific things that happen to her. Instead, she tends to imagine herself as a free agent, operating within an intriguing field of possibility, rather than the victim of sexual and physical abuse (she is also that, of course).

She gets no farther from home on her journey to the south than the dangerous city of La Ceiba, Honduras ('este paisaje horrible que parece salido del realismo socialista chileno' 'this horrible landscape that looks like it came out of Chilean socialist realism' loc 135), and no further north than the no less dangerous city of Tijuana ('Podía haberse llamado de otra manera, la ciudad a la que va, Beijing, Budapest, y a ella le habría dado lo mismo' 'it could have gone by any other name, the city she's going to, Beijing, Budapest, it would have made no difference to her' loc 131), and while these Latin American cities are both tourist destinations, they are far less exotic ones for the reader than Kyoto or Beirut. For Lía, of course, the cruel, cruddy environment changes very little as she moves from one toxic location to another. She does not arrive to either of these cities as a tourist, but rather as a member of a group of itinerant migrants who are precariously employed

DOI: 10.4324/9780429356421-6

and consistently exploited by international visitors and exiles to these cities. Despite this situation, and perhaps by contrast with the profoundly poverty-stricken environment of her Mexican border hometown, she sees hopeful prospects in each of them. This novel, then, lays out the intersection of inhumanity and illegality in conditions of extreme marginalization, but refuses to wallow in the abject. Instead, Villafuerte continually pulls us up short with her bracing, astringent perspective.

The use of a child's perspective to uncover a harsh reality is not innovative, of course. Many authors have done so, from Mexican Juan Rulfo's magnificent short story, 'Macario' to Irish-Canadian Emma Donoghue's novel *Room*, as well as Villafuerte herself in other tales. For instance, the first chapters of *Por el lado salvaje* rework the story of an adolescent prostitute named Elena/Helena and her transvestite lover/pimp Glen/Glenda, as told from Glenda's perspective in the novella 'Te gusta el latex, cielo?' (found in the collection of the same title).[2] Villafuerte's focus on child/adolescent figures in her narrative reminds us in a very particular, very practical way of how often the melodramatic stories we tell ourselves secure a specific imaginary context for making ethical statements, for emitting judgments that have life and death consequences. Coviello writes:

> Nothing seems to speak so directly of what we value – of what kind of world we wish to make – as how we imagine children. . . . Freighted with the burdens of purity, innocence, varieties of nostalgia and self-memorialization, as well as with the burden of unforeclosed possibility – of futurity itself – children have offered a vehicle for meaning that is compelling for the range of affects it can speak to all at once. . . . One of the things this has meant is that children are *useful* to us: we use them, often quite ruthlessly, to tell ourselves things we need to believe.
>
> (135)

The image of burdening and the word 'ruthlessly' stand out here, and seem to me eminently appropriate to describe as well Villafuerte's exacting use of children in her tales of missteps, abuse, and minimal survival. Her characters too are weighted down with unrealizable expectations, while at the same time a ruthless aesthetic cuts through any inclination towards nostalgia: 'las historias deben ser breves como los alkaseltzers, incómodas con las resacas' 'stories should be as short as Alka Seltzer, as uncomfortable as hangovers,' she writes (*Por el lado salvaje* loc 1752). Among the questions Coviello asks us to consider is how the story of the innocent child (a story that we do not believe, although we pretend that we do) is integral to the story of the nation we need to keep retelling obsessively in order to consolidate languages of belonging and mutuality (153). For him, the image of the menaced child is key to this inherently unstable conception of nation. National cohesion derives from a shared understanding of the child's vulnerability and the commitment of the nation to protecting its innocent, menaced future (137). Nothing, argues Coviello, more strongly speaks to the national need for that burdened, damaged child than the evocation of scenes of sexuality, 'not least because sex remains one of the most reliable catalysts for the evocation of scenes of shock or trauma or loss. For a number of reasons, such scenes have come to stand at the center of American self-conception' (138).

I would add, further, that this sense of a national narrative derived from the sexually vulnerable child can also be extended to a larger context, in which the burdened child figures as a powerful metaphor for exploitative globalization. The general modes of recognition relating the innocence of the child to the future of the nation become twisted and strange in the border context, where the migrant child's innocence is suspect, and hence presages the wrong kind of future, becoming, in essence, a threat to liberal security and the national self-concept.[3] In that larger context, curiously, the vulnerable child can easily flip to its opposite, the dangerous child, where 'burdened' changes to 'burden', and 'menaced' becomes 'menacing', like a rhetorical analogue to the Rubin's vase optical illusion, which flips from vase to face.

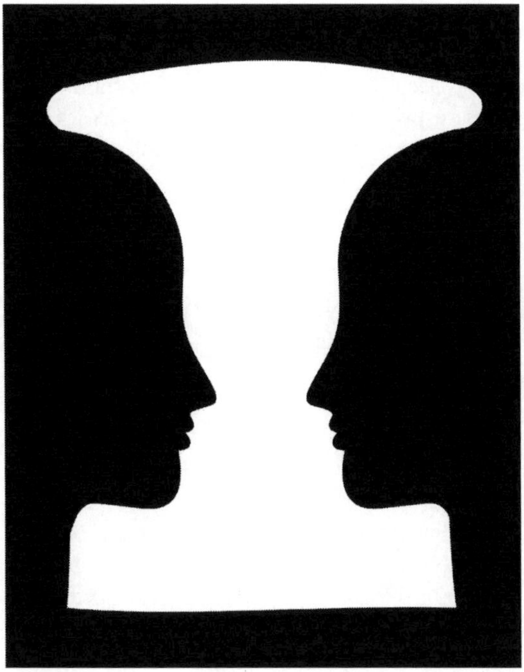

Figure 3.1 Rubin's vase.
Source: Opensource image

In her research for this novel, Villafuerte says she 'realized that violence against women is doubly visible: for their condition of being migrants, and as well as their condition of being women' (Bruic). The increasing awareness of gender-based violence alongside other drivers of immigration like climate change on Central Americans has become especially palpable in discussions of the immigration crisis since the second decade of the 21st century, and Villafuerte's novel seems even more prescient today than when it was published in 2011. In the 2016 interview with Audra Bruic she comments,

> I think it was in 2014 that this crisis became palpable – the crisis of children sent by parents, or their families, to the northern borders to cross over, often into the United States. And I think this crisis of the children is symptomatic of our economic moment that we're living in.

Thus, this novel, which was based on Villfuerte's imaginative retelling of a series of crimes committed in the 1980s in her home region of southern Mexico, speaks a long history of transphobia and violence against women and children in her country, while also – lamentably remaining exceptionally timely in our current moment.

One of the most important underlying considerations for Coviello, as well as other scholars who write on the human rights implications of a focus on children, is that, in general, under the law children formally have less rights than animals (Brysk 32),[4] but this lack of rights tends to remain invisible because of the presumption that the family (and in its absence, the state) will care for the minor child. Thus, for example, Brysk adumbrates how the policy of 'best interests of the child' forecloses autonomy and agency, in effect nullifying legal personhood (36).

For Elizabeth Povinelli, who theorizes state relations to marginalized peoples in her book *Economies of Abandonment*, care is a key concept, and her work complements that of Coviello and Brysk in important ways. Care is socially constructed and has important, if ill-defined, parameters, akin to the parameters Coviello intuits in his understanding of the imaginary vulnerable child as an allegory of nation; likewise, 'care' is an imprecise measure (similar in that sense to the rhetorical reliance on the 'best interests of the child') for rights-based analysis. Povinelli writes:

> To care for others is to make a claim; it is a small theoretical gesture. To care is to embody an argument about what a good life is and how such a good life comes into being. . . . In the first instance, the question is, what do we believe care to consist of, such that when we experience a form of relating to one another socially, we experience that form of relating as a form of caring for others? (160)

This ethical and theoretical gesture comes under pressure in contexts where we normatively believe we should care (i.e. care for/about children) but do not want to care, where two different social structures come into friction, or where we see a conflict between care within the context of our own social structure and care for the undesired, menaced/menacing child. Povinelli continues,

> when the waters recede and the ground stops shaking, empathy also evaporates as ethical sense settles back into doxic accounts of poverty, its causes and consequences. Cost reemerges as a central issue for how to calculate who can or should be protected, relocated, cared for.
>
> (162)

And – I would add – who can legitimately make a claim on 'our' concern.[5] One current example is the incoherence of much of the discussion around the Central American refugee children in the United States, which touts family reunification as the correct, humanitarian solution, even when it means sending the children back into the war zones to the families, who in the first instance sent them north to get them out of harm's way, but at the same time prevents family reunification when the child's family resides in the United States, in which case the child has no right to family (e.g. Brysk 41). Povinelli asks, acutely: 'What does care consist of such that when a form of creating harm for others is thought of and experienced as a form of caring for others?' (58) This question of a failure of care – its theoretical structure and its implications – will, in essence, occupy me for the rest of this paper.

Por el lado salvaje, like all complex, meaty novels, is difficult to summarize without turning it into a caricature; as one of the characters writes:

> esta historia no es la de una puta en ascenso que tarde o temprano acaba muerta o chapaleando en el mismo desagüe que la engendró. De hecho, esta historia comienza cuando termina. Y los relatos nunca terminan, están llenos de huecos, pistas falsas, contradicciones 'this story is not about a whore on her way up who sooner or later ends up dead or back swimming in the same sewer that gave her birth. In fact, this story begins when it ends. And tales never end. They are full of holes, false clues, contradictions.'
>
> (loc 3410)

The central point-of-view characters are Lía (later called Bonnie), a southern Mexican mulatta adolescent, and, to a lesser extent, a marginally employed poet and graffiti writer called Spiderman, from Tijuana, who loves superheroes and John Donne in equal measure (loc 1668). Lía is first convinced by Glen/Glenda (a South American transvestite biologist in charge of an

Honduran insectarium) to follow him/her to La Ceiba, where she works as Glenda's maid and mistress, something both of them see as a completely normative combination of duties.

Glenda describes herself as 'una pésima imitación de Madonna, si usted quiere, una Madonna sudaca' 'a terrible imitation of Madonna, if you like, a greaser Madonna' (loc 171), indicating her own insecurities, and is first attracted to the child because of Lía's deformity (she is missing one arm) and her toxic provenance: 'una sirena tullida saliendo de las aguas contaminadas (desechos tóxicos, petróleo, químicos, sustancias radioactivas construyendo el destello marino que tanto inspira a los poetas)' 'a crippled mermaid arising out of polluted waters (toxic wastes, petroleum, chemicals, radioactive substances shaping the oceanic gleam that so inspires poets' (loc 220). Glenda, who has been amusing herself on the side with sexual relations with another minor, a boy in a drugstore, soon tires of the girl and passes her to Bardem, an exiled Italian pornographer drawn to paedophilia and violence. Bardem, in turn, sells her to a Vietnam veteran called Draco, who sends her to Tijuana with a shoebox of torture photographs for his own obscure purposes. Along the way, a central section of the novel is dedicated to Lía/ Bonnie's relationship with Spiderman in Tijuana; he writes obscure messages on public spaces and she makes anonymous phone calls with obscure sayings (loc 1615). Eventually, she begins to take her own photographs and send 'postcards', which include short narratives about a Colombian in the United States, two Pakistani sisters in Mumbai, and a Philippine terrorist in Cavite, among others.

The importance of the visual referent, especially photography, and to a lesser extent, graffiti art, is crucial in this novel, as it serves as the central point of departure to define Villafuerte's aesthetic project. In the novel, Bardem identifies the subjects of his controversial photographs as Belina, Aldo, and Sera, his children, and the novel describes them as portrayed in nude, often sexually compromised poses. Lía flips through the images: 'Desnúdate' 'Strip naked', Bardem orders her (loc 381), reproducing in this adolescent's body further pornographic images. In context, the relationship between Bardem and Lía, which echoes that of Bardem and his biological children, in turning explicitly exploitative and pornographic responds to a specific imaginary construction of the female child that combines attraction and dread. There is a fascination with the girl child's forbidden sexuality, her potential for waywardness, an image in literary circles often associated with Nabokov's *Lolita*. Precisely because the child should *not* be associated with sexuality, for Bardem, as for Nabokov's protagonist, the two notions are inextricably linked. In Villafuerte's case, however, not only is the child unconscionably knowing, she also suffers under a further triple marginalization: poor, southern Mexican, black.

Bardem's photographs, the reason for his exile to Honduras, are also fundamentally a Rubin's vase evocation of the menaced/menacing child. These photographs of his children are a direct citation of celebrated US photographer Sally's Mann's controversial 1992 series of photographs of her children, Jessie, Emmett, and Virginia, in *Immediate Family*, the book which essentially made her famous. Mann's stunningly beautiful pictures include many in the nude, taken in a rural landscape, playing between a child's grasp of freedom, and an adult's almost inevitable jump to – and refusal of – a more sinister reading, which is both tantalizing and perverse, echoing a parent's worst nightmares about/for their children (abduction, sexual abuse, murder). Lía is attracted to the images, sees their pathos and their burdening: 'son criaturas semejantes a mí: quieren aletear pero no pueden, tal vez no lo hagan nunca' ('they are similar creatures to me; they want to fly but can't, maybe they never will': note how this sentiment reverses Sally Mann's comment about her children, echoing the idea of flight in a very different register. Mann describes the pictures as 'gifts to me from my children; gifts that come in a moment as fleeting as the touch of an angel's wing' 6).

Mann was virulently attacked for these powerful and unnerving images, and her most effective response in silencing the critiques was basically to play the mommy card, a position already intricately laid out in her introduction to the book. In later interviews with her and statements about these pictures, she has consistently decried the darker interpretations of the series, emphasizing her own naïveté in wanting to share their Edenic, playful, joyous qualities, highlighting the innocence of the children and her photographs of them. At the same time, it must be noted that her aesthetic inclination, seen in the context of her larger body of work, tends to be drawn to those extremes where beauty and disgust meld together, playing off contradictory affects (e.g. 2010's *Body Farm*, with its eerie photographs of disintegrating human bodies), thus making her disclaimer about the earlier work seem disingenuous, a quality that Villafuerte picks up on and exploits, with her mental experiment of attributing the same photographs to a father.

Many of the images from *Immediate Family* can be seen on Mann's personal website. One of the most famous and controversial of all the pictures in the book, and often pointed out as the most beautiful of them all, is 'Rodney Plogger at 6:01'. This photograph was famously plagiarized by James Cameron for *Titanic*, appearing as a sketch in Leonardo DiCaprio's character's sketchbook (Bowe), and shows a naked adult man, with his hands framing the abdomen of a tiny naked girl, Mann's daughter, Virginia (www.sallymann.com/new-gallery-1).[6]

The often-ambiguous titles of the photographs belie Mann's protestation of her naïveté: 'Candy' undercuts the overly mature gaze of the preadolescent girl holding the cigarette and turns it into a game that we believe/do not believe; 'Dirty Jessie' plays off expectations of a prurient reading, while insisting that it is about nothing more than a child's revelling in the muddy terrain. Likewise, 'Damaged Child' hints at abuse, when the context is the swelling of Jessie's face due to an insect bite. More mysterious are

'Rodney Plogger' and 'Last Light', where Virginia's tiny body is captured (cradled) between a man's legs and arms. It is worth pointing out here that much of the success of the photographs is due to their technical high quality (their luminosity, the play of chiaroscuro), and part of their attraction is attributable to the beauty of the children themselves, who are not just passive objects of her lens, but spunky, sullen agents in their own right; Mann describes them as collaborators in this book, 'spinning a story of what it is to grow up' (6).

There is another thread to the moral panic adduced by Mann (or Bardem), one that Shannon Walsh accurately defines: 'it seems an easy criticism to level at Mann that she is being negligent to portray her children as sexual beings for the world to see (and implicit in this criticism: "for men to locate, stalk, or potentially abduct")' (Knabe 93). In other words, the children are menaced precisely because of the way in which their parent negligently violates taboos about the care for children and the child's best interests. The anxiety Walsh intuits is precisely the anxiety that Lía identifies early in the novel – that of abduction. The accusation against Mann is one we see frequently in social media contexts a generation later, which defines a menacing world of sexual stalkers and kidnappers as a normative national context, and abduction as the threatening reality that every parent has to guard against. The fantasy of extreme violence, then, forces/allows the readers/viewers to confront (or to repress) their desires towards these children, whose attraction increases because of their presumed helplessness, their inability to consent to anything at all, while at the same time (another Rubin's vase), the children are more delectably exploitable, more desirably abductable, because of their complicity.

In the US national imaginary, the innocent child is generally and tacitly figured as white; here too we measure the impact of Mann's photographs, and their compelling, dreadful ambiguity. The demand that we take the images literally, as Edenic play, rubs up against their spectacularity, against their transgression of cultural norms about white children. Villafuerte, of course, adds race and transnational sex trafficking into the mix, pairing Bardem's lovely, pornographic images with their unlovely darker (in all senses) counterparts. The aesthetic project masks a crime that needs to be revealed and the perpetrator punished. Bardem's dilemma, put in such lurid melodramatic terms, also starkly outlines more obscure issues. How do we trace the limits of caring (for the child) when it flips into desire? How do we desire not to desire? Or, in other terms, how do we parse the ethical dilemma of how not to want (at least in certain public circles) what we desperately want?

One of Villafuerte's signal achievements is the exposure of unsavoury desires as an outgrowth of stunted care, both in a transnational construct and as a consequence of deliberate policy. Her geographically specific southern border perspective also evokes the individually precise borders of the inhabitants' bodies, and especially the bodies of the undesired/undesirable migrant child who experiences violence and also commits violence against others. In Bardem's case, abuse of his own children is ameliorated by aesthetics (though it also provokes an ethical response in some circles) whereas the ordinary suffering of less beautiful bodies creates little interest and falls back into oblivion. Late in the novel, a first-person narrator who sympathizes with Bardem comments about Lía, for example:

> 'yo supe, desde que la vi, que esa niña iba a acabar mal. El origen siempre es el fin. . . . Lía iba a terminar en un sanatorio público o su cuerpo acabará destazado por estudiantes de una facultad de medicina.' 'I knew, ever since I saw her, that the girl was going to end up bad. The origin is always the end. Lía was going to end up in a public insane asylum or her body would be dismembered by students in a medical school'.
>
> (loc 2816)

The narrative 'I' who confirms 'en algo, repito, en mucho me parezco a Bardem', 'in some ways, I repeat, in many ways, I am like Bardem,' also notes that the story that has been told, in the novel that is near to ending, for all its complexity, is less than a third of what the narrator knows, 'pero ya no importa' 'but it no longer matters' (loc 3057). In this respect, the narrative devolves from the spectacular to an ordinary sequence of events, and one not, or no longer, worth our further attention. The child/children whose stories are garbled and bodies have been lost have henceforth no call on our care. That care is implicitly reserved for the desired (and differently burdened) children who participate in the imagined futurity of the nation, whereas Lía and children like her from the toxic wastelands of the global south fit only into a discourse of disposability. They are excessive, finally, not in their narrative potential but only because they are population in excess.[7]

Villafuerte takes as the epigraph of her novel a poem by E.E. Cummings. The original poem is called 'Being' and begins like this:

> being
> twelve
> who hast merely
> gonorrhea (65)[8]

Almost half of the poems about childhood in Cumming's collected works are dark or satiric in ways that echo this poem: in this case focused through the double valence of 'being', both noun and verb, and linking the diminutive qualities of 'merely', 'weeness', and 'tiny' that resonate against the only polysyllabic words in the poem: 'ambitious' and 'gonorrhoea'. The poem, ultimately, is less political than coldly disciplinary – as Villafuerte's translation more overtly posits: What history needs to be uncovered, what can death add to the image of a 12-year-old child with gonorrhoea?

One of the important points that Povinelli would add to this reckoning is that a discussion of accountability needs also to include an analysis of the corrosive effects of toxicity, what she calls the ordinary cruddiness of precarious life anywhere on the margins of dominant civil society: 'Any discussion of the relationship among ordinary exhaustion, quasi events, and endurance in the late liberal governance of difference must be situated within the various ways that eventfulness is distributed.' In this respect, she argues forcefully, claims made based on Giorgio Agamben's theory of 'bare life' are unhelpful (133).

The photographs circulating since Summer 2014 of Immigration Service detention camps capture some of this cruddy, ordinary exhaustion. They are taken in spaces that are overcrowded, underheated, or undercooled; the children have been abandoned in bleak warehouse settings. Reporters and human rights activists have decried the difficulty of gaining access to these children, and when access is achieved, they express dismay at their lack of understanding of their rights, because no one has bothered to inform them about their eligibility for asylum claims. In general, these reporters find the children have less legal support than adults in detention. This treatment of refugee minors has been condemned by Amnesty International, as the processing of minor immigrants frequently includes confinement with criminals, shacking, and strip searches (Brysk 45). We might see how this chaotic processing follows naturally from a failure of care, but also from a legal context in which someone else's children do not achieve full human capacity, hence there is no legitimate call on our obligation to care.

Certainly, these many photographs of children in immigration prisons have been much reproduced, much linked, and they tend to highlight that quality of a lack of care. The children in detention are less individual subjects than a mass of bodies covered with foil heat blankets, almost already cadavers, and certainly without full humanity.

The second important set of photographs in Villafuerte's novel details scenes of torture in Central America: 'cadaveres exhibidos sin pudor, con el descaro del pornógrafo' 'corpses exhibited without shame, with the coldness of the pornographer' (loc 733). Even though Bardem has been fleeing prosecution in Italy as a pornographer who exploited his own children, and has behaved equally reprehensibly in Honduras, these photographs shock and embarrass him. They are, he finds, more pornographic than anything he imagined shooting himself. These are the photographs in the shoebox, the contraband that Lía carries with her to Tijuana, following the author's conceit that trafficking in these images is exactly parallel to human or drug trafficking: just as illegal, just as attractive, just as addicting. Bardem and

Draco's goal is to make money by selling them in the United States, where 'ya los historiadores y restauradores se encargarán de exhibirlas, de llevarlas al altar y multiplicar su precio. No hay nada más fresco y eternamente joven que el horror' 'already historians and restorationists will be taking charge of exhibiting them, of taking them to the altar and multiplying their prices. There is nothing fresher and more eternally youthful than horror' (loc 3113).

In this respect, universities in the United States are an especially attractive market, since they can cover their financial interest with a veneer of historical pieties (the use of the word 'altar' is not coincidental in defining the archive/museum space). Horror sells well in the youth market, and the competition among universities for a piece of this terrific history will drive up the prices for the black marketers of the images, while at the same time ensuring that the history is both attended to and forgotten. And, for university trustees, the photographs represent a good investment, one that will only appreciate over time. As the narrator's friend in Austin comments, 'Las universidades extranjeras compran este tipo de archivos. Fotografías para explicar la historia y para sustituirla' 'foreign universities buy this type of archives. Photographs to explain history and substitute for it' (loc 3234). When the photographs move into the university archives or museum space, they then enter into a second level of exchange. Coviello accurately describes the mode for public consumption of stories like these of damage and suffering: 'the chief occasions for public acts of compassion, because they are staged through the organs of national culture, are virtually always ones in which no immediate course of ameliorative action suggests itself to the individual subject'. In the case of these public exhibitions, for the observer, feeling badly becomes a proxy for action. Without much effort feeling extremely badly becomes the only possible action, such that ethical response is exhausted in the expression of affect (156–157). Feeling badly, then, becomes another way of erasing history, substituting the somatic response of the consumer body and mind.

Balancing the poverty of ethical response is the equally compromised aspect of aesthetic appreciation, the Rubin's vase of these images. For Villafuerte's cynical characters, who are marketing the photographs abroad, the very intensity of the marks of violence on these anonymous Central American bodies heightens their value, since, as they have observed, the greater the violence, the more artistry that is ascribed to them (loc 745). Catastrophe, as more than one scholar has noted, is closely allied with the sublime. Weighed against the unbalanced feeling of shock, of feeling badly, is the intellectual appreciation of the beautiful composition, a second-level reading of the photograph that allows the consumer to feel good.

The photographic provenance is murky, and the obscurity of the story is part of the point: the history is told so as to be forgotten, so that only the eternally youthful and horrible images remain to please our aesthetic senses and excite our feelings of pathos. When Villafuerte gets around to telling it, she outlines a multiply mediated tale set in Nicaragua, and related by the first-person narrator, as derived from Bardem's unreliable version of the story, supposedly told to him by Liz Manero, the wife of a secretary to a Nicaraguan general, who gets it partly from her husband and partly from the general's wife. When, upon perusing the photographs, Bardem asks Liz who is the author, she responds, '¿a qué se refiere? ¿a quien captó las imágenes, o a quien cometió alguna de las torturas ahí representadas?' 'What are you referring to? Who shot these images or who committed any of the tortures represented in them?' Liz succinctly defines the knotty central issue: the murdered captives were doubly captured, first by the artistry of the torturer, then by that of the photographer. More mundanely, in the context of the novel, the (non)answer to the first question is the general's wife, New York born Gilda Zeligson, whom Bardem and the narrator suspect is a fictitious invention of Liz's. The answer to the second question, is, of course, the general himself: General Urtrizo (or Urtizo, or Urquizo, or Urquiza): the narrator notes the inconsistency in Bardem's attribution of the general's last name as one more index of the unreliability of the background story (loc 2878).

Povinelli asks us to think about 'What are the various relationships informing social imaginaries and concepts?' (41). With respect to the torture photographs, the context within Latin America necessarily consists of the long history of US-supported authoritarian regimes, and the shorter, more recent history of Truth and Reconciliation Commissions and memory projects; that is, in Villafuerte's caustic terms, 'restregar la herida con el argumento de para no olvidar' 'dig into the wound with the argument about not forgetting' (loc 727). Outside of Latin America, however, the peoples most affected belong to groups consigned to 'the imaginary waiting room of history' (Chakrabarty 8), existing only when they come to the attention of metropolitan centres and evaporating otherwise. This is what Povinelli discusses in terms of 'the parts that have no part' (77), a social spacing of projects and peoples that are neither inside nor outside the politics of recognition. From the metropolitan perspective, within these bracketed spaces, coopted 'counterworlds are picturesque scenes of glorious resistance and wells of creative discovery' (Povinelli 99) – what Lía has early identified as the tourist destinations of international caring. They inhabit the tense of the other, a conditional past that has only a limited claim on our attention. Or, as Villafuerte puts it: 'Hay lugares que no deberían existir, Bardem, y este fundo de estiércol llamado Latinoamérica es uno de ellos' 'There are places that shouldn't exist, Bardem, and this shit sack called Latin America is one of them' (loc 2944)

Villafuerte clearly plays aesthetics against rights, in contexts where aesthetic wants/desires can thwart care, and rights may include the consumer-citizen's right to forget. Lía says at one point about herself and her friend

Spiderman: 'Ambos apostamos por ver cuál de las dos es más inversosímil, cuál la más triste, o la más olvidable' 'We gamble on which of the two is most unbelievable, which is the saddest or the most forgettable' (loc 1241), and later Spiderman adds: 'olvidar, deberíamos darnos el derecho a olvidar' 'Forgetfulness. We should give ourselves the right to forget' (loc 1759). Yet, it is evident that the right to forget flourishes in the context of privilege, since only the (relatively) privileged can exercise it. The marginalized are in this novel condemned to memory, albeit the contradictory and fragmented memory of the dislocated, as they are likewise condemned to a limited aesthetic representation created by and for consumption by those forgetful others, those of us who care about such things. We buy the photographs, and send the children 'home'.

Notes

1 Villafuerte (Tuxtla Gutiérrez, Chiapas, 1978) studied music and journalism in her home state. She is the author of the short story collections *Preludio* (2002), *Barcos en Houston* (Ships in Houston, 2005), *Presidente, por favor* (President, please, 2006), and *¿Te gusta el latex, cielo?* (Do you like latex, sweetheart? 2008), as well as this novel. She generally focuses her work on the harsh realities of border life, especially the southern Mexican border with Guatemala. She has been supported by the Programa de Apoyo a Jóvenes Creadores del Fondo Nacional para la Cultura y las Artes and the Fundación para las Letras Mexicanas. She has recently been receiving deserved attention through scholarly articles by Coulon, Cuevas Velasco, Villalobos, and Ward, the latter of whom, in addition to interviews and scholarly work, has also translated Villafuerte's stories into English.

2 In the novella, Glenda exploits the Mexican adolescent as a prostitute; she becomes a drug addict, and is eventually recruited by corrupt politicians to kill the candidate to the presidency, with the promise of legal papers to set her up in the United States. After the candidate's murder, the politician has Helena killed in a house outside the Otay border crossing in order to wrap up loose ends.

3 Like Villafuerte, I would argue that much of the heightened rhetoric in Summer 2014 around the refugee crisis of unaccompanied minors fleeing Central American violence (numbers went up from about 7,000 in 2011 to an estimated 90,000 in 2014; see Nazario) can be profitably explored through this nexus. Unlike adult immigrants, children are not an immediately economically exploitable population, and furthermore, as tainted by the violence they are fleeing, they point towards what many Americans see as an undesired future. At the same time, they also pose an ethical conundrum – protests calling for immediate deportation are matched by protests calling for asylum. These numbers, of course, do not include the tens of thousands turned back within Mexico who never reach the United States (see, e.g. Brysk). This crisis has become even more acute in recent years, leading to the 2018 migrant caravans, created for self-protection against violence, and the harsh restrictions on asylum claims inaugurated by Donald Trump and continuing into the Biden presidency of the United States.

4 Brysk cites examples from the United States (state and federal law) with its emphasis on the ambiguous category of 'best interests of the child' as the foundation of family law. She also discusses countries ranging from the Dominican Republic to Afghanistan, Bangladesh, Nepal, Egypt, Japan, Russia, Bhutan, and Niger.

5 For example, when both Mexico and Honduras, like the United States countries with birthright citizenship laws, refused to register the births of children to Salvadorans and Guatemalans in refugee camps in the 1980s, leaving these children officially stateless (see Brysk 33).
6 See also 'Titanic Movie Mistakes' YouTube: http://youtu.be/heaNQfcmwt0
7 In this respect (as well as many others), the novel intersects with current debates in Mexico and elsewhere about human trafficking, especially of minor girl children. See, e.g. Martínez.
8 The Spanish translation cited by Villafuerte is, in effect, an interpretation: 'Tú que tienes/doce años/y padeces simplemente/gonorrea//Criatura/de viejos ojos, a/la ambiciosa pequeñez/de unas botas diminutas//¿qué/añadirá/la/muerte?' Coincidentally, Sally Mann also has a series of photographs, taken between 1983 and 1985 and published as an album titled *At Twelve: Portraits of Young Women* (1988).

References

Bowe, John. "Legal Affairs: The Rip-Off Artist." *New York Magazine* 1998. http://nymag.com/nymetro/news/crimelaw/features/2825/

Bruic, Audra. "Mexican Author, Narrator Nadia Villafuerte Discusses Migration, Gender and Literature." 11 November 2016. NPR (KGOU). www.kgou.org/world/2016-11-11/mexican-author-narrator-nadia-villafuerte-discusses-migration-gender-and-literature

Brysk, Alison. *Human Rights and Private Wrongs: Constructing Global Civil Society.* New York: Routledge, 2005.

Chakrabarty, Dipesh. *Provincializing Europe: Postcolonial Thought and Historical Difference.* Princeton: Princeton University Press, 2000.

Coulon, Ana Luisa. "Sobre la extrema violencia en la vida cotidiana: 'Por el lado salvaje' de Nadia Villafuerte." *Romance Notes* 54 (2014): 85–92.

Coviello, Peter. "The Sexual Child; or, This American Life." *Raritan* 27.4 (2008): 134–157.

Cuevas Velasco, Norma Angélica. "'Frontera de Sal,' engarce para un tríptico de la identidad migrante en la narrativa de Nadia Villafuerte." *Liminar* 19.2 (2021) https://doaj.org/article/080314affac0477d9f29ea12155a27e4

Cummings, E.E. "Being." *Tulips & Chimneys* (1919) New York: W.W. Norton, 1996.

Donoghue, Emma. *Room.* New York: Little, Brown, 2010.

Kiefer, Michael. "First Peek: Immigrant Children Flood Detention Center." *azcentral.com* www.azcentral.com/story/news/politics/immigration/2014/06/18/arizona-immigrant-children-holding-area-tour/10780449/

Knabe, Susan. "Suffer the Children: National Crisis, Affective Collectivity, and the Sexualized Child." *Canadian Review of American Studies* 42.1 (2012). 82–104.

Mann, Sally. *At Twelve: Portraits of Young Women.* New York: Aperture, 1988.

———. *Immediate Family.* New York: Aperture, 1992.

———. Website: http://sallymann.com/

Martínez, Sanjuana. *Se venden niños.* Mexico: Planeta, 2009.

Nazario, Sonia. "The Children of the Drug Wars." *New York Times Sunday Review* 13 July 2014. 1, 6.

Povinelli, Elizabeth. *Economies of Abandonment: Social Belonging and Endurance in Late Liberalism.* Durham: Duke University Press, 2011.

Rulfo, Juan. "Macario" *Revista América* 1946, republished in *Llano en llamas.* (1953) www.literatura.us/rulfo/macario.html

Villafuerte, Nadia. *¿Te gusta el latex, cielo?* Mexico: Tierra adentro, 2008.

———. *Por el lado salvaje.* Mexico: Ediciones B, 2011 (ebook).

Villalobos, Elizabeth. "Cartografías corporales: la violencia travesti como recodficación de la masculinidad en la frontera sur de México en '¿Te gusta el latex, cielo' de Nadia Villafuerte." *Chasqui* 45.1 (2016): 54–64.

Ward, Julie. "The Other Southern Border: Mexico's Forgotten Frontier in Nadia Villafuerte's *Barcos en Houston* (2005)." *Revista de estudios hispánicos* 53.1 (2019): 59–75.

4

WITNESSING AND THE TRANSFORMATION OF SELF

Borders and the Violence of 'Evidence'

Kavita Panjabi

Introduction

On 8 January 2011, India and Bangladesh woke up to the news of the bullet-ridden body of a 15-year-old Bangladesh girl, Felani Khatun, spread-eagled high above the barbed wire border between these two nations. Felani had been shot dead on 7 January 2011 while she was returning from India to Bangladesh with her father. As she tried to climb over the barbed wire fence along the Anantapur border in Kurigram, the Indian Border Security Forces fired at her.

Global Voices, citing Mahmud Faisal, reports:

> Her father managed to cross the barbed wire, but Felani's clothes got stuck in the wire and she started screaming in fear. Noticing her [the] BSF shot instantaneously and a bullet went through her body. But she did not die. If [the] BSF wanted [they] could end her misery by putting more bullets into her. But they waited four hours to be sure that she [had] stopped screaming and [was] dead. She was screaming 'Water, water' while… hanging on the barbed wire, hurt. Nobody listened to her and [the] BSF finally took away her dead body. After 30 hours she was brought back to Bangladesh [hanging like] a dead cow (on a pole).

The woman's body has been a site of brutal violence in the communal and national conflicts in the very making of the nation-states of the Indian subcontinent.[1] So, the fact that this 'crucifixion' of Felani, a young Muslim girl, by the forces of a now Hindu majoritarian nation-state, vanished from public memory in India with rapidity should be almost as shocking as the image itself, but is not. For Bangladeshi migrants compelled to cross the border

DOI: 10.4324/9780429356421-7

into India in search of work for their survival not only accrue trans-border identities but also risk inequities of power, privileges, and rights.

This international boundary is largely considered as a site of national security and 'Islamic terrorism' in India rather than as a zone of cohabitation, and as Malini Sur points out, Felani's proximity to this border 'obliterated any claims to Felani as an Indian Muslim subject or even a Bangladeshi migrant whose killing merits protest' (34). Constable Amiya Ghosh of the Indian BSF, accused of shooting and killing Felani, was tried and exonerated by the General Security Force Court in 2013. Two years later, a revision trial too acquitted him. (Dasgupta). The rhetoric of othering, cast in the discourse of national security and majoritarian integrity, is such that it has the potential to inhibit the claims of justice of trans-border people like Felani, who cross borders without documentation and experience state violence.

In contrast, the Bangladeshi posters of her covered a range: from close shots of a vulnerable child's face and chest torn apart by the barbed wire and stitched back in to place in the corpse, to the political symbolism on the nationally familiar poster of a distant shot of her hanging from the wire and the lines 'It's not Felani who hangs, it's Bangladesh that hangs' or 'simply', 'India hangs Bangladesh'. The former finally found its way to the report of Dhaka-based Odhikar, a human right's organization that articulated the conscience of the subcontinent on its cover (Dasgupta).

Such silence, as Felani's killing met with in India, as well as erasures of torture and abjection from public memory are of course not unique to the India–Bangladesh border, and cross-border scholarship not only recognizes this, it also does call for engagement with the precarity of such transnational lives. As Sur points out, 'Felani Khatun's tortured form connects many dots across geographies of violence', from the Indo-Bangladesh border to the Mediterranean waters to the U.S.–Mexico border and

> reminds us that the figures of those migrating under precarious conditions rise alongside legally protected travellers and compel us to recognize that scholarship and protests must engage with complicated and transnational lives that link home, workstations, and trading hubs straddling border fences.
>
> (35)

The border violence and the impunity of the Border Security Forces are both critical concerns here. My question, however, is somewhat different – given that it is photographs that bring us the 'evidence' of border violence, what is the status and reception of such 'evidence' in the depiction of the violence in trans-border people's lives? *Without the photographic image we would not have had evidential knowledge of Felani on the wire; because of it we become complicit in the nation-state's jingoistic assertion of power.* What is the function of the photographic image today that, rather than provoking political action, it catalyses the disappearance of the event? Why did the images of Felani fail to move most people in India beyond the initial horror? Does the reason lie in the aestheticization of suffering in the photograph? What is the nature of the 'truth claim' that the photograph makes – why is it antithetical to responsible action? Or is it something about our 'ways of seeing' that ensures that such photographs, and collaterally the reality of Felani's murder, be rendered into oblivion?

Debra Castillo's essay in this volume offers one way of approaching such erasures of precarity. Drawing upon Povinelli she observes that when stories of suffering are disseminated through the organs of national culture, they are staged as occasions for public acts of compassion, not ameliorative action. In such cases, feeling bad becomes a proxy for action, such that 'ethical response is exhausted in the expression of affect'. Feeling badly, then, according to Castillo becomes another way of erasing history.

The expunging of such violence and suffering from public memory may well have already become the norm in statist and majoritarian contexts; yet such obliterations do raise disturbing questions about how our modes of seeing – and erasure – adjust to statist and majoritarian identities, in slow but sure elisions of ethicality. Positing the question of the ethical responsibilities of spectator towards visual suffering in our mediatized age, Lilie Chouliaraki states that 'the mediation between spectator and sufferer is a crucial political space because the relationship between the two of them maps on to distinct geopolitical territories that reflect the global distribution of power' (22).

The inherent meaning of the image is not as important as

> how it intervenes in the world, how it helps to shape notions of community, subjectivity, political engagement and empathy by bringing to the surface a range of emotions and reactions that reflect the sentiments, fears, hopes and aspirations of the time.
>
> (Evans 2)

The fact, that India and Bangladesh's responses to the image of Felani spread-eagled on the barbed wire shape communities in terms of dominating and resistant identities, makes it evident that the same image can intervene in opposing ways when it is of violations and suffering at the borders. The context and the politics of reception are crucial.

Supriya Chaudhuri also draws our attention, via Sontag, to a perverse aesthetics represented by the twinning of power and lust. She reminds us that in *Regarding the Pain of Others* (2003), as well as in a later essay called 'Regarding the Torture of Others' written after the circulation of the Abu Ghraib photographs, Susan Sontag notes that 'photographs, especially photographs of atrocities, have lost their power to disgust or appall: rather, there is *an erotic charge, a lust of viewing*, that affects the viewer as it appears to have affected the photographer on the scene'. The possibility of connecting with the suffering of violated is subverted by an erotic aestheticization that has the potential to transform the viewer into a consumer of eroticized suffering.

What would an alternative 'ethics of seeing' involve, and what kind of lived engagement with the real world and ourselves would it take to develop such an alternative? Hariman raises another interesting question regarding such images; he says they provide remarkable resources for 'thinking about what it means to see and be seen, and about how we might live well together in a world connected by lines of sight'. What does it take to 'live well together', then, in a world connected by lines of sight but separated by borders?

In the modern world in which the local has given way to the global, physical presence has given way to the visual media, and witnessing to spectatorship. The photograph has thus accrued central importance as 'evidence' of faraway events; and it also plays a critical role in the construction of a territorial and bordered national imaginary. Visual media representations are a predominant mode of accessing seemingly reliable knowledge of people and events at borders that demarcate modern nation-states, and that, for reasons of national security, are normally inaccessible without permission. Yet, as Sontag asserts, despite 'the presumption of veracity that gives all photographers authority...the work that photographers do is no exception to the usual shady commerce between art and truth. Photographs are as much an interpretation of the world as painting and drawing are' (6–7).

What we have then, in place of direct witnessing, is an interpretation of an interpretation. The photograph in itself is an interpretation, and our reception of it is a second level of interpretation, twice removed from the actual experience of the reality. The knowledge that the photograph transmits to us is 'self-evident' by virtue of the mimetic power of the photograph; but the event and people photographed are rendered simultaneously into objects of consumption. Central to this bordered modernity, then, is the violence of such photographic representation of our geopolitical margins, and the centre's spectatorship of trans-border people becomes a prism of this transformation.

The epistemological matrix in which the complex linkages between perception and understanding are embedded has undergone a transformation: individual human values have been overwritten by the dominant ideology of the nation-state, and this is what controls perception. The human understanding of a perceived reality begins to give way to the dominant political understanding – the individual human beings perceived transmute, in the process of such understanding, into subjects of the nation-state, or its enemies. In the context of borders such photographs then feed into as well as shape territorial nationalist ideologies – the value of that human being gives way to an unquestioned aura of the nation-state.

Debra Castillo also raises, via Povinelli, the question of the various relationships that inform social imaginaries and concepts. She draws our attention to a social spacing of peoples, and her mode of locating them applies to Felani and her people too, who cross borders without documentation, experience state violence, but also 'work the border' – they too are 'neither inside nor outside the politics of recognition'.

This alienating politics of (non)/recognition buttresses the modes of otherization at the borders. In her recent work Cruel Modernity, Jean Franco argues that contemporary modernity is premised on the institution of borders that, in their ever-intensifying otherization, compels large numbers of people to shed the taboo against hurting others. One may not be held accountable for violence against those who are 'neither inside nor outside the politics of recognition'. Add to this, the fact that excessive familiarity with images of horror banalize horror makes it seem ordinary, even remote, so the 'ante keeps getting raised-partly through the very proliferation of such images of horror' (Sontag 19). In this ever-escalating scale of horror and simultaneous insensitivity to another's horror, can the photographic image ever enable us to transcend the borders, to feel another's pain as one's own again?

Photography: 'Anaesthetization by Evidence'

Photographs aestheticize reality, and as they become means of mass manipulation and political domination, the result is 'a society of spectacles and scopic regimes where citizens are converted into both passive spectators and objects of surveillance' (Hariman and Lucaites). In the face of such passivity, it becomes imperative to reflect on our role as spectators, to retrieve and recast agency.

The photograph of Felani nailed high on the barbed wire fence makes us complicit in the 'possession' of the young woman's body as symbolic object of conflict; it makes us symbolic accomplices in the enactment of the shift from the nation inscribed on the body of the woman during the partition to the spectacle of the body of the woman now exhibited high on the borders of the nation. It interpellates us as collaborators in a figurative 'defence' of our boundaries about which we are insecure, of triumphant assertion of 'supremacy' of 'our' nation, India, in a conflict-ridden subcontinent.

Do we continue to submit to the ideological significance that a collective, public reading of these photographs entail, i.e. the ideology of a violent, gendered, national supremacy? Or may we relate to Felani's suffering? Sontag also elaborates the difference between the direct experience of suffering and the remote consumption of photographs of that suffering: 'To suffer is one thing, another thing is living with the photographed images of suffering, which does not necessarily strengthen conscience and the ability to be compassionate' (20). The way Sontag explains this inclination towards passivity is as follows: 'Images transfix. Images anaesthetize. An event known through photographs certainly becomes more real than it could have been if one had never seen the photographs....But after repeated exposure to images it also becomes less real' (20).

What then is the range of truth *foreclosed*, the quality of experiential responses to suffering *elided*, by the privileged 'truth claim' of evidence? What is the status of the 'truth claim' of the photograph that converts the experience of suffering into a representation of evidence?

Photographs furnish evidence – there is a certain truth claim attached to the photograph, but what is rarely considered is that it is only part of a much larger truth. The historical and political context of the immediately visible 'truth' do not find representation in the photograph. They have to be narrated, the photograph can lay claim to a larger truth only when contextualized in a narrative, be it visual or verbal. The nature of the evidence is thus shallow by virtue of the very nature of the photograph as an individual entity. When one witnesses an event, however, the evidence is not required; so what then constitutes the truth of witnessing? Human presence catalyses a range of affective significations and motivations that the privileging of evidence completely elides. How does one then overcome the anaesthetizing effect of images of suffering that stand in for the activity of actually bearing witness to suffering? Can there be an ethics of seeing that can break through such 'anaesthetization by evidence'?

Truth Telling

What would an alternative 'ethics of seeing' involve? At the very least it would call for an analysis, after Foucault, of 'the relation between truth games and games of power, where truth is seen as a weapon and discourse as an assembly of polemical and strategic facts' (3). For 'the problem is that of knowing ...what are the different games of truth and falsehood that are established, and according to what *forms* they are established' (20).

In Wrong-Doing, Truth-Telling, the structure of which has been compared to that of a Möbius strip, the editors draw attention to Foucault's announcement that the problem that preoccupies him has two aspects. The first is political: 'knowing how the individual finds himself tied, and accepts to be tied, to the power exerted over him' (18). The second is philosophical: 'knowing how subjects are effectively tied within and by the *forms* of veridiction in which they are engaged' (19). The former perpetually recalls the latter, and the latter the former (4).

The new element in these formulations relates to how one speaks the truth about oneself; and the new object introduced into the game 'is the relation to oneself' (4). It involves the obligation not just to know the truth of ourselves, but also 'to tell, manifest and authenticate it' (5). This notion of a conscience transparent unto oneself. In this sense, it involves examining both, the philosophical tradition and scientific discourse, for an avatar of the imaginary relation humans bear to the conditions of their existence (6).

Witnessing versus Viewing

Witnessing has given way to viewing. This shift from witnessing to viewing has created a critical chasm in the nature of our engagement with what we view – and even more so if the object of our 'seeing' is already marginal, already at the borders of both, our existence and our consciousness. The essential qualifications of a witness are knowledge of the fact at issue and truthfulness: s/he must be an eye-witness and trustworthy. A witness is a witness by virtue of something he or she has experienced.

There are two acts: the act of witnessing and of bearing witness. Kosten observes that the two acts imply two different modes of address:

> the role of being a witness demands a simultaneous relation with two 'you's': the 'you' that is presently being witnessed and the 'you' of some sort of an audience, or more specifically, a community that is virtually present in the act of witnessing the first 'you'.

The experience of witnessing, however, is not something easily communicable in contexts of suffering. The loss of the act of witnessing is a sign of an alienation from human faculties; the 'otherization' of human beings at and across borders is grounded in an alienation from the wholeness of being. Veena Das reflects on the importance of finding ways to speak about the experience of witnessing: that if one's way of being-with-others was brutally damaged. This knowledge, she asserts, can be engaged only through a knowing by suffering. This knowing is akin to what Benjamin refers to as *Erfahrung* in comparison to *Erlebnis* in his writings on Baudelaire, the last lyric poet on the watershed of modernity – this knowing involves not just having a cognitive knowledge of something, but being transformed by the knowledge. Witnessing, according to Das, is an intervention, a relating that involves a transformation of one's own self. And Foucault's mode of Truth Telling points the way to it – a mode of a conscience transparent unto itself, grounded in the obligation not just to know the truth of ourselves, but also 'to tell, manifest and authenticate it'.

Das cites Martha Nussbaum to explain a knowing that goes beyond the intellect, that reaches the depth of lived human knowledge, in emotions, imagination, and behaviour:

> There is a kind of knowing that works by suffering because suffering is the appropriate acknowledgement of the way human life, in these cases, is. And in general: to grasp either a love or a tragedy by intellect is not sufficient for having real human knowledge of it.

> Agamemnon *knows* that Iphigenia is his child all through... But because in his emotions, his imagination and his behaviour he does not acknowledge the tie, we want to join the Chorus in saying that his state is less one of knowledge than one of *delusion*. He doesn't *really know* that she is his daughter. A piece of true understanding is missing.
>
> (26)

The photograph thus cannot be just 'seen' as evidence; it has to be embedded in a narrative of one's own making, of one's *knowing*. The ethical responsibility rests with the photographer, and with the viewer. Connecting with the other across borders becomes an act of connecting with oneself.

Note

1 Cf. Urvashi Butalia: *The Other Side of Silence*, Ritu Menon and Kamla Bhasin: *Borders and Boundaries &* Jasodhara Bagchi ed. *The Trauma and the Triumph*, vols 1 & 2, and innumerable other studies of the partition of India and Pakistan; and Nayanika Mookherji's *The Spectral Wound* is the latest in a series of important studies of the mass rapes of Bangladeshi women by the Pakistan army published in the last two decades.

References

"Bangladesh, India: Human Rights Hanging on the Border Fence." Global Voices, January 12, 2011. https://globalvoices.org/2011/01/12/bangladesh-india-human-rights-hanging-on-the-border-fence/

Berger, John. *Ways of Seeing*. London: Penguin, 1972.

Chaudhuri, Supriya. "'Marked Unsafe': Women, Violence, and the State of Risk." In Eds. Paula L. Ellman, Jhuma Basak, and Gertraud Schlesinger-Kipp: *Psychoanalytic and Socio-Cultural Perspectives on Women in India: Violence, Safety, and Survival*. London: Routledge, 2021.

Chouliaraki, Lilie. *The Spectatorship of Suffering*. Thousand Oaks, CA: Sage, 2006.

Das, Veena. "Language and Body: Transactions in the Construction of Pain." *Daedalus* 125, no. 1 (1996): 67–91.

Das, Veena. "The Act of Witnessing: Violence, Gender, and Subjectivity." In *Life and Words Violence and the Descent into the Ordinary*. Berkeley: University of California Press, 2006. pp. 59–78.

Dasgupta, Rajashri: "With SC Set to Hear Petition, Killings at Bangladesh Border Back in Focus." *The Wire*, March 5, 2020.

Evans, Jennifer V. "Introduction: Photography as an Ethics of Seeing." In Eds. Jennifer Evans, Paul Betts and Stefan-Ludwig Hoffman: *The Ethics of Seeing: Photography and Twentieth-Century German History*. New York: Berghahn Books, 2018. pp. 1–22.

Felman, Shoshana and Dori Laub. *Testimony: Crises of Witnessing in Literature, Psychoanalysis, and History*. New York and London: Routledge, 1992.

Foucault, Michel. *Wrong-Doing, Truth-Telling: The Function of Avowal in Justice*. Eds. Fabienne Brion and Bernard E. Harcourt Translated by Stephen W. Sawyer. Chicago and London: University of Chicago Press, 2014.

Franco, Jean. *Cruel Modernity*. Durham: Duke University Press, 2013.

Hariman, Robert and John Louis Lucaites. "Rethinking Photography, Spectatorship, and the Public Image." *Witness*, December 8, 2016, https://witness.worldpressphoto.org/rethinking-photography-spectatorship-and-the-public-image-c106b1b4d997

Korsten. "Frans-Willem the Rhetorical Structure of the Act of Witnessing." www.being-here.net/page/2234/the-rhetorical-structure-of-the-act-of-witnessing

Laub, Dori Ed and Andreas Ed Hamburger. *Psychoanalysis and Holocaust Testimony: Unwanted Memories of Social Trauma*. London: Routledge/Taylor & Francis Group, 2017.

Povinelli, Elizabeth A. *Economies of Abandonment: Social Belonging and Endurance in Late Liberalism*. Durham: Duke University Press, 2011.

Rose, Jacqueline. "I Am a Knife." *London Review of Books* February 22 (2018): 3–11.

Sontag, S. Regarding the Pain of Others. New York: Picador, 2003. pp. 3–24.

Sontag, Susan. *"In Plato's Cave." On Photography*. New York: Farrar, Straus and Giroux, 1977.

Sur, Malini. "Divided Bodies: Crossing the India-Bangladesh Border." *Economic and Political Weekly* (2014): 31–35.

Part III

CINEMATIC REPRESENTATIONS

Vulnerability as Experience and Metaphor

5

THE ATLANTIC BORDERLANDS

Container Politics, Social Death, and the Countercultures of Mexican Migrants

Melissa Castillo Planas

> El Norte es como el mar… Prefiero pensar que nunca fui a Estados Unidos y, cuando escucho hablar de aquel país, muy pronto me acuerdo del mar; he ido al mar, pero nunca me han dado ganas de bañarme, ni de comer ahí siquiera, por eso pienso cuando uno va de ilegal, pues va de cola o basura, yo me imaginé como el mar que toda la basura la arroja afuera, dije, a lo mejor aquí también estoy en el mar y entonces me esta arrojando pa'fuera cada rato. Lo que sí es cierto es que antes de ir al Norte, el mar se me hacía muy bonito, aunque nunca me he bañado, ahora ¡ni ganas me dan de pisar la arena![1]
> A quienes se quedaron en medio de ninguna parte[2]

The final image of Alex Rivera's 'Visible Border', is a haunting x-ray of immigrant bodies hiding in a container (*The Borders Trilogy*). Starting as a blurry silvery screen, the image, captured at the Mexico/Guatemala border by American Science and Engineering, Inc, a contract development firm for the US government, including support from the Department of Defense, represents the newest x-ray technology. As the image slowly comes into focus, during the less than 3-minute video, the voice-over comments on the technology's novelty and appropriateness for detecting 'large scale border crossings'. Particularly, this voice tells us, these new technologies have a wide variety of uses; they are able to distinguish any number of 'materials', from 'cocaine' to 'plastic explosives' to 'the human body'. In the end, we are left with a clear image of immigrant bodies huddled compactly in a shipping container, disguised as and surrounded by bananas.

Composed of three 2–3-minute videos, *The Borders Trilogy* begins with 'Love on the Line', a transnational border picnic (or 'dia del campo' as the participants describe it) at Border State Park in San Diego/Playas de Tijuana. This video emphasizes the personal and familial effects of immigration laws

DOI: 10.4324/9780429356421-9

in traditional documentary style. It is a familiar face of immigration, one that represents the realities of the border as a physical and emotional '1,950 mile-long open wound/dividing a *pueblo*', as Gloria Anzaldúa has described (24), and the personal losses that result. Following this, however, with the mockumentary styled 'Container City', Alex Rivera juxtaposes this humanistic view of the immigrant with a perspective held by the US government. Set in Newark NJ, the immigrant becomes invisible and is replaced by shipping containers. In this way, the film brings attention to the contrast of tightening border restrictions on people (such as the militarization of the wall, increased border patrol, increasingly restrictive anti-immigrant laws) with the welcoming of free trade. Residents here are fighting off a 'container invasion' that is creating a community eyesore as more and more iron boxes pile higher and higher around this modern-day port. In using the same language of invasions used on immigrants (alien invasion), Rivera draws attention to the language of consumer desire and denial.

In bringing together the container and the immigrant body in this final haunting and yet immobile image of global labour and economy, another equally horrifying image also arises. The visual similarities of these government-sponsored x-rays to abolitionist pamphlets that incorporated naval style drawings of slave ships is startling. Specifically, images like 'Description of a Slave Ship, Society for Effecting the Abolition of the Slave Trade, 1789', were exemplars of naval drawing's precision for schematic diagrams, in this case, of seven numbered sections, each filled with tiny darkened figures representing the bodies of slaves. Though meant to demonstrate the immoral horror of the slave trade, these images also offered a voyeuristic view of the slave trip in a way that reduced slaves to faceless, nameless, black outlines. Like the bright white x-rayed images in Rivera's video, there are no distinguishable individuals, men or women. They all just become interchangeable labouring bodies that must be transported and/or deported.

In *The Black Atlantic: Modernity and Double Consciousness*, Paul Gilroy uses the 'image of ships in motion' as his central organizing principle for understanding and analysing what he terms 'the Black Atlantic'. Beyond the slave ship's central importance as a symbol for the experiences and legacies of the middle passage, Gilroy further theorizes the significance of the ship through the roles of African sailors, maritime themed artwork, novels, pan-Africanist communiqués, and other sources (13). In other words, the movement of the ships back and forth across the Atlantic serves Gilroy as a way to expand commonly held perceptions of black diaspora and identity from one of slavery to one of community and creation. As he describes, 'I want to develop the suggestion that cultural historians could take the Atlantic as one single, complex unit of analysis in their discussions of the modern world and use it to produce an explicitly transnational and intercultural perspective' (15). Thus, Gilroy counteracts an essentialist conception of black American cultural and political histories by including the multiple ways in which the African diaspora was and is experienced through the bringing together of diverse communities in North and South America, the Caribbean, Europe, and Africa.

In highlighting the similarities between the current-day situation of immigrant transfer in containers (both as actual bodies and as represented by products), and the legacies of the middle passage, *The Borders Trilogy* not only brings attention to new ways the borderland is being represented and imagined, but also the impact and importance of the legacies of slavery on these conceptions. It is significant, of course, that Alex Rivera titles his work *The Borders Trilogy* and not 'The Border Trilogy', reflecting the multiplicity of images both past and present that he references of the borderlands as both an analytic and real site. In doing so, Alex Rivera and other artists and intellectuals wrestling with what I have termed the 'Atlantic Borderlands' consciously tie the current-day plight of immigrants to a longer legacy of brown and black bodies as commodities – interchangeable labouring apparatuses inseparable from the goods they produce. Temporally, this highlights the American role in a long history of global racialized capitalism based in the exchange and exploitation of black and brown bodies.[3] This long history allows the concept of the 'Atlantic Borderlands' to demystify a system that captures both the legacies of slavery and the systemic racialization and disenfranchisement of Mexican Americans in the Southwest, the areas that were once Mexico. Conceptually, it ties together both black and Latinx scholarship on the consumption of people as racial capitol. As such, geographically precarious and reflection of cultures constantly in conflict or in flux, the term itself reflects the lives black and brown bodies in motion.

At the heart of Gilroy's Black Atlantic subject is the double experience of being rooted and routed, of 'trying to face to (at least) two ways at once', a descriptor which in many ways has been used to discuss people of the borderlands and Latinx more generally (3). There are numerous parallels, for example, between the experience of Black Britain's' as described in Gilroy's text and Mexican Americans–the sense of 'othering', the perception of illegitimacy and in authenticity both to countries of origin and residence, the portrayal as a danger to the culture of the nation-state, the long histories and legacies of colonialism, the application of scientific racism, an insider/outsider relationship to state institutions, a continual a historical treatment (Gilroy 5–11), and the struggle for representation in academic institutions. The list could go on and on.

But this chapter does not mean to argue that the Mexican American and Black British or Black American experiences are parallel, or use Afro-Mexicans like Lucy Parsons or John Murillo as an obvious black-Mexican link within the Black Atlantic. What I propose here is that reading together these two structures of analysis – that of the Borderlands and that of the

Black Atlantic, two influential and foundational modes of thinking, now over 20 years old, highlights important considerations about how the brown/black labouring body in movement is being replicated and responded to today. It is an attempt to bring the Black Atlantic into the modern-day borderlands. In this sense, the 'Atlantic Borderlands' offers a contemporary unit of analysis, in which what I describe as 'container politics' and 'container culture' form a postmodern means of critique of the commodification of brown bodies.

Part II of *The Borders Trilogy* features comments by Peter Zantal, General Manager for Strategic Analysis and Industry Relations at the Port Authority of NY & NJ. Through Zantal, Rivera makes three main points about containers. First is their physical size, either 20 or 40 feet long, seven feet wide and eight feet long. They are consistent, replicable, and easily replaceable. Second is their mobility. They are meant to be mobile 'vessels', constantly in transit from factory to truck to train to port to boat and across seas. Finally, these containers reflect a particular moment of postmodernity[4]; the evolution of the container, as Zantal points out, reflects a change in the US global economy. In this postmodern age of capitalism, not only are goods highly mobile, but so is labour. The mobility of goods and labours – is not new – but in this moment, its scale and speed are hard to fathom. In fact, capitalism is so mobile that US industry itself has gone oversees and so have container production (China is the major producer). As such, there is a problem when they arrive in the United States, since instead of circulating, the containers come to stay: two containers come in for one container that moves out. The US consumes more than it produces. It wants more than it is willing to give. These are the 'abandoned containers' that 'are slowly taking over', the voice-over reflects (*The Borders Trilogy*).

The irony, of course, clear from the mockumentary style of the second film, 'Container City', is that this is the same language used to describe the threat of immigration – specifically immigration from Mexico and Central America – to the United States. In bringing affordable products from all over the world, shipping containers represent a postmodern global economic system that would not exist without a global system of labour. These migrants are following trade routes, then making new roots in the United States. This is not new; slave ships played a similar role for the modern age. As Gilroy notes,

> Ships also refer us back to the middle passage, to the half-remembered micro-politics of the slave trade and its relationship to both industrialization and modernization. As it were, getting on board promises a means to reconceptualise the orthodox relationship between modernity and what passes for its prehistory. It provides a different sense of where modernity might itself be though

> to begin in the constitutive relationships with outsiders that both found and temper a self-conscious sense of western civilization. (17)

Likewise, Alex Rivera's work underscores the relationship between containers, 21st century immigration, and postmodernity. In hiding in containers, migrants facing an increasingly hostile and treacherous borderlands are also reflecting on their postmodern status. Global commodities, not global communities, are what are welcomed.

The Atlantic Borderlands clarifies important aspects of a current moment in US–Mexico relations and the resulting influence on the borderlands' identity, one that is nevertheless built on these racialized capitalist foundations.[5] First, it reflects a certain moment in US economic history in which de-industrialization is buttressed by a service sector economy supported by immigration.[6] Secondly, it identifies an ambivalent treatment of labour in which the US consumer both desires cheap products brought in by containers at the same time that the containers themselves are seen as unsightly, undesirable eyesores. Here the simultaneous desire and disgust for shipping containers serves as a metaphor for how violence of the borders may be studied through objects that move across borders. In other words, they reflect a 'container politics' of dis-identity and disassociation. In an effort to distance consumer from the brown labouring bodies, the labouring body becomes invisible within the process of production. Not once are labourers, either those overseas, or those forced to migrate, such as represented in 'Love on the Line' mentioned in 'Container City'. They have been replaced by goods. This is the horror, the eeriness represented by the stylistic and stereotypical horror film music choices of 'Container City'. If 'containers are taking over', how does their invasion reflect a postmodern view of labour?

In an attempt to address these container politics, Mexican journalist Jorge Ramos centres his discussion of immigration reform on the container. Recounting the deaths of 19 Latin American migrants who died from asphyxiation, dehydration, and heat after being packed with at least 54 others into a truck trailer, his book *Dying to Cross* is significantly subtitled 'The Worst Immigrant Tragedy in American History'. I say *significantly* because thousands have died at the border, but for Ramos the tragedy of the container is particularly unsettling. The events of *Dying to Cross* took place on May 2003, during which at least 73 undocumented immigrants who had already crossed the US–Mexico border travelled from Harligen, Texas to Houston. Ramos, using testimonies from four of the survivors, recounts both the hours in the truck, the migration histories of the individuals, and the subsequent trials against the coyotes and truck driver, who failed to activate air conditioning on one of the hottest days of the year and then abandoned the trailer itself after seeing dead and near-dead state of its travellers. One chapter specifically focuses on the heart breaking death of five-year-old Marco Antonio (Kindle location 1001).

Clearly, it is a narrative meant to arise sympathy and outrage. Nevertheless, for Ramos, this case presents several particularities about migrant deaths in the borderlands. He writes:

> In addition to the fact that this case set a new record for the number of immigrants dead in one single incident, it is also significant in terms of legal precedents; this was the first time that immigrant traffickers could have been sentenced to death.
>
> (Kindle Location 122)

Although this death toll is significant, as is the possibility of capital punishment (which did not end up occurring), his focus on fatalities points to Ramos' aim as well. The Atlantic Borderlands has become a cemetery and few are visiting the dead.

What these deaths establish, as does Ramos' emotional narrative response, is a larger and more alarming trend – the death toll at the border has increased and US policies enacted in the 1990s are the cause (Soto 44). In what is now established practice, in an attempt to deter migration, immigration officials decided to 'funnel' migrants into the longest, most dangerous, and most isolated paths.[7] Of course, deterrence has never been an effective policy on people fleeing death and so for 30 years immigration enforcement has idly watched the death toll rise. In 2009, for example, the American Civil Liberties Union sponsored report by Maria Jimenez, 'Humanitarian Crisis: Migrant Deaths at the U.S.-Mexico Border', which analysed bodies recovered in the deadliest section of the border found that the risk of dying was 1.5 times higher in 2009 than in 2004 and 17 times greater than in 1998, meanwhile the total number of rescues has diminished over the years from 2,537 in 2005–2006 to 964 in 2008–2009 (8–9). And while the US Border Patrol has recorded over 7,000 migrant deaths along the US–Mexico border between fiscal year 1998 and 2020, others estimate the numbers to be at least 10,000 just between 2000 and 2012 (Soto 44). What is clear from these harrowing statistics is that despite the recent surges from Central America, overall, in the past decades, fewer migrants have been willing or able to make the trip, while those that do so are in more desperate situations, and in the eyes of the US government, their lives are less and less valuable. Often times, families are not even given the dignity of repatriation of their loved ones' remains – as there is no centralized database for locating a relative, the search may take months or years. In fact, only about 75 percent of the recovered bodies or remains are identified, which is quite low when compared to 99.5 percent for US citizen deaths (Jimenez 10). Already, in the first three months of 2021, more migrants died trying to cross the border than in all of 2019 according to the Missing Migrant Project (Fry).

Ramos' outrage at the 2003 tragedy, unfortunately, reflects the commonplace fact of death on the borderlands today. The description of the immigrant experience inside the container, hour after hour, is then what it is particularly disturbing about this text. As the narrative begins:

> The immigrants did not fit comfortably in the truck trailer. Some people remained on their feet, leaning against the walls, while others squatted, and others sat with their legs pressed against their chests. The metal floors in this kind of trailer are not smooth; they are lined with very thin metal bars that run down the entire length of the trailer, from front to back, to facilitate the manipulation of heavy cargo loads. These bars and indentations make the floor an extremely painful place to sit. Truck trailers are not exactly made from transporting cramped human cargo.
>
> (Kindle location 653)

Desperate for air, the passengers clawed at the doors, breaking out the taillights to circulate some air, and bloodying themselves in the process (Kindle Location 690). Some hyperventilated, while others vomited only to die in their own bodily waste (Kindle Location 710). For three hours they signalled with shirts and baseball caps to other cars on the road through the holes they had created with injured hands. They even tried to call 911 but were not transferred to a Spanish-speaking operator (Kindle Locations 750–770). The invisibility of their lives and coming deaths was palpable. Drenched in sweat, and in complete darkness, some managed to drink their own urine to survive (Kindle Location 811). Ramos describes:

> Some of the passengers had begun to feel cramps in their extremities and a strange uncomfortable sensation around their mouths. So much sweating had depleted their bodies of salt and this, in part, was what brought on the cramping. Due to the excessive, constant heat, a rash of little blisters had begun to break out on their necks and hands. But when they tried to scratch at the rash, their fingernails turned black from the combination of sweat and damp skin cells. Their breaths per minute continued to rise as their bodies continued reacting to the lack of oxygen. Some say they had an easier time breathing down by the floor, while others say they preferred to remain standing. In the darkness, there was no way they could tell, but their skin had already turned an extremely pale, grayish-bluish hue.
>
> (Kindle Location 896)

Not only is this image of brown bodies piled on top of each other in various states of death and dying clearly reminiscent of the middle passage, but moreover, it reflects a new state of migrant terror.

Key to Gilroy's analytics of the Black Atlantic is the shared experience of 'terror' based in slavery. This terror is an important root of transnational black identity, but it is also an integral part of a transnational trade system integral to modernity, and this memory lives on (60). This connection between trade and terror is implicit in Ramos' critique as he profiles the migrants' plans and desires to work in the United States within this horrifying narrative. In the final hour of their journey, Ramos describes the following scene: 'The dead were stretched out across the floor, strewn among those who had fainted and those who had fallen asleep, but there was no real way to tell who had died and who had just passed out' (Kindle Location 917). The dead and living become interchangeable, equally invisible. Posing as commodities in route for consumer consumption, their terror as they helplessly flag cars and attempt 911 calls is their realization that they are not human in the United States. For it is one terror to die in open air, and another to die in a container; it is a death with a different sort of haunting. It is a death in which an identity has been captured and imprisoned within the confines of product and production. This is death lost in blind transport, a death completely without knowledge or control of where one's final words are spoken. Moreover, due to the ghastly inhumanity of the circumstances, it is a type of death that haunts the community memories.

Saidiya Hartman's work *Lose Your Mother* provides a clear example of this memory of terror at work. Her journey to and through Africa reflects a desire not to return in a final sense of the word, but to seek out memories. She finds these memories are no longer rooted in Africa but have been routed throughout the diaspora. In these memories, she finds disconnection from massive slave death and, as such, makes the connection between death and commerce crystal clear.

> Death wasn't a goal of its own but just a by-product of commerce, which has had the lasting effect of making negligible all the millions of lives lost. Incidental death occurs when life has no normative value, when no humans are involved, when the population is, in effect, seen as already dead. Unlike the concentration camp, the gulag, and the killing field, which had as their intended end the extermination of a population, the African trade created millions of corpses, but as a corollary to the making of commodities. To my eyes this lack of intention didn't diminish the crime of slavery but from the vantage of judges, juries, and insurers exonerated the culpable agents. In effect, it made it easier for a trader to countenance yet another dead black body or for a captain to dump a shipload of captives into the sea in order to collect the insurance, since it wasn't

> possible to kill cargo or to murder a thing already denied life. Death was simply a part of the workings of the trade.
>
> (Hartman 31)

In a similar vein, the transformation of borderlands into a stateless space where those that dare traverse are left to die reflects a development in migrant identity. In a postmodern world, the Atlantic Borderlands demonstrates a container politics that sees migrant deaths as normative, as an acceptable by-product of an age of trade dependent on the movement of goods in shipping containers. Migrants, unlike slaves, are not seen as already dead, but neither they are seen as living.

In *Social Death: Racialized Rightlessness and the Criminalization of the Unprotected,* Lisa Marie Cacho forcefully argues that in the eyes of society, personhood is premised upon the unchallenged devaluation of criminalized populations of colour. The undocumented worker is a key figure in her study, as a member of a population who under neoliberal arguments of worth is considered not a deserving member of society. According to Cacho, this valuation replicates, creates, and normalizes states of social and literal death. According to Cacho:

> To be ineligible for personhood is a form of social death, it not only defines who does not matter, it also makes mattering meaningful. For different reasons, undocumented immigrants, the racialized poor of the global South, and criminalized U.S. residents of color in both inner cities and rural areas are populations who 'never achieve, in the eyes of others, the status of "living."'
>
> (6–7)

Accordingly, while 'container politics' represents one aspect of social death, the Atlantic Borderlands is not solely geographically located either in the shipping container ports around the world or the US–Mexico border, but extends imaginatively to a particular non-status of invisibility.

As both Cacho and Hartman conceptualize, social death is a state that cuts across borders and oceans. Hartman, for example, extends the notion of social death originally introduced as a fundamental aspect of slavery by Orlando Patterson in 1982 to the present-day condition of black diaspora. She writes:

> We may have forgotten our country, but we haven't forgotten our dispossession... We stay there, but we don't live there . . . Staying is living in a country without exercising any claims on its resources. It is the perilous condition of existing in a world in which you have no investments. It is having never resided in a place that you can say is yours. It is being 'of the house' but not having a stake in it. Staying

> implies transient quarters, a makeshift domicile, a temporary shelter, but no attachment or affiliation. This sense of not belonging and of being an extraneous element is at the heart of slavery.
>
> (87–88)

Like in Cacho's analysis, for Hartman, this state of transience is not just a state of unbelonging and homelessness, but also a lack of living. It connects the histories of the black diaspora born out of slavery to the modern-day African American second-class status. While Hartman reflects on the master's words, 'stay put', the US border patrol's 'get out' rings in a dialectical but symbiotic way. If they were never alive, their deaths are inconsequential. Heavily documented with precision, little seen in any other subject area of the times, this realm of knowledge about the control of the bodies of people of colour has been passed from generation to generation. From slave codes to Jim Crow laws, from convict leasing to the prison industrial complex,[8] from the robbery of Mexican lands, to the deportations of thousands of Mexican American US citizens in the 1930s, to the creation of the Bracero Program (1942–1964) of legalized exploitative contract labor, these forms of containment have been altered to fit the times but not the intention. The intention for the US economy has never been clearer: to get the most labor for the least amount of money via racialized subjugation and exclusion. Following this history, Michelle Alexander's *The New Jim Crow* explores the outcomes of the vast imprisonment and criminalization of African Americans due to the racialized War on Drug policies. One particularly detrimental result is an increasingly large population of black men and women who are left with a criminal record that makes legal, or even authorizes, discriminatory practices 'in employment, housing, education, public benefits, and jury service' (141). This modern-day form of 'social death', is essentially a way to strip African Americans of their citizenship. In other words, it makes them like immigrants.

Although few narratives exist around the experience of the middle passage, especially those written by slaves themselves or from their perspectives (Diedrich, Gates, and Pedersen 19), these passages in Ramos and Hartman as well as the questions explored in Rivera's films about these experiences of disembodiment, dehumanization, and erasure hundreds of years later, nevertheless have an eerie echo of what the feeling of being confined among death must be like.[9] Perhaps this is why the slave ship and the container reflect similar scenes of terror, and the Ramos and Rivera texts echo the writers and intellectuals Gilroy analyses in *The Black Atlantic*.

As already mentioned, ships are central to a Black Atlantic, because in that orientation to the middle passage, multiple meanings of movement are mobility that are also referenced. Just as Rivera's container politics reflect a parallel emphasis on trade, (post) modernization, and (de) industrialization, Ramos' text demonstrates a concern for a different aspect of passage along the Atlantic Borderlands. In his focus on the death of the boy, he inverts the standard cliché that 'our children are our future', reflecting the social death of migrants, and the spectacular terror of the container. Even children are amongst these non-people, lost in 'the middle of nowhere' (*Desiertos*).

A similar turn can be seen in Hugo Alfredo Hinojosa's play *Desiertos* (*Deserts*), one of the first plays to directly address the situation of migration via container. Hinojosa, an actor, theatre director, and essayist from Tijuana, Mexico provides another response to 'container politics'. *Desiertos* is a mosaic of fragmented intertwined stories each addressing different aspects of immigration. These voices include such diverse characters as a girl who was sexually abused by her father, undocumented migrants in the dessert, a sniper trying to kill border crossers, a life insurance salesman, a preacher talking to a coyote, and women mourning migrant deaths. One of these stories, or rather vignettes, centres around a group of 17 men and a boy trapped in a container. An epigraph[10] to his play cites the same events that Ramos reports on in *Dying to Cross*.

The first scene in the container centres on the panic of being trapped and the different responses that ensue. The audience hears only the voices of the 17 men and a boy as they express discomfort, rage, and fear at being hot, without air and facing death. The father tries to keep his son calm as the men squabble over trying to force the door open, or stay still and try to conserve air, or light a match. The scene is presented in complete darkness until one man lights a match and then a second as the young boy calls out for his father. These increasingly brusque exchanges between men are juxtaposed by the boy's exclamations of 'mamá' and then 'papá'. The matches burn out and the men are left again in darkness (Hinojosa 13–14).

In the second appearance, we encounter the men below ground. This time, the child's voice is the first that the audience hears. He says, 'Había un navío cargado, cargado de... comida' (there was a ship, load with, loaded with ... food). In a tragic game, over the course of the scene, the boy adds to the items on his imaginary ship – saints, water, clouds, salvation, dreams, money, heat, and thirst. Meanwhile the men's comments are increasingly disjointed and irrational expressions of emotion and memory. The boy's imaginary ship and its items, then, punctuate and give organization to a scene that is otherwise filled with the men's growing realization of their fatal predicament (Hinojosa 25). Moreover, the items the boy lists also poetically define the archetypal immigrant baggage – 'De todo lo que no hay', ('everything there is not') as the boy continues – what is given up in crossing. These are the items there is no room to bring in the container, items like 'mi mamá que no está' ('my mother who is not here') (Hinojosa 26). As the men become alternately angrier and more resigned to their fate, the boy continues filling his ship with water, exhaustion, 'this little thing called death', 'little angels', desperation, and finally the boy's and the scene's last line, 'De silencio... ¡papá!' ('of silence ... daddy!') (Hinojosa 26). As silence falls on the container, Hinojosa reminds us that the ship from the boy's imagination should be a nuclear family home, the game is no longer child's play, and the migrant child faces a particular form of containment and stunting in this in-between stateless space.

In the final scene, the men, again below ground, occupy an ambiguous space between life and death. The child disappears to the background as the men aggressively posture against each other in a final form of masculine expression. In a sexually charged scene several ask for kisses to alleviate their thirst, while some call others 'faggots', and still others demand silence and stillness. In this climate the father becomes increasingly protective of the son, as the men toy with the boy asking for food. We learn that the container has stopped moving and has not moved for some time (41–45). The boy's games and the dreams are over, they too have been abandoned to die.

In these scenes, Hinojosa is not trying to recreate the experience of the container realistically as Ramos does in *Dying to Cross*, rather what his work along the Atlantic Borderlands reflects is a developing 'container culture'. Building from Alex Rivera's film critique employing parody and dark humour, Hinojosa's play is an attempt to counter the dehumanization of the migrant and the erasure of the labouring body by making them visible again even within the container that suffocates them. Here the importance of shifting the politics of representation within the container becomes clear. While Rivera draws attention to the ironies of the US 'container politics' and the representation of migrants that encapsulate their lives into disposable x-rayed figures, Hinojosa enters the container to give voice to migrants and demonstrate the creativity that also springs from terror.

As previously mention, Gilroy's focus on the ship in motion stresses the importance of the middle passage as symbolic of the relationship between labour, capital black bodies. However, he also emphasizes the ship's role in the black diasporic imaginary no longer shackled[11] (4). He writes,

> The image of the ship – a living, micro-cultural, micro-political system in motion – is especially important for historical and theoretical reasons. . . . Ships immediately focus attention on the middle passage, on the various projects for redemptive return to an African homeland, on the circulation of ideas and activists as well as the movement of key cultural and political artifacts.
>
> (4)

Likewise, Hinojosa's focus on the container goes beyond Ramos' 'container politics' to an exploration of the imaginary. Hinojosa's reflection does not just emphasize the traumas and terror of a tragedy like the one in Texas 2003 (and that have since become so commonplace so as to warrant minimal news attention), but how the container as an image is altering the narrative of the borderlands to consider migrant creative responses to this neoliberal global phenomenon informed by geopolitical borders.

In particular, it highlights a peculiar immobility that emphasized Hinojosa's dedication '*A quienes se quedaron en medio de ninguna parte*' ('To those who remained in the middle of nowhere') (2). In *Desiertos* these lives in transit, as the term 'migrant' itself implies, are ironically physically and emotionally confined. Thus, Hinojosa adds a second catastrophe to the little boy's death in the trailer as described by Ramos, the death of innocence, dreaming, and imagination. Over the course of the container scenes, the one site of imagination, the boy, is tragically suffocated as well.

Like Hartman's and other literary and artistic conceptions of the middle passage, the image of the container powerfully asserts not just the impossibility of return, but a state of immobility and confinement that is not a complete existence, but rather a suspension between places and lives. According to Gilroy, African American writers and intellectuals have nurtured 'redemptive critiques' of the middle passage and slavery through a 'hermeneutics of two interrelated dimensions – it is both a hermeneutics of suspicion and a hermeneutics of memory' (71). Among the literary works he examines, Toni Morrison's *Beloved* functions as critical response to slavery as foundational violence that helped to establish the modern Euro-American white subjectivity. In the novel, Morrison represents the middle passage as a space of narrative void. Consequently, passages which directly engage with the trauma of the middle passage are represented by fragments in which language and syntax collapse, gesturing toward the impossibility of representation.[12,13] A similar gesture toward unrepresentability comes forth in *Desiertos*. The specifics of the event which inspired the scenes, and the reality of entrapment in a container itself, slowly dissipate as the play progresses into fragmented thoughts, emotions, and sentences until we are left, like the migrants, in the chaos and confusion of the unsayable.

Contemporary black authors have developed a 'slave sublime' that attempts to represent the 'unsayable' experience of slavery (131). This 'slave sublime' is not just an attempt to recover a past which can never be fully recovered and the recognition of the impossibility of representing the middle passage, but also as a form of refuting the modern belief in 'reason' against the 'irrationality' of Africans and the diaspora:

> In particular, [the desire to pit Euro-American modernity against 'bestial' slaves] is formed by the need to indict those forms of rationality which have been rendered implausible by their racially exclusive character and further to explore the history of their complicity with terror systematically and rationally practiced as a form of political and economic administration.
>
> (220)

Hinojosa's expression of 'container culture' not only reflects the unrepresentability of this borderlands state, but also posits alternative forms of knowledge. In many ways, this is an extension of Gloria Anzaldúa's borderlands, a site of new knowledge production through a mestizo rhetoric of revisionist history ('autohistoria-teoria') and the embrace of 'irrational' spirituality ('*la facultad*'),[14] but one that reflects the new importance of the container on the borderlands' psyche. For many, Gloria Anzaldúa has become 'the representative' for conceptual and geopolitical study of 'the border', in Latinx theory and Chicano/a literature. For Anzaldúa the jagged wound of the border is inflected by the precise local geographies of her birthplace of El Paso, where the border is crossed and defined by bridges over the Río Bravo. In this project, however, 'border' is more than a simple geopolitical divide. In addition to moving beyond the lands surrounding the physical border, it signals a space for multiple and even seemingly contradictory meanings and identities in relation to a real site of US–Mexico division. It is also a border that incorporates not just questions of place, but questions of language, gender, culture, race, and history, particularly the legacies of slavery on modern-day race relations and state modes of control.[15] 'Container culture' as a collision of borderlands and Black Atlantic theory expands these temporal, geographical, and conceptual boundaries to reflect today's geopolitical borders which simultaneously invite and discard, diversify (product) and confine, terrorize and welcome.

Gilroy's 'slave sublime' is also echoed in Alicia Schmidt Camacho's term 'migrant melancholia'. According to Schmidt Camacho:

> The material and psychic hungers that propels migrants to abandon the most basic elements of sociality – residence, kinship, language, culture and landscape – in short, home, for wages exert a violence that immigration scholarship and state discourse have yet to full address. The condition or status but rather entails the active conversion of the migrant into a distinct category of stateless personhood. This peculiar status emerges with the contradiction between market demands for mobile labor and consumable goods and the immobility of rights beyond the bounds of the nation-state. Mexican migrants, like other displaced peoples, continually invent forms of agency within that space of opposition. It is a melancholy task. Stories of border orality and disappearance are means to narrate the other kinds of death…the leave-taking that extinguishes one form of connection to make way for another. In this ritual of departure, the family enacts, in intimate form, the migrant's detachment from the state, a severing a citizenship that is also a death, a death that produces.
>
> (302–303)

This 'peculiar status' begins to take shape through the image of the container. Unsayability is central to containers, as is immobility, trauma, terror, and social death. They are a reality today of neoliberal global capital, but they are also new sights of artistic and literary response. What I would add to the notion of 'migrant melancholia', is the ways in which this 'stateless personhood' is very much gendered. Ramos makes it a point to highlight that only men died in the container at Victoria. Likewise, only men are present and die in the container *Desiertos*. In reality, both men and women have died and suffered in containers and on slave ships, but it is a suffering that is clearly gendered.

It is significant to note that containers are a crucial part of the maquiladora industry (assembly plants operating along the border in a zone exempted from import and export duties and tending to employ young women for low wages) story. The Border Industrialization Program initiated in 1965 to supplement the end of the Bracero Program facilitated the establishment of *maquiladoras*, where Mexican, mostly female labour assembled Asian-made components into products that were then moved across the border to warehouses and stores. These operations clearly could not have succeeded if it were not due to the low transportation costs that resulted from the introduction of the shipping container (54) As McCrossen notes, 'The container was to global production of consumer goods what the moving assembly line was to Ford's organization of factory production' (54–55) or, as I would add, the trade and slave ship to cotton production in slavery times. In fact, the efficacies of containers lowered shipping costs in most instances to less than 1 percent of the total cost of production and distribution (McCrossen 50).

Consequently, one of the most striking, and maybe most disturbing, insights gained on the Atlantic Borderlands when thinking through the model of container politics is that international labour is not only feminized but also sexualized. Structurally speaking, a young woman in Juárez has three options: an assembly worker; a domestica (maid), if she has insufficient education to be accepted at a factory; or prostitution, if she can't produce a recommendation for a maid position. On the borderlands, women's bodies are contained and interpolated onto specific labor sites. Yet securing a factory job is not always the end of the story, as low salaries force many women to seek supplementary income from prostitution on weekends, putting them at higher risk for sexual predators and murder (Biemann 7). Sexual and labor markets interpenetrate within this economic order, and both rely on a category of brown labouring bodies treated as less than human. Biemann adds:

> Their racialized, gendered figures become the articulators of the border, that fragile line marking the fringe of the national body. It is here, according to national(ist) discourse, that all disease, illegality,

> contamination, and poverty come from. This is the most vulnerable, penetrable site, the place where anxieties tend to concentrate. What better site to localize the panic of national identity? Above all, U.S. customers need to be assured that the offshore female bodies are not out of control.
>
> (Biemann 4)

As Biemann suggests, this new model of borderlands relies on people simultaneously kept under control and in movement. According to this logic, disposable men and boys die in the non-space of container transit, disposable women die in the maquiladora spaces of border feminicide. This mobility and immobility then form two ends of the same chain, two ways of dying, and two types of disposable bodies.

Ships and containers expose the limits of the nation both as geographical form and as ethical project: 'It should be emphasised that ships were the living means by which the points within that Atlantic world were joined. They were mobile elements that stood for the shifting spaces in between the fixed places that they connected', Gilroy clarifies (16). In the same way that ships provide a chance to explore connection and disjuncture between different ports on either side of the Atlantic, containers reflect the way global commerce has formed links that leave many migrants in a state of nowhere. As Alicia Schmidt Camacho notes, 'The transborder region is best understood as a social form distinct from that of the nation, a form that is alternately a place of exception from the nation and subject to its domination' (10–11). It is within this site of domination then that a Border Atlantic perspective helps to uncover concurrent forms of response, which I have described as 'container politics' and 'container culture'. As Rivera demonstrates, containers are both 'cultural and political units' (Gilroy 16) creating scenes of community memory while effecting US views on immigration. Containers and their stories are also a 'means to conduct political dissent' (Gilroy 16) as Ramos' narrative choices and perspective demonstrate. Lastly, containers provide a lens to analyse 'distinct modes of cultural production' (Gilroy 17) through the Atlantic Borderlands as Hinojosa's imaginative and creative text highlights. 'Either through immigrant dreams, as reflected in the boy's ship game, or men's immigrant nightmares, as reflected by the migrant testimony that opens this paper', these are journeys that are traumatic but part of a community memory. Like the crossing of the Atlantic, they are imagined as much as lived.

The Atlantic Borderlands brings together Mexican American experiences and black diaspora not as a comparison but in recognition that colonialism, interracial and interethnic contact through trade, migration, and slavery are all part of the same capitalist economy and technological development that today manifests at least in part, via the container. Today, this can no better be witnessed than in New York City, the centre of the US financial and trade industries from the times of slave-produced cotton and since the 1990s home to hundreds of thousands of Mexicans, the fastest growing Latinx population in the City, and one that is rapidly closing in on the long historical groups, Puerto Ricans and Dominicans. As the recent discovery of the African Burial Ground in Lower Manhattan reminds us, New York City's significance as the racial capitalist entryway to the United States for both people and goods, past and present should not be overlooked, but often is. Under the shadow of a false Statue of Liberty welcome, are buried stories of black labour, are hidden stories of brown labour. Through the reference to the middle passage, we are reminded of slavery as a trade and particular moment of industrialization and modernization. But the Atlantic Borderlands is also a way, like Gilroy's project of black diaspora, to expand notions of Mexicanidad that go beyond labour and immigration, without unlinking those critical narratives. The Atlantic Borderlands then is also a step outward to include black diaspora in postmodern Mexicanidades, a fact of Mexican existence but one that is often overlooked in battles over identity politics.

Notes

1 From Durand, Jorge. *El Norte es como el mar: Entrevistas a trabajadores migrantes en Estados Unidos*. Guadalajara: Universidad Autonoma de Guadalajara Press, 1996, p. 28.

> The North is like the Sea… I want to think that I never went to the U.S., and whenever I hear of that country, I remember the sea. I have gone to the sea, but I've never swum in the beaches, or eaten there. So, whenever one goes there undocumented, one is like trash. I imagine myself like the sea, all trash is thrown out. So, I'm better here than at the sea. Before I went to the North, I believed the sea was beautiful, even though I never swam. Now, I don't even want to step on the sand.
>
> (my translation)

2 From Hinojosa, Hugo Alberto. *Desiertos*. Mexico City: Programa Cultural Tierra Adentro, 2010, p. 2. 'To those who remained in the middle of nowhere' (my translation).

3 As Cedric Robinson extends in *Black Marxism: The Making of the Black Radical Tradition*, colonialism, imperialism, and racial capitalism have long worked in tandem (2–3). Racism is more than just an aspect of a capitalist system but also a 'material force' and 'historical agency' of capitalism (2–3). Similarly, capitalism was not an economic system that broke with older forms of marginalization, but one that evolved alongside racism to produce a modern world system which captures not just people of African descent in the United States, but migrants as well. For scholars of the borderlands such as Natalie Molina and others, Mexicans' lack of racial capital reveals the extent to which Mexicans remain racially suspect in the US – 'foreign until proven otherwise' – and thus valued in certain racially charged ways ('The Long Arc' 446).

4 My use of the term 'postmodern' is not meant to invoke vast debates about culture, but to identify an economic moment which Frederick Jameson and David

Harvey have linked with late capitalism or flexible accumulation. This stage of late capitalism is characterized by highly mobile labour and capital as well as a 'time and space compression' two characteristics that reflect the role of the container on the borderlands (Harvey 47).

5 Along the long historical route of racial capitalism, the Brookes Ship and Rivera's 'The Visible Border' again overlap. Here, the concept of 'racial capitalism', rejects treatments of race as external to a purely economic project and counters the idea that racism is an externality, or aberration from the workings and structures of capitalism. Moreover, for legal scholar Nancy Leong, racial capitalism is not just a system of economic injustice or marginalization but also a measure of value. According to Leong, racial capitalism is 'the way that white people and predominately white institutions derive value from nonwhiteness' (2154). In other words, the way nonwhiteness is commodified and monetized whether as labouring bodies or as the goods produced from labour and circulated in shipping containers around the world. Of course, the practice 'of using nonwhiteness as a justification for the commodification of nonwhite individuals is older than America itself', as the history of slavery brutally demonstrates (Leong 2155).

6 Saskia Sassen helps conceptualize the trend of service industry growth in the United States. As she describes in 'Global Cities and Survival Circuits', the debt and debt-servicing problems of the 1980s, along with the economic crisis of the 1990s and the structural adjustment programs implemented by the IMF and World Bank that followed have contributed to a vast increase in unemployment and poverty in the developing world (266–267). The resulting influx of immigrants to the United States then, bolstered a trend toward the services industries that began in the 1960s but which really accelerated since the 1980s, with an increase of approximately 60 million employees in the 1979, to a high of over 115 million in 2008 (Short). As Sassen points out, this development has serious implications for the treatment of workers in late capitalist global economies more generally. She argues,

> It seems, then, that we need to rethink two assumptions: that the postindustrial economy primarily requires highly educated workers, and that informalization and downgrading are just Third World imports or anachronistic holdovers. Service-dominated urban economies do indeed create low-wage jobs with minimal education requirements, few advancement opportunities, and low pay for demanding work. For workers raised in an ideological context that emphasizes success, wealth, and career, these are not attractive positions, hence the growing demand for immigrant workers. But given the provenance of the jobs these immigrant workers take, we must resist assuming that they are located in the backward sectors of the economy.
>
> (Global Woman 261)

Thus, these largely immigrant workers are workers who are incorporated into what has become the dominant engine of the US economy, the service sector, and yet are not seen as full members of an economy which they ultimately sustain. Instead, these largely women and immigrants who perform the tasks of low-wage clerical and service workers, maids and nannies, or restaurant workers represent a profound change in the way low-wage workers are perceived in today's global US economy. No longer is employment in growth sectors a source of worker empowerment, but the cause of worker isolation and invisibility.

7 See, for example, the work of De León.

8 For more about the system of convict leasing, see Blackmon and Mancini. See Alexander and Davis for a fuller description of race and the US prison system.

9 One of these rare narratives is that of Olaudah Equiano, also known as Gustavus Vassa, a slave in the West Indies. His description of the middle passage is similar to the testimonies in *Dying to Cross* in numerous aspects including the smell, heat, and lack of space. According to Equiano's narrative,

> The stench of the hold while we were on the coast was so intolerably loathsome that it was dangerous to remain there for any time, and some of us had been permitted to stay on the deck for the fresh air; but now that the whole ship's cargo were confined together, it became absolutely pestilential. The closeness of the place, and the heat of the climate, added to the number in the ship, which was so crowded that each had scarcely room to turn himself, almost suffocated us. This produced copious perspirations, so that the air soon became unfit for respiration, from a variety of loathsome smells, and brought on a sickness among the slaves, of which many died, thus falling victims to the improvident avarice, as I may call it, of their purchasers. This wretched situation was again aggravated by the galling of the chains, now become insupportable; and the filth of the necessary tubs, into which the children often fell, and were almost suffocated. The shrieks of the women, and the groans of the dying, rendered the whole a scene of horror almost inconceivable.
>
> (23)

10

> Un camión en el que viajaban 18 inmigrantes fue interceptado hoy por las autoridades cerca de Victoria (Texas), la localidad donde el pasado miércoles aparecieron muertos otros 18 inmigrantes que viajaban en las mismas condiciones. (...) El caso se produce dos días después de que 18 inmigrantes de México y Centroamérica, entre ellos un niño, murieran asfixiados cuando viajaban en un remolque, que fue abandonado en Victoria. (...) los inmigrantes estuvieron encerrados en la parte trasera del camión durante un día y medio.
>
> Periódico Frontera. Tijuana, Baja California, 17 de Julio del 2002.

11 Ironically, the number of Mexican-born immigrants who left the United States for Mexico rose sharply from 2005 to 2010, even as the flow of new immigrants to the United States from Mexico fell steeply, according to a Pew Hispanic Center analysis of data from both countries. As a result, net Mexican immigration to the United States is at a standstill. These developments represent a notable reversal of the historic pattern of Mexican immigration to the United States, which had risen dramatically over the past four decades. In a 2020 report, the Pew Hispanic Center notes that there are now more apprehensions of non-Mexicans than Mexicans at the border.

12 Another example of this literary unrepresentability of the middle passage can be found in the antinarrative poem *Zong* in which memory, history, and law collide and collapse into a haunting lament for the forgotten and space of forgetting.

13 These hermeneutics are also heavily represented in black arts. Cheryl Finley, for example, examines the way contemporary artists of the African diaspora have resurrected the 18th century abolitionist icon, starting with prints of 'Descriptions of a slave ship'.

14 One of Anzaldúa's biggest challenges to the academia is her refusal to become a prisoner to western rationality. 'Like many Indians and Mexicans, I did not deem my psychic experiences real', she writes.

> I denied their occurrences and let my inner senses atrophy. I allowed white rationality to tell me that the existence of the 'other world' was mere pagan superstition. I accepted their reality, the 'official' reality of the rational, reasonable mode which is connected with external reality, the upper world, and is considered the most developed consciousness – the consciousness of duality.
>
> (Borderlands 59)

In this other consciousness, rationality exists but it also incorporates dreams, imagination, soul, and spirituality at the same time. While a Western brain may split these two sides, Anzaldúa develops '*la facultad*' to inhabit both at the same time. It is 'the capacity to see in surface phenomena the meaning of deeper realities, to see the deep structure below the surface' (Borderlands 60).

15 Here I am referencing works like *The New Jim Crow* by Michelle Alexander and *Are Prisons Obsolete* by Angela Davis.

References

Alexander, Michelle. *The New Jim Crow: Mass Incarceration in the Age of Colorblindness.* New York: The New Press, 2012.

Anzaldúa, Gloria. *Borderlands/La Frontera: The New Mestiza.* Third edition. San Francisco: Aunt Lute Books, 2007.

Biemann, Ursula. "Performing the Border: On Gender, Transnational Bodies, and Technology." *Globalization on the Line: Gender, Nation, and Capital at U.S. Borders.* Claudia Sadowsky ed. New York: Palgrave, 2002.

Blackmon, Douglas. *Slavery by Another Name: The Re-Enslavement of Black Americans from the Civil War to World War II.* New York: Anchor Press, 2009.

Budiman, Abby. "Key Findings about U.S. Immigrants." *Pew Hispanic Center.* 20 August 2020. www.pewresearch.org/fact-tank/2020/08/20/key-findings-about-u-s-immigrants/. Accessed 14 September 2021.

Cacho, Lisa Marie. *Social Death: Racialized Rightlessness and the Criminalization of the Unprotected.* New York: New York University Press, 2012.

Davis, Angela. *Are Prisons Obsolete.* New York: Seven Stories Press, 2003.

De León J. *The Land of Open Graves: Living and Dying on the Migrant Trail.* Oakland: University of California Press, 2015.

Diedrich, Maria, Henry Louis Gates, Jr. and Carl Pedersen eds. *Black Imagination and the Middle Passage.* New York: Oxford University Press, 1999.

Durand, Jorge. *El Norte es como el mar: Entrevistas a trabajadores migrantes en Estados Unidos.* Guadalajara: Universidad Autonoma de Guadalajara Press, 1996.

Equiano, Olaudah. *The Interesting Narrative and Other Writings: Revised Edition.* Vincent Carreta ed. New York: Penguin, 2003.

Finley, Cheryl. "Schematics of Memory." *Small Axe.* 35 (July 2011): 96–116.

Fry, Wendy. "Tougher Border Security Measures Have Led to More Death and Injury for Migrants." *The San Diego Tribune.* 26 March 2021. www.sandiegouniontribune.com/news/border-baja-california/story/2021-03-26/migrants-dying-border-security. Accessed 14 September 2021.

Gilroy, Paul. *The Black Atlantic: Modernity and Double Consciousness*. Cambridge: Harvard University Press, 1993.

Hartman, Saidiya V. *Lose Your Mother: A Journey Along the Atlantic Slave Route*. First paperback edition. New York: Farrar, Straus and Giroux, 2007.

Harvey, David. *The Condition of Postmodernity: An Enquiry into the Origins of Cultural Change*. London: Wiley-Blackwell, 1989.

Hinojosa, Hugo Alfredo. *Desiertos*. Mexico City: Conaculta/Programa Cultural Tierra Adentro, 2010.

Jimenez, Maria. "Humanitarian Crisis: Migrant Deaths at the U.S.-Mexico Border." American Civil Liberties Union San Diego and Imperial Counties. 1 October 2009. www.aclu.org/immigrants-rights/humanitarian-crisis-migrant-deaths-us-mexico-border. Accessed 23 November 2013.

Leong, Nancy. "Racial Capitalism." *Harvard Law Review*. 126.8 (June 2014): 1251–2226.

Mancini, Matthew. *One Dies, Get Another: Convict Leasing in the American South, 1866-1928*. Raleigh: University of South Carolina Press, 1996.

McCrossen, Alexis ed. *Land of Necessity: Consumer Culture in the United States – Mexico Borderlands*. Durham: Duke University Press, 2009.

Molina, Natalie. *How Race Is Made in America: Immigration, Citizenship, and the Historical Power of Racial Scripts*. Berkeley: University of California Press, 2014.

Morrison, Toni. *Beloved*. New York: Knopf, 1987.

Passel, Jeffrey S., Cohen D'Vera and Ana Gonzalez-Barrera. "Migration between the U.S. and Mexico." *Pew Hispanic Center*. 23 April 2013. www.pewhispanic.org/2012/04/23/ii-migration-between-the-u-s-and-mexico/. Accessed 24 November 2013.

Patterson, Orlando. *Slavery and Social Death: A Comparative Study*. Cambridge: Harvard University Press, 1982.

Philip, NourbeSe M. *Zong!* Middletown: Wesleyan University Press, 2011.

Ramos, Jorge. *Dying to Cross: The Worst Immigrant Tragedy in American History*. New York: HarperCollins ebooks, 2005. Kindle.

Robinson, Cedric. *Black Marxism: The Making of the Black Radical Tradition*. Second Edition. Chapel Hill and London: University of North Carolina Press, 2000.

Sassen, Saskia. "Global Cities and Survival Circuits." *Global Woman: Nannies, Maids, and Sex Workers in the New Economy*. Barbara Ehrenreich and Arlie Russel Hochschild, eds. New York: Henry Hold and Company, pp. 254–274.

Schmidt Camacho, Alicia. *Migrant Imaginaries: Latino Politics in the U.S. Mexico Borderlands*. New York: New York University Press, 2008.

Short, Doug. "Charting the Incredible Shift from Manufacturing to Services in America." *Business Insider*. 5 September 2011. www.businessinsider.com/charting-the-incredible-shift-from-manufacturing-to-services-in-america-2011-9. Accessed 15 December 2012.

Soto, Gabriella. "Absent and Present: Biopolitics and the Materiality of Body Counts on the US–Mexico Border." *Journal of Material Culture*. 26.1 (2021): 43–63.

The Borders Trilogy. Dir. Alex Rivera. Producer Alex Rivera, 2003. Online. http://alexrivera.com/project/the-borders-trilogy/

6

WHAT IS THE KID DOING AT THE BORDER?

Some Thoughts on Representations of Children in Indian and Latin American Border-Themed Cinema

Sucheta Bhattacharya

Kabir Khan's 2015 movie *Bajrangi Bhaijaan* made business worth 626 crore rupees (US $93 million) after an investment of 90 crores in its making. It is believed to be so far the second highest grosser in the Indian film history. The director who is noted for his earlier works involving cross-border narratives (*Kabul Express* in 2006, *New York* in 2009) struck gold with this movie which tells the story of the rescue and return of a six-year-old mute Pakistani girl Munni who accidentally gets lost in India. She is restored to her parents by an uncompromisingly honest and not-too-bright but devout Hindu young man nicknamed Bajrangi who travels to Pakistan occupied Kashmir without visa/passport or permit of any kind, with a bit of help from a not-too-competent Pakistani TV journalist and the internet. He does get arrested but as his story gets publicity on the net put out by the enterprising Pakistani journalist, popular opinion in Pakistan and India ensures Bajrangi returns to India under dramatic circumstances.

Movies dealing with India–Pakistan relations have, as a rule, done well at the Indian box office, but even by that standard *Bajrangi Bhaijaan's* success is phenomenal. The success can be attributed to some obvious reasons: the charisma and popularity of Salman Khan who plays the eponymous hero, the unbelievable cuteness of Harshaali Malhotra who dons the role of six-year-old Munni with aplomb, and the messages of tolerance, goodness, sympathy, etc. that the movie advocates. The other reasons for its success are not so obvious but at the same time equally important. Mainstream Bollywood movies dealing with border issues basically tend to be of fixed kinds. Overtly jingoistic (like the 1997 movie *Border*), or cross-border romances like *Gadar*, *Ek Prem Katha* (2001) and *Veer Zaara* (another box office hit in 2004), both having takers along the length and breadth of the

 DOI: 10.4324/9780429356421-10

subcontinent, both telling stories with bold brush strokes (I apologize for the mixed metaphor), either stoking fires of nationalism or not-so-gently nudging us to look beyond the political and religious divides and to discover, assisted by the movie, to look for humanity. Melodrama remains the main element in both kinds. There had been movies of the other kinds also, more cerebral and finer-nuanced not only dealing with the trauma of partition but also issues of the India–Pakistan border post-partition. One is reminded of M. S. Sathyu's *Garam Hawa* based on a relatively less-known story by Ismat Chughtai, the celebrated Urdu author, where the sins of partition are visited upon the future generation (1973); or Shyam Benegal's 1994 film *Mammo*, based on the journalist and author Khalid Mohammad's autobiographical account of his childhood years, where the issue of divided identity of individuals after the partition of India is treated with unparalleled sympathy and insight. Shyam Benegal's film was not a box office success, not because by 1994 the pain of partition of 1947 has started becoming a distant memory for both Indians and Pakistanis with both nations becoming dominated by a generation which had not experienced the direct pain of partition, but because it was too subtle in its portrayal of victimhood of individual citizens under a mechanical and sympathy less legal, political, and governmental structure, in short, because of its shortage of melodrama quotient. Deepa Mehta's 1998 film *1947: Earth*, which won more critical acclaim and better commercial reception was supported by a storyline which while keeping the focus on a particular historical event also managed deftly to show the interplay of sexual jealousy and violence which erupts in the background of political and religious violence. *1947: Earth* had another dimension to it, the story of corruption and destruction of innocence of Lenny, the child protagonist of Mehta's movie.

The child as an observer or a victim of a border, whether geopolitical, economic, or cultural, has often been represented in popular culture, particularly in cinema. Most often the child is turned into an adult by its experience of crossing the border, the geopolitical border often turning into a signifier for an experiential border on the other side of which lies disillusioned adulthood. Such is the case of Lenny in Bapsi Sidhwa's *The Ice Candy Man* which was made into *1947: Earth* by Deepa Mehta. Lenny's happy, protected world is torn asunder by the violence of Indian partition. Her Hindu ayah is kidnapped by a Muslim mob and her paradise is lost forever. Lenny's adorable precocity before her traumatic experience, her secret half-knowledge of the adult world fall like a house of cards when she experiences prematurely the real adulthood as the confusion of the partition hurls her into the tornado of violence. The movie is narrated in retrospect by the grown-up Lenny whose memory now gets sublimated losing its edge into a nostalgia for a lost Eden but also a newer realization of the lack of her subjectivity back then and now, which is symbolized perhaps by her physical disability. By contrast in Munni's case no corruption takes place. She faces no physical abuse, no emotional trauma. She gets lost in an 'enemy' country, she meets a stranger whose goodness she recognizes instinctively and is restored to her parents, against all odds. That is the 'stoff' of *Bajrangi Bhaijaan*.

Kabir Khan's *pièce de resistance* addresses, however, quite a number of issues which perhaps can only be addressed in the garb of a comedy, because they are too close to the Indian reality for comfort. The machoism of the male protagonist expressed through his devotion to *Bajrang* (*Hanuman*, the celibate monkey-god who was a devout follower of *Rama*) and his obsessive honesty are being constantly undercut by real situations where he has to forget and unlearn much of his received wisdom.[1] *Bajrangi Bhaijaan* is an extremely political film, a tongue-in-cheek criticism of the attempted saffronization of India, questioning all the prejudices that neoliberal India is being forced to swallow in the name of a return to Hindu tradition. It is a protest against backtracking into a projected world by powers-that-be which is completely antithetical and alien to the cultural and spiritual ethos of India. It talks about India's multiculturalism, polytheism. Munni's entry into Bajrangi's life is a border crossing for him of sorts. Yet, the movie gives hint about what the actual border crossing may involve for a child. One of them being the potent threat of being trafficked, from which Bajrangi saves her. On an even darker side, Munni's recovery and restoration is a throwback to the earlier incidents of 'recovery and restoration' (of abducted women) in the context of the history of Indian partition.[2]

Even if there is always an artistic and intellectual justification for centring a child in a narrative of borders, it is arguably the appeal to the emotions that matters more in such narratives. Hume talked about sentiment itself being a kind of aesthetic response, and it is nowhere more applicable than in films dealing with borders. Border issues are complex and complicated ranging over economic, political, cultural, and much more, yet, the movies that leave imprint on the viewer's mind appeal to the emotions, not the intellect. Yet, the affects related with all borders are not of the same nature. If Indian border themes have changed their thrust over the years, the themes of Latin American border narratives have changed in other directions. The Indian border themes often still focus on the issue of return to one's home with a certain directional change over the last few years. Whereas previously, in the years following immediately the partition of 1947, the uncertainty of new political and national identities made the notion of home problematic for the characters, and the major image was the image of rupture, in recent times, the entrenchment in the sureness of one's national identity often makes the story of homecoming a circular experience.

The basic difference between Indian and Latin American border movies lies in the nature of the issues involved. For the latter it is economic primarily. From economic it invariably leads towards the criminal like trafficking and smuggling. Law and legality become major themes too.

In *La Misma Luna* (2007) Patricia Riggen's movie dealing with the story of nine-year-old Carlitos crossing the border from Mexico into the United States to look for his mother Rosario who works as a maid there, has a similar pattern like that of *Bajrangi Bhaijaan* with certain inevitable differences. Carlitos is an older and savvier child compared to Munni. He is extremely articulate, able to converse in two languages, prepared, and waiting to go over to his mother once she has enough money to pay for his papers. His grandmother's death throws him into an unplanned journey negotiating a path ridden with risks of violence, injustice, incarceration, and betrayals. Depending on unreliable guidance including an elusive father who unsurprisingly betrays him, but exercising his agency he manages to reach his mother. Carlitos gains experiences, information, knowledge, in short, some kind of subjectivity during his journey, yet his innate innocence and honesty are preserved, very much like Munni's.

Munni's journey is circular and a return to the point of the start as the meaning of home has changed over the last few years in the Indian subcontinent. Yet Munni gains a second home in India as she calls out 'Mama' (which in Hindi means mother's brother) breaking her silence at the end of the movie as Bajrangi leaves for India, leaping into his arms in the no man's land between the borders of India and Pakistan. Their reunion hints at an ideal possibility of an understanding between two nations based on people's understanding of the artificiality of political divide. It is significant that they meet midway outside borders.

Carlitos' journey in contrast is linear, unidirectional, aspirational – underlining the nature of economic transaction between the United States and Mexico. The other threads remain loose. The main reason behind Rosario's migration to the United States had been economic. Her economic condition remains unstable despite her utmost attempts. There is a big question mark which remains hanging over Carlitos' and Rosario's future which does not come into the ambit of the plot of the movie, but nevertheless would make any sensitive audience wonder about.

Not all children are as fortunate as Carlitos or Munni, however. Innocence and illusions don't get protected for all. Enrique and Rosa, the teenage brother and sister in Gregory Nava's *El Norte* (1983) escape from violence-ridden Guatemala to the United States via Mexico through a rat-infested sewer pipe with the dream of having a safer and freer life in the North, a utopia that everyone back home had talked about. Temporarily, they settle down into a comfortable life. But law is the first thing that catches up with them, introducing anxiety and insecurity which are as unshakeable as the insecurity at home. Then come Rosa's inability to deal with a foreign, mechanized, 'sophisticated' culture, and her subsequent illness, a bad attack of typhus, which kills her (the effect of the rat bites she suffered in the abandoned sewer pipe through which they had entered the North). Rosa dies with the realization that they are unwanted, they don't have any space either in or out of Guatemala, that the hospitality and freedom of the North are after all a miasma. Enrique is reduced to the status of an illegal farm labourer, unable to use the opportunities the North puts before him, as he becomes saddled with his ill sister.

Children once more become the major protagonists in *Al Otro Lado* (2004), Gustav Loza's film covering three separate narratives in three countries involving three children: Prisciliano in Mexico, Àngel in Cuba, Fatima in Morocco, all three looking for their fathers who had gone over to their respective norths as migrant labourers. Prisciliano's father leaves just before his ninth birthday for the North crossing the Rio Grande. The child attempts to cross the river in a small boat which capsizes and he is saved by the spirit of Ereneida, a mythical Indian princess who had died trying to escape from a conquistador. Àngel tries to sail to the United States to look for a father he had never known crossing the Gulf of Mexico in a makeshift boat which capsizes drowning his friend but he escapes with a guilty secret that he cannot share with anyone. Fatima from Morocco looking for a ship to take her to her father in Malaga (who is working as a labourer in a shipping firm in Spain), gets trafficked but is saved by the conscience of the woman who runs the trafficking network and is reunited with her father.

Prisciliano does not get to go over to his father, but he realizes that he has to assume the responsibilities of his father in his absence. Àngel's father of his imagination remains illusory, but he learns to appreciate his mother and grandfather whose care and love he had not considered inadequate and against whose imperfections he had set up the image of the absent father (he carries a tattered photograph of Robert de Niro in his wallet) as the paradigm of goodness and haven of security. Fatima braves the murky and unknown world of smuggling and trafficking and locates her father and saves him from an illicit relationship and brings him back home.

All the children cross borders in this movie: between innocence and experience, hatred and love, childhood and adulthood. They are saved and are saviours. They redefine the significance of borders and home. At the same time, they become socialized. They are tamed to the concept of social identities too early through their border experiences.

However, the question I raised in the title of the chapter as to why children become so often the focus of films dealing with the concept of border remains difficult to answer. Is it because children are often seen as pure and uncorrupted and therefore as sites, both psychological and physical where the trauma and lessons of border experiences can be seen clearly written? This assumption would take us to two related assumptions: the first one the child being seen sentimentally and even romantically with the concept of it being the carrier of a native innocence which external circumstances cannot corrupt but whose body often like that of Christ would carry the marks of the wound, but never the mind or the spirit; the other more sinister assumption being the child seen as an experimental subject by the filmmakers, a cleaner subject than a complicated and complicit adult, on whom the effects of the border can be clearly marked and analysed.

As a critical spectator one cannot help wondering, however, if often the images of the children as objects and centres of these movies are not being exploited once more. Their innocence is taken for granted, their misfortune and pain and also their nobility used merely to reconfirm certain popular prejudices about children. In most cases the children are victims or victimized. Their subjectivities in most cases are erased. Do these representations tell us anything new about border realities apart from what we already feel as adults?

To go back to the starting point of my essay, by the end of *Bajrangi Bhaijaan*, it becomes clear that the movie is not about Munni, or Bajrangi or even the India–Pakistan border. It is about contemporary India, a criticism of the attempted saffronization of India. Munni is just an excuse and a narrative necessity for Kabir Khan's vision of India. The real child is never there.

Which, however, is not to deny the artistic autonomy of the director of a feature film. It is simply that in the plethora of child-centric border movies the child too often seems relegated to victimhood or the symbol of the defeat of the modern world by divisive forces. They symbolize our future. Perhaps thereby the movies also become self-critical texts.

However, it is too easy to play the devil's advocate and use a logic which is a polar opposite to what I have focused on so far, for another kind of problematization. If in a paradoxical manner in these movies, art simply becomes a true reflector of reality, if it is taken for granted that children are victims in real life, more so in context of borders and for any movie to show any change in this reality would be falsification and distortion of reality, (a reality fortified by the powerful and all-pervading image of the three-year-old Syrian baby Aylan Kurdi lying dead on the beach in September 2015, dressed nattily in red t-shirt, blue jeans, and tiny sneakers, drowned in the Mediterranean trying to cross illegally into Europe with his family), if therefore these films constitute non-reactive reflection of reality, then where does art end up or what vision do the movies offer?

I would argue that children here are symbols of our own confusion regarding borders. They project often the adult's defeat in an increasingly bordered society. They embody our hopes, our despair, our fight, as well as symbolize our exploitation of the border, which willy-nilly is always happening despite our unease regarding borders as well as our resistance to them. Their innocence and vulnerability are our own. Suffering childhood becomes an acuter experience of experiencing borders.

If representations in popular culture can be seen as one of the significant contributions to 'border pedagogy', if movies dealing with border issues can be seen constituting a particular genre, one needs to examine how these movies are carrying out those responsibilities. Emma Wilson in her introduction to *Cinema's Missing Children* says that many films on missing children 'can be seen to conjure the fears and phantoms of our culture which offer no easy solutions or redemptive closure' (Wilson 4). She goes on to say that such refusal of (re)solution and often of action opens up a space for reflection and imaginative, emotive viewing. In these movies both the director and the spectator tend to think 'through' the child rather than about it. This to my mind sums up the whole psychology behind the portrayal of the child in 'border' movies.

There are some exceptions to this general practice, however. *Trade* (2007, Dir: Marco Kreuzpaintner) is a movie the story of which deserves, I think, a bit of exposition as the question of a child's subjectivity is rather powerfully addressed in this thriller. The movie tells the story of Adriana and her brother Jorge. Thirteen-year-old Adriana from Mexico is abducted into the United States and sold into an international sex-trafficking racket which does trade through the internet. Her seventeen-year-old brother Jorge chases her and her abductors through the terrains of Mexico, crossing the border illegally and travels through the breadth of the United States helped in his attempt by a US investigator who is troubled by his own demons from the past. It is found that Adriana is to be auctioned off as a virgin on the net and Ray, the investigator, pretends to be a customer and buys her from the syndicate which runs the setup. However, when he goes to collect his purchase, his behaviour makes the woman, in whose house Adriana has been installed, suspicious who insists that the first sexual intercourse with the girl must take place in her house so that she can be sure he is a 'genuine' buyer and not a cop masquerading as a buyer. Locked in the bedroom with the girl, Ray has to take a quick decision, from which dilemma Adriana saves him by rupturing her hymen with her own finger and showing the blood-stained bedclothes to her confiner as proof of her lost virginity. Jorge returns to Mexico with his sister but then goes out and stabs to death the man in his neighbourhood who was the contact for the kidnapping ring.

Trade is one of those rare movies where children grow up and exhibit their subjectivity. Jorge's refusal to lose his sister has a lot of heroism about it but he is not satisfied with getting the sister back. He turns into a murderer at the end presumably doomed to carry another identity for the rest of his life. Adriana returns unraped, but not unmolested or a virgin. Her physical and mental innocence is irreparably gone when she de-virginizes herself. Taking control of her own life is what distinguishes Adriana from Rosa of *El Norte*. She does not suffer passively. She protects her virginity by losing her virginity, which paradoxically is given such a premium value by the flesh racket. The whole tension in the movie is built up as much by the suspense of the uncertainty of Jorge's ability to rescue her sister, as by the suspense of the strong possibility of Adriana's rape. Veronica, the young mother of a child whom she has left in Poland, and one of the women getting trafficked along with Adriana gets raped first and then gets raped again and again as she tries to protect Adriana, sometimes even offering herself, till she cannot take any more and commits suicide. Veronica's maternal/Christ-like protection extended to the virgin throws in sharp contrast Adriana's vulnerability but also her superior position as a virgin in the spiritual and moral capacity valourized by our culture. Adriana seems to place herself finally in a situation where the goddess-whore polarity is invalidated. Or is it?

The figures of children that I have looked in my rather rambling survey of some of the movies from both India and Latin America show some definite features: firstly, the children can be divided into two groups, pre-teens and teens. Rosa, Enrique, Jorge, Adriana, the teenagers have some amount of agency, if merely of physical movement, between borders perhaps. Their motives and actions are analysable by adult understanding. Whereas the rest of the children are too young, too vulnerable, lose too much. Apart from Carlitos of *La Misma Luna* who shows a stronger subjectivity, the others are at the receiving end of the system, whether political or economic, which like the Grecian fate govern their lives. But then has Carlitos ever been a child in the movie? His childhood seems to have disappeared long ago with the departure of the mother to the north. He acts as a guardian to his ailing grandmother, in his spare time helping with an agency to get people across the border. The true gainers seem to be Munni in *Bajrangi Bhaijaan* and Fatima in *Al Otro Lado*. Coincidentally both children are mute in effect. Fatima does not speak or understand Spanish at all, and Munni cannot speak. In his introduction to *What Maisie Knew*, Henry James pointed out, 'Small children have many more perceptions than they have terms to translate them; their vision is at any moment much richer, their apprehension even constantly stronger, than their prompt, their at all producible, vocabulary' (James 1908). One cannot help wondering if in Fatima's and Munni's case that is what is happening. Without feeling the need to translate their needs and their desires into the language of the adult where they would be reasoned with and made helpless, they depend solely and unconsciously on the power of their own conviction and they go and get what they want.

The children seem to escape the grasp of the filmmaker, the fleeting experience of childhood that the adult cannot hold on to cannot be exactly rendered in the language or rhetoric of the adult world. In the movies the children are usually seen to be in the process of becoming adults, which perhaps facilitates the adult understanding of what the child experiences or thinks. Rendered mute, the children are used as symbols of other experiences, transformed into markers of adult anxiety. In Inarritu's 2006 *Babel*, Mike, the little American boy as he is driven into Mexico innocently says to his nanny Amelia, 'Mom says Mexicans are liars'. On the way back as Amelia gets stranded in the blazing Texan desert with two white children and tries to navigate the way back, Mike turns to her, crying, confused, and scared and parrots his absent mother saying with equal amounts of viciousness and helplessness and fear, 'you are a bad person'. The adult's black and white world already imprinted on the back of his mind, his mother's consciousness takes over his own, and the fear acts as the catalyst turning Amelia as the 'other' erasing all her other identities for him.

The relationship in movies between the child and the adult entered into whether as a director or as a spectator is uneasy, tension-fraught. As Lucia Rabello do Castro says, 'the child's identity is conceived as a *difference* in respect to the adult's identity: what the adult is, the child is not yet, but will be; what the adult was, and has successfully overcome, the child is' (Rocha and Seminet xii). At the same time, it is also true, what being a child is, the adult forgets, and the child does not *know* how to be an adult except by imitating the adult. The children at the border perhaps are similar refracted adults or in the process of becoming one. Often the psychological borders that the child is seen as crossing along with the geopolitical ones reflect an adult's ideological concerns. Whether, or if at all, movies made by adults can represent the child's anxiety, fear, helplessness, as well as resilience remains a moot question – because in most movies the child does not participate, it remains an object and an extension of an adult's own psychical process.

Notes

1 Bajrang Dal (the Army of Bajrang or Hanuman) is a militant Hindu organization which came to be in 1984, in the wake of resurgence of the Hindu identity after the extreme right wing came to power for the first time since India gained independence. This group was banned temporarily in 1992 immediately after the demolition of Babri Masjid by militant Hindus, as it was seen as encouraging incendiary activities against non-Hindus, particularly Muslims and Christians. The character of Bajrangi in the movie is basically composed of two irreconcilable elements: his devotion to Bajrang as a die-hard Hindu, and his Gandhian dedication to truth and nonviolence. A contradiction which is apparent in the title of the movie too: *Bajrangi* means a follower of Bajrang/Hanuman, tagged to the word *bhaijaan* (brother), which is a typically Muslim address.

2 India and the newborn Pakistan jointly framed an Act known popularly as the 'Recovery and Restoration Act' in 1949 to rescue persons abducted immediately before or after the month of Independence, i.e. August 1947. Abducted, raped, forcibly converted children and women of the North and West of India were mainly to be brought under its ambit. Camps were set up on both sides of the border to house the 'rescued' women who were known or suspected to have been abducted, with the intention of returning them to their families. The results were not happy leading to confusion, heartbreak, emotional trauma for the persons affected. *Pinjar* and *Gadar, Ek Prem Katha* are movies which are based on narratives centred on this act. Fortunately, it was in operation only till 1951.

References

Emma Wilson, *Cinema's Missing Children* (Wallflower Press, London, New York, 2003).

Henry James, *What Maisie Knew* (Penguin Classics, 2010).

Olsen Debbie (ed), *The Child in World Cinema* (Lexington Books, 2018).

Maguire and Randall (eds), *New Visions of Adolescence in Latin American Cinema* (Palgrave Macmillan, 2018).

Martin Deborah, *The Child in Contemporary Latin American Cinema* (Palgrave Macmillan, 2019).

Rocha and Seminet (eds), *Representing History, Class and Gender in Spain and Latin America* (Palgrave Macmillan, 2012).

Rocha and Seminet (eds), *Screening Minors in Latin American Cinema* (Lexington Books, 2014).

Soledad Paz-Mackay and Rodriguez (eds), *Politics of Children in Latin American Cinema* (Lexington Books, 2019).

Part IV

AUDIO/VISUAL LANGUAGES OF PERCEPTION

Humour and Satire – Subversion as Resistance

7

HUMOURIZING TENSION

Bengali Identity, Partition, and Borders

Parthasarathi Bhaumik

The question of Bengali modernity in the 19th century made self-reflection and ruthless self-analyses imperative as both these activities were linked integrally to a larger issue of nation formation. The newfound western notions of nationalism and its concomitant ideas of shared past, good citizenship, and cultural homogeneity necessitated a re-evaluation of one's own socio-cultural and moral locations comparable to those of Europe. But it never had been an easy proposition for many Bengali elites who took up this cudgel voluntarily for various reasons as the entire endeavour of implementing the western concept of nationhood in India dashed against the colonial reality. Colonialism in India, which was considered to be one of the facilitators of so-called 'Bengal renaissance' by a number of Bengali thinkers and elites, also turned out to be one of the major stumbling blocks as there remained a non-negotiable gulf between India and a concept of a western state. Their search for a shared historical past and identity as a morally upright and free citizen of a noble nation encountered an unresolved complication: the mutually exclusive nature of the western notion of free and good citizenship, and subjugation to a colonial power. The Bengali intellectuals, in such circumstances, invented an ingenious way of addressing this problem: instead of asking questions against the colonial enterprises fair and square, they redirected them against themselves, instead of censuring the colonial authority, they censured themselves. The reason behind the proliferation of Bengali satires and self-criticism and simultaneous enthusiasm for social and religious reforms in Bengal during the 19th century might be traced, among many other reasons, in the Bengali reluctance and inability to negotiate the overwhelming and much difficult question of blatant colonialism straightaway. In most of the cases, the seriousness of such issue was masqueraded behind public humour and self-irony, which continued to be one of the Bengali ways of responding to any crisis too complicated to negotiate. If a gruesome colonial rule was to be presented, responded, and negotiated, let it be done in a funny way. So

DOI: 10.4324/9780429356421-12

there came, for instance, *naksās* in its dual capacities as a Bengali term: a pattern or plan, and a literary genre of humorous prose.[1] This is, in psychological term, a sweet lemon situation, a Bengali defence mechanism: when one has to eat a lemon, let us pretend that the lemon is sweet. The Bengali tradition of humourizing tension and conflicts in the time of crisis can also be seen as an exploration of selfhood and self-consciousness. This study intends to engage with the issue of masking violence and displacement with humour during and after another moment of Bengali crisis: the partition of Bengal in 1947, and explore its subversive attempt at all political high drama associated with the event. It will try to understand how this tradition exposes the moment of creating political and geographical border as a redundant historical incident, the border was created much earlier albeit all the euphoria of a unified Bengal and Bengali identity. Besides, it would also study the role of such humour to stereotype and institutionalize various Bengali identities, undermine or uphold the idea of nation-state in the south-east Asian contexts.

I

Ghoti and Bāngāl: Constructing a Cultural Binary

The Bengali identity as a race, like many others, is not unitary and homogeneous, and there always exist divisions not only on the basis of general markers like class and gender, but also on the geographical locations within Bengal. Bengal as a geographical space was changed several times in its historical course, and in the popular parlance of Bengali culture, the inhabitants of the eastern and the western parts of Bengal are called *Bāngāl* and *Ghoti*, respectively. Before 1947, there was no definite demarcation between these two parts, and the division was more of a construction on the basis of some cultural modes including language, food habits, rituals etcetera rather than a geographical reality. Though in 1905, Bengal Presidency was divided by the colonial administration, and a separate Eastern Bengal province was created, and it merged with Assam. The Partition of Bengal of 1905 was significant as it raised a number of important issues which would dictate the course of history for South Asia in future. For examples, the communal division between the Hindus and Muslims, rise of cultural nationalism, assertion of Bengali-ness as a marker of national identity, the emergence of Swadeshi and Boycott as tools for political resistance etcetera emerged as defining issues of the South Asian political and cultural history.[2] The Partition of 1905 was revoked in the face of intense protests; Bengal was 'reunited', and the 'border' drawn by Lord Curzon, the then Viceroy, was erased. This short-lived Partition of Bengal of 1905, however, left an indelible legacy which the Partition of 1947 followed meticulously. But the Partition of India of 1947 provided a concrete, tangible, and permanent marker of division in the form of a 'border' running between West Bengal and the then East Pakistan, and so, what had been an ideological construction now got tangibility.

The easy binary of East Bengal and West Bengal officially came up in 1947 when the 3rd June Plan of Viceroy Lord Mountbatten was actualized and political border was drawn. The official nomenclature of 'East Bengal' existed for 24 years (1947–1971) as an administrative unit until it became independent Bangladesh. For these 24 years, 'East Bengal' or *Pūrba Bānglā* had a concrete geographical space to define itself, and it needed no imperative reference of binary to 'West Bengal' or *Paschim Banga*. But before 1947 and after 1971 (when Bangladesh as a sovereign state was born), 'East Bengal' remains as a profound example of the cartography of affect; it neither had a demarcated boundary/border prior to this period, nor an official definition after it.[3] But '*Pūrba Banga*' refused to cease merely because of the want of geographical definitions, it remains a construct, a construct of memory, assumptions and expectations, and subsequently there has been innumerable definitions. Syed Mujtaba Ali, one of the finest Bengali writers tried to define '*Pūrba Banga*', a place he was very passionate about, cryptically as '*Padmār hei pār*' (that side of Padma) leaving an implicit definition of '*Paschim Bangā*' (West Bengal) as '*Padmār ei pār*' (this side of Padma). The difference between '*hei*' and '*ei*' is not merely about the occurrence and non-occurrence of the glottal sound /h/; it encompasses a rich array of cultural experiences including language.[4] What is noticeable in Mujtaba Ali's attempt to locate '*Pūrba Bānglā*' in terms of 'this' and 'that', 'ei' and 'hei' is that the frame of reference is invariably that of this side or the western part of Bengal, a privileged space to stand on to inspect around.

Notwithstanding its etymological association with more holistic notions of '*Bānglā*' *(Bengal)* and '*Bāngālī*' (Bengali), *Bāngāl* comes to represent only a fraction of 'semi-civilized' population of Bengal. The Samsad Bengali Dictionary defines *Bāngāl* as 'a native of east Bengal, an unrefined rustic'; a much older Bengali Dictionary *Calantikā* of Rajshekhar Bose puts forth its adjectival form as '*Bāngāle*' (বাঙালে, Bangal-like), which came to much use to denote the *Bāngāl* characteristics in a nutshell. The Samsad Dictionary gives a fine example in '*Bangale gon*' (বাঙালে গোঁ a *Bāngāl*-like stubbornness). All these pejorative associations, and a deeply run tension between two types of Bengalis charted out on some assumed and fictive geography, were the outcome of some socio-economic and cultural factors whose relative arbitrary values were accentuated by the colonial administration. The industrial and administrative growth around Calcutta and the subsequent prominence and significance of the western part of Bengal privileged its populace over its agrarian counterpart on the eastern side of Bengal. Moreover, the power of letters was also more with the western side. According to the *Blumhardt Catalogue of Bengali Books* published in 1886, and a *Supplementary Catalogue* of the same of 1910, an overwhelming majority of the books were published only from Calcutta. The same was also true for journals and newspapers. A complete sway over the written letters and publications privileged a particular cultural pattern over other patterns, including language.

Long before the partition, the western side of Bengal remained a privileged space compared to its eastern part. There are quite a number of literary evidences in Bangla literature to illustrate that *Bāngāl–Ghoti* division had existed long before the Partition, and, much like the post-Partition scenario, it was a source of laughter, and in most of the cases, *Bāngāls* were made the subject of humour and ridicule. Shri Brindaban Das (1507?–1589?) in his *Srichaitanyabhāgavat* narrated how Srichaitanya, in his younger days, loved to make fun of the east-Bengal people, mimicking their language though he himself was from *Shrihatta*, a place in East Bengal.[5] He continued to irritate them until they became infuriated and chased him madly (*Srichaitanyabhāgavat* 107) (Das 107). The Bangla theatre, a tradition initiated in the 19th century and flourished primarily in the colonial city Calcutta, also portrayed *Bāngāl* characters on the stage as sources of laughter and hilarious examples of incongruity. Dramatists and playwrights, like Dinabandhu Mitra (1829–1873), Dwijendralal Roy (1863–1913), Amritalal Bose (1853–1929), used *Bāngāl* characters on stage much to the delight of contemporary urban audience.

Lost in Laughter: *Bāngāl* Language and Its Linguistic 'Incompetence'

Sharadindu Bandyopadhyay (1899–1970), a significant writer of historical fiction, pushed *Bāngāl–Ghoti* incompatibility to an 'ahistorical' time of fairy tales in his story *Tandrā Haraṇ*[6] (Abduction of Tandrā) where the princess Tandrā was reluctant to marry the prince of Prāgjyotiṣpur because he belonged to the eastern part of Bengal, or in short, he was a *Bāngāl*, and the worse part of this good-looking young prince was that he spoke an 'obscene' Bānglā (Bāngāl Bānglā) in ridiculously affected way. But love, as it happens in all ahistorical or historical times, won over the differences, Princess Tandrā fell in love with this good-looking but foul-mouthed *Bāngāl* prince. At the end, princess not only changed her heart for this rustic young man, she, most importantly, changed her language too, and started to talk in Bāngāl Bānglā (Bandyopadhyay).

Accepting a *Bāngāl* and his language is much easier in fairy tales than in real life situations since *Bāngāl* stands for uncouth barbarity. The language of the *Bāngāl* has been a source of great humour for the rest, and behind such an apparent innocuous humour lurks the implication of the inferiority/superiority of language. Amongst different forms of Bangla language spoken in different regions of Bengal, the east Bengal variations are considered hilarious by their own merit. In the article *Chattogrāmer Kathyabhāṣā* ('The Spoken Language of Chittagong') published in the Bangla journal *Prabāsī* in 1945, one Sri Subodhranjan Roy discussed the absurdity of the language spoken in Chittagong, a place in East Bengal, and made the following observation:

> The unintelligibility of the language of this remote region [Chittagong] still raises, as it did in the past, a contemptuous curiosity among the people…The educated people of Chittagong (particularly those who are socially sensible), if they have willingness and self-effort, could even pick up the spoken language of this great metropolis [Calcutta] transcending the influences of their own speech and verbal gestures… One of my Calcutta friends once wanted to know out of innocent curiosity whether the husbands and wives of Chittagong express their love and romance in this very language…Perhaps he had an impression that no tender conversation of sweet romance was ever possible in such an unintelligible language.
>
> (Roy)

The author is further apprehensive that the swiftness of their speech might provoke other people to call the inhabitants of Chittagong '*boyangsi*' meaning birds, because their speech is nothing but the meaningless chirpings.

As discussed earlier, the Bangla spoken in and around Calcutta happened to acquire prestige for extra-linguistic and political reasons and stood to represent the standard Bangla, and the Bangla spoken in places far away from Calcutta were subjects of 'contemptuous curiosity' of the educated elites. The Bāṅglā language written in books was a particular register of many available versions of Bāṅglā used by the educated elites. Other versions of Bangla language, including a vast array of versions spoken in east Bengal, in want of printing opportunities and accommodation in academic discourses, are reduced into a 'corrupt' and 'rustic' form of the 'standard' Bangla which is not only unsuitable as a language for a good literature, but it is incompetent to express noble human sentiments. Krishnabihari Gupta in his article '*Banga Sāhitye Bāṅgāl*' (Bāṅgāl in Bengali Literature), published in the Bangla journal *Bicitrā* in 1932, pointed out that even the writers of the East Bengal never considered their Bangla good enough for literary purposes, and so they all wrote in 'western Bangla' (782). He wondered about its reason since there were examples in English literature where writers like Robert Burns and Walter Scott composed many of their much-celebrated works in Scots language. The reason, he found ultimately, was that the language of East Bengal was essentially hilarious, and thus if any literary work was at all possible to be composed in such a language, it must be a humorous one generically. On the other hand, if any serious sentiment was conveyed through this language, it would lose its seriousness and reduce soon into comic stuff. Krishnabihari quoted a song of Rajanikanta Sen (1865–1910) which had high philosophy about the useless struggle and pain one must endure in this world, and, unlike his other songs, this particular one was written in *Bāngāl* language. Rajanikanta was a renowned composer of many popular devotional songs of the 19th century, and a '*Bāngāl*' by birth. Krishnabihari comments, 'Even when a *Bāngāl* sings the song[7] in utter renunciation of the worldliness, you can't help but laugh at the incongruity of the seriousness of the theme and its silly linguistic expressions'. Mukundaram Chakraborty's *Candimangalkāvya, (*16th c), for another instance, reveals that the dying laments of *Bāngāl* boatmen of a capsizing boat 'would arouse among us emotion which is far removed from compassion or pity' (Gupta 783).

The question now remains about the transferred epithet: how far the 'comicality' of a language may be transferred to the general characteristics of its speakers. It opens up two possibilities: firstly, language does shape its speakers, or the characteristics of the speakers are already taken as a priori, and their language is subsumed into it. The modern linguists would argue that there is close connection between the language one speaks and her social behaviour. Leaving the first possibility outside the scope of this paper, it acknowledges that the popular perceptions about *Bāngāl* were contingent upon socio-political and economic imperatives, and were ideological rather than cartographical. *Bāngāl* is a cultural construct, and notions of humour were so obviously integrated into this identity that *Bāngāls* were denied the status of victimhood. It was the *Bāngāls* who had to leave their ancestral places, endured all kinds of violence and pain only to become shelterless refugees in India as India was divided in 1947. But their sufferings became a matter of humour; their painful struggles to resume their lives in alien places as refugees in the post-Partition time became the endless sources of public comedy.

II

Navine Murshid made an interesting comparative observation between *Bāngāl* settlements in India and the Muhajir settlements in the West Pakistan and their concomitant consequences. According to him, since the size of migration from the east Punjab (India) to the west Pakistan was twice the size of migration from west Pakistan to India, and similarly the size of the migration from East Bengal to India was twice the size of the migration to the opposite direction, there were rise in net population in West Pakistan and West Bengal (India). So in the context of increased population, both in West Pakistan and West Bengal the *Muhajirs* (Migrants from East Punjab to Pakistan's West Punjab) and *Bāngāls* (migrants from East Bengal to West Bengal) faced discrimination as they had to compete with the locals for their sustenance. *Muhajirs* later emerged as a potent political force in 1978, initiated Muhajir Quami Movement (MQM) and later Muttahida Quami Movement which still have great impact on Pakistan politics. In the general election in 2013, MQM held 24 seats in the National Assembly [MQM did not participate in 2018 election] and they have considerable sway over the state policies (Murshid 100). But nothing of this sort happened for Bāngāls in West Bengal; they never built any political platform of their own to voice their concerns and ensure their participation in national politics. But it does not mean that the *Bāngāls* did not struggle collectively. They encroached private and vested land, squatted on empty houses collectively, and ran refugee colonies under their own organizations. But all these efforts were not translated into full-fledged political organization. Murshid comments,

> [Their (*Bāngāls*)] cohesion did not have a political platform but found expression in local football, where the Bangali team, East Bengal loved to play Mohun Bagan, the local (Ghoti) team. Bangal pride in West Bengal also rested partly on claims to intellectual superiority reinforced by Amartya Sen's Nobel Memorial Prize in Economic Sciences, for example.
>
> (Murshid 101)

What could have been a blatant conflict between the refugees and the locals was thus channelized/sublimated into competitions at various cultural sites. Laughter and public humour were essential ingredients to claims of such competitiveness between *Bāngāls* and *Ghotis*, as innumerable witty innuendos, jokes, sharp ridicules flooded Bengali life aiming at each other, and are still continuing in some form or other.

Language is just one of many cultural sites where the *Bāngāl–Ghoti* division works in binary ways, and in most of the cases, *Bāngāl* ways of life would be a matter of great hilarity in contradistinction to the life of *Ghotis* which would be a yardstick for 'normal' ways of life. *Bāngāls* are uncouth, rough, never bothered much about civility. They are impulsive, quarrelsome, stubborn, and rustic, against which the *Ghotis* would be implied as civil, urbane, sensible, and thoughtful. Hilarity springs forth from the proximity of these two opposites, when *Bāngāl* and *Ghoti* interact, argue, and wonder at each other's 'ridiculous' ways of life. Before the Partition, the possibility of proximity was temporary and ideological, but after the Partition when about 3 million *Bāngāls* came from East Bengal to live permanently with *Ghotis*, and compete with them for survival, the humour on both sides ceased to be a harmless jovial exercise.

'Laughter' and 'Unlaughter': Subjectivity and/or Assertion of Bāngāl Identity

Humour is not a unitary entity; it is not oriented to a single cause and effect. Laughter, which is taken to be natural outcome of humour might not be an innocuous affair. With every laughter, there may be an 'unlaughter' lurking behind the arras, a term coined by Michael Billing in his book *Laughter and Ridicule: Towards a Social Critique of Humour*. Billing finds out three essential paradoxes of humour: one of them is that 'humour is both social and anti-social: it can bring people together in a bond of enjoyment, and by mockery, it can exclude people' (Billing 175–176). Laughter is also a language, and just like a spoken language it is a rhetorical communication. The paradoxes of laughter are similar to the paradoxes of verbal languages. Billing argues,

> Like language and other aspects of rhetorical communication, laughter has to be learnt and taught. The rhetorical nature of laughter helps us to understand why humour might be paradoxical. Language is paradoxical to the extent that it enables us to perform contrary discursive acts: we can assert, because we can deny; we can question because we can answer; we can criticize because we can justify, and so on. Because laughter is rhetorical, it cannot be a single, simple thing that can be considered apart from the rhetoric of communication. So the rhetorical opposite of laughter, [is] termed 'unlaughter'. Laughter and unlaughter are very much part of the processes of learning and imposing the disciplines of social life. In this respect, the social links between humour and laughter take us to the heart of serious living.
>
> (Billing 177)

Presenting the life of East Bengal in 'non-serious' manner, making its speech as a source of comic, and a stereotyping *Bāngāl* character as a combination of weird and harmless behaviours, constitute a perfect recipe for comedy. In literature, children's stories, plays, and particularly post-Partition Bangla films, *Bāngāl* characters were assigned to play the role of some sort of a buffoon; they were the objects of ridicule with their accent, customs, and food habits. They were misfits with all kinds of clumsiness in the new surroundings. But at the same time, they would be good-hearted but with no consequence over the ultimate action. A *Bāngāl* could not be either a hero as he was too uncouth for this, nor can be a villain as he is ineffectual, he never initiates, nor has he the ability to finish off, he only lingers in between. He is ridiculous, and 'ridicule, even when framed as amiable teasing is still ridicule: it proceeds from an assumption of cultural inferiority', an assumption embedded in the historical processes of Bengal long before the partition (Sarkar 159).

The famine of 1943, which saw a steady flow of hungry people to Calcutta and Decca, and ugly deaths of 3 million people, many of whom died literally on city streets, and once again in 1947 the unwelcome refugees from East Bengal and the sight of *vastuhārā* (homeless) colony, a term which would soon become pertinent with another political register '*Sarbahārā*' (who has lost everything, proletariat) towards a particular political orientation, vehemently disturbed the idyllic universe of West Bengal *bhadralok*. By the end of 1949 more than a million refugees came to West Bengal, the first four months of 1950 alone created another million, and the 1951 census shows a total refugee population in West Bengal was over 2 million. This was much more than West Bengal was capable of accommodating. Moreover, for a far long time the refugees believed that one day they would return to their home and claim back their property easily. Their stay in West Bengal was merely a temporary affair. Ashoke Mitra observes, 'This resulted in transforming the East Bengal refugees into listless dole-seekers, fawning and militant by turns, willing pawns in the hands of political manipulators, averse to enterprise and bereft of pride' (Mitra 143). The ugliness of the refugees became synonymous with *Bāngāl*, and *Bāngāl* rhymed excellently with the Bangla word '*Kāngāl*' (beggars).

During 1950s and 60s the proliferation of romantic melodramas and the tremendous popularity of superstar screen couple Uttam Kumar and Suchitra Sen, perhaps for the first time, gave the Bengalis a flight of fantasy from the ordeal and ugliness of post-Partition trauma or a not-so-old memory of famine in 1943. Any melodrama is a necessary medium of negotiating the social unrest within a private space like home, and imposes order and discipline by the resolution of the crisis (Sarkar 144–145). On the fantastic flight of Bengali wish-fulfilment over the sordidness of immediate crisis and anxiety over sharing resources with uprooted people, the films showed a remarkable strategy for laughter: the poignant cultural differences and 'affected' Bangla, some insignificant conflicts arising out of '*Bāngālpona*' (attitude of a *Bāngāl*) and a complete resolution of all crises. The good audience would feel better that in spite of differences the *Bāngāl* can be assimilated into main stream of things.

The first debut film of Uttam–Suchitra pair, a romantic comedy *Sāre Chuāttor* (Seventy-four and half) is about Bengali life in a boarding house. Boarding house or in Bangla *messbāri* was a significant addition to Bengali life in the post-Partition time particularly when finding accommodation in Calcutta was becoming increasingly difficult. The most hilarious and conspicuous character in the film is Kedar, an East Bengal chap. The role was played by actor Bhanu Bandyopadhay (1920–1983) who earned his fame as an actor and leading comedian from his specialized acting of *Bāngāl* roles. Kedar typifies all the characteristics of a typical East Bengal boy:

> who seems forever famished: as soon as his friend returns from home after vacation, he hastens to see if he brought back homemade ghee; he frequently visits people who serve good quality tea; smelling freshly made dessert, he runs around looking for the source. He is the jocular friend of Rampriti (played by Uttam Kumar); but once they start wooing the same girl, Ramala (Suchitra Sen), he turns into a scheming fiend. Of course, he is too inept to cause any serious

> damage: his pathetic attempts to win Ramala's affections produce more hilarity. Failing both in romance and villainy, the *Bāngāl* is reduced to a harmless clown – a comic plot device.
>
> (Sarkar 159)

Similar instances can be cited from other films like *Orā thāke odhāre* (They live on the other side), once again featuring romantic duo Uttam–Suchitra, which is a story of two families, one from East Bengal, and the other from West Bengal. They live together with funny and absurd bickering over their own cultures but at the same time retaining mutual love and trust. They share one iron, one radio, one sewing machine. This *Bāngāl* family speaks *Bāngāl* Bangla, but their daughter (role played by Suchitra Sen, the heroine), speaks 'chaste' Calcutta Bangla, and thus saves her status as a heroine.

Partition as a violent rupture had its repercussions on life in Bengal in terms of divided identity, and mutual suspicion between the refugees and the permanent residents, there were struggles on either side to assert one's self-dignity. As native inhabitants of West Bengal struggled to maintain their position less, they slip into the economic and social chaos created by the Partition, on the other hand, the refugees wanted to tell the stories of their erstwhile life on the other side of the border to let the world know that they had never been so what they were. Even if a family was out on the pavement or living in a slum, it could assert its entitlement of respect.[8] The popular humour on *Bāngāls* exaggerating their wealth and being a little bit imaginative in ascertaining the quantum of land they left behind might be a case in point. But, however, the struggle for cultural assertion and the question of superiority–inferiority matched with *bhadralok* Bengali identity was not the outcome of Partition of 1947, the pattern was woven much earlier and humourizing the latent tension of difference also started in the late-19th and early-20th centuries. Bengal Partition, in this respect, was a redundant historical event; it only sharpened some of its prongs like deep anxiety for uncertain economic future.

In the year of the Partition, an old Bangla journal (now extinct) *Sacitra Bhārat* published an article named 'Bangabhanga O Ghatī-Bāngāl Samasyā' (The Partition of Bengal and *Ghoti–Bāngāl* Crisis) written from an assumed perspective of a *Bāngāl* which put forth the impossibility of any reconciliation between them much in the spirit of Rudyard Kipling's '*OH, East is East, and West is West, and never the twain shall meet*'. It argues,

> You are *Ghoti*, and we are *Bāngāl* though both of us live in Bengal as Bengali. You are *Ghoti*; and so you are the West. We are *Bāngāl*; and so we are the East. Our sun rises early, and your sun sets late. Our land is green and fertile while yours is barren and malaria infested.... [Your] Calcutta is the present capital of Bengal under

> the British rule, and [our] Dhaka was the former capital of Bengal under the Mughal Empire. The British glory rose in Calcutta, and the Mughal glory went down in Dhaka.
>
> (Shishir 17)

What is noticeable here is a rereading of history from the perspective of the *Ghoti–Bāngāl* divide, where West (*Ghoti*–Bengal) appears to be emerging, privileged site of power, and the East (*Bāngāl*–Bengal) is a reminiscent of an erstwhile glory. This division is not ontological, it is temporal, one stands for the presentness of the present and the other is the pastness of the present, and each temporal location is viewed through the grid of possibility and loss.

It would be a simplification of the fact if *Bāngāl–Ghoti* humour is viewed only as repercussion of snubbing by *Ghotis* at their erstwhile compatriot, and now turned refugees from the East Bengal. It was not merely an expression of their self-acclaimed 'superiority' over their 'inferior' counterparts from the eastern region. This humour is double-edged, it not only caricatures *Bāngāls* as rustic crass, plain speakers, and reckless risk takers, but on the other side, it never fails to portray the *Ghotis* as indolent mass busking on erstwhile glories of their forefathers. The idea is that in the post-Partition scenario of sharp competition, the *Ghotis* were fighting a losing battle against die-hard, pragmatic *Bāngāls*. The differences between a *Bangal* and a *Bangalī* (i.e. Ghoti), one of the most recurrent themes of *Bāngāl–Ghoti* humour, *Bangal* is called 'masculine' whereas Ghoti is 'feminine'.[9] The differences, far from belittling the hapless *Bāngāl* refugees in West Bengal, started to assert *Bāngāl* identity in vigorous manner, and in post-Partition time *Bāngāl* identity became a matter of pride. Movies, audio cassettes, humorous books took *Ghoti–Bāngāl* debate as a commercially successful commodity and became popular equally to the Bengalis belonging to both 'warring' camps. The humour about *Bāngāls* and its acceptance among the *Bāngāl* refugees became, in a way, a consolidation of identity and enhanced the formation of groups in a difficult time when losing one's identity and history in a new homeland was not a distant possibility.

The relevance of *Bāngāl* might not be too ostensible today and the cultural rift might be blurred apparently in the neo-liberal contexts of globalization, at least apparently, but such humour is still popular because the tensions and anxieties are there in Bengali society. The *Bāngāl* identity has assumed new names; new nomenclatures have come into being; new political demands are being asserted. The issue of citizenship to *Bāngāl* refugees has been an important one for many political parties in all recent elections. The homogeneous notion of *Bāngāl* of earlier time has been splintered into various groups woven into complex patterns of identity politics. The emerging subaltern movements in West Bengal on and around the issues of equality and citizenship rights are, in most of the cases, integrally related to the Partition and refugeehood. Recent Bengali movies are still using *Bāngāl–Ghoti* stereotypes with much popular success. The history of fractured Bengali identity is continuing, and the best or the worst part is that the humour and the laughter refuse to die even in the most painful situations.

Notes

1 *Hutom Pyancār Nakśā* (1861) by Kaliprasanna Singha, for instance, was one of the most popular *nakśās* of its time, and is still read for its use of spoken Bangla language and great humour. It smacked vigorous attack against the Bengali *Baboo* culture, its profligacy and moral decadence, while the venom of severe satire was often hidden under apparently innocuous humour.

2 For detailed documents pertaining to the Partition of Bengal of 1905 and its various cultural implications, see the database created by the author in the British Library. www.bl.uk/projects/partition-of-bengal-1905-and-rise-of-nationalism.

3 The official nomenclature 'East Bengal' first came into effect on 16 October 1905 when Bengal was partitioned by the colonial authority into two provinces 'Bengal' and 'Eastern Bengal and Assam'. The colonial government, however, was initially reluctant in using the word 'Partition' in this regard, they preferred 'redistribution'. The decision was revoked in 1912 under much public agitation.

4 In 'standard' Bangla language '*ei*' means 'this', and '*sei*' means 'that'. '*Sei*' in East Bengal is often pronounced as '*hei*'. There is no dearth of humour about Bāngāl preference for this glottal sound.

5 সভার সহিত প্রভু হাস্য-কথা-রঙ্গে।/কহিলেন যেনমতে আছিলেন বঙ্গে।।/বঙ্গদেশী-বাক্য অনুকরণ করিয়া।/বাঙ্গালেরে কদর্থেন হাসিয়া হাসিয়া।। (107) [The Lord (Srichaitanya) talked jovially with the congregated people. He was telling them about how he had lived in Banga. He mimicked the language of Banga, and made fun of the Bāngāl people laughingly.]

6 Sharadindu Bandyopadhyay, *Sharadindu Omnibus*, Vol. 5, Ananda Publishers, pp. 277–279.

7 চারদিকে থনে পাগলা তেরে ঘিরিয়া ধরছে পাপে,/ অ্যাহন, মইষেরে সিঙ্গে মারবে গুত্তা, বাচাইবো কে নে বাপে?

8 In an audio comedy, Bhanu Bandyopadhyay, the afore-mentioned Bengali actor, who became synonymous with Bāngāl humour, was found to write his name on nameplate as 'Lord Bhanu Bandyopadhyay'. Surprised by this strange honorific, when his friend asked him for a clarification, Bhanu answered that he was a 'Landlord', but he lost his 'land' in the Partition only to hold the remaining part of the word. Now as a refugee he was living with whatever little he could save for him.

9 In Bangla language, the feminine word generally ends with inflection /ī/ sound, and the word marks its difference from its corresponding masculine counterpart by this /ī/ prefix. For example, *nandan* means son, whereas *nandinī* means daughter. So, by the same rule, it is jovially argued that 'Bāngal' is masculine and 'Bāngalī' is feminine.

References

Bandyopadhyay, Sharadindu, 1953. *Sharadindu Omnibus, Vol. 5*. Kolkata: Ananda Publishers.

Billing, M., 2005. *Laughter and Ridicule: Towards a Social Critique of Humour*. London: Sage Publications.

Das, Brindaban. (Atulkrishna Goswami ed.), 1985. *Srichaitanyabhāgavat*. Kolkata: Goudiya Baishnab Sammilan.

Gupta, K., 1339 BS (1932 CE). 'Bangasāhitye Bāngāl. *Bicitrā,* Issue Poush, pp. 781–785.
Mitra, A., 1991. *The New India, 1948-1955: Memoirs of an Indian Civil Servant.* Calcutta: Popular Prakashan.
Murshid, N., 2014. *The Politics of Refugees in South-Asia: Identity, Resistance, Manipulation.* New York: Routledge.
Roy, S., 1352 BS (1945 CE). Chattogramer Kathyabhāshā. *Prabāsī,* Issue Kartik, pp. 91–92.
Sarkar, B., 2009. *Mourning the Nation: Indian Cinema in the Wake of Partition.* Durham: Duke University Press.
Shishir, 1947. Bangabhanga O Ghatī-Bāngāl Samasyā. *Sacitra Bhārat,* 12(6), pp. 17–18.

Websites

Bhanu Bandopadhyay Comic Music Box www.youtube.com/watch?v=hxOsyb-HJvgs accessed on 10 September 2016.
Bhaumik, Parthasarathi. *Partition of Bengal (1905) and Rise of Nationalism,* www.bl.uk/projects/partition-of-bengal-1905-and-rise-of-nationalism accessed on 23 October 2021.

8

CHHITMAHAL

Subjectivity, Resistance, and Identities

Sawon Chakraborty

It was 8 September 2016. I was entering Mashaldanga for my field study. The *toto*[1] was running through the road. This path ends at Shalmara, the border of India. It has always been part of the Indian territory. The farmlands beside the road were nicely covered with various shades of green paddies. It is impossible to recognize that once these lands were excluded from India, that these were Bangladeshi territories. These were enclaves, locally known as 'Chhit'. Some people were standing there on those lands in an odd manner. No, I was wrong. These were scarecrows, mounted in a way that imitate local people. Something was inscribed on their heads and chests. I went close to those scarecrows to read that and found, it was inscribed 'ami'/'I'. Strange! Who is this 'I'? This question had been on my mind ever since and catalysed my curiosity about the people of Chhitmahal.

I first met Belal Hussain at Mashaldanga. He is a farmer by profession. They don't have much to do during this time of year. A few other people of Chit Mashaldanga were sitting there. They were passing their time by chatting about how much crop would finally grow that season! I could not resist my curiosity anymore. I started to arrange to interview them. I asked them, 'Why did you inscribe these scarecrows as "I"?' My curiosity was vividly expressed in my gesture of questioning. They started laughing because of that. I joined them too. Belal started telling me about the tales of their struggle. His stories indicated how the word 'struggle' is a nuanced one and carries a lot of meanings in it!

> What's scarecrow? It's merely a distorted imitation of a human being, of one who is not fully a human. A scarecrow doesn't own the field, it guards it. It protects the crops from birds and other unwanted beings, but doesn't get a share of its own. Being an ephemeral figure, it loses its shape with time. Such a sacrifice! But what do they get in return? Absolutely nothing!

 DOI: 10.4324/9780429356421-13

Taking a long breath Belal started again,

> After the enclave exchange program, we, the people of enclaves, have not got the documents of our own land and properties yet. The crops, you are seeing now, are the crops of our labour. Before the exchange program, when we had to enter Indian markets to sell our crops, either we were looted by the local people of the mainland or had to sell our crops at a very lower price than the actual market value. What was our fault? We were the people of Chhit. So, like scarecrows we got nothing in exchange for our labour. And now, even after the enclave exchange program, we don't have any official acknowledgement of the ownership of our lands which belong to India now. The local people of the mainland have never treated us like as human beings.

It is clearly evident how the enclave dwellers were dehumanized as the 'other'. Enclaves, by its traits, otherized the enclave dwellers from mainland dwellers via access to the state provided security and validation. It therefore pronounced an unequal power relation between them, one standing as exploiter, another exploited. On 28 October 2015, at the same place Akbar Ali, another Chhit dweller, told me, 'We led our lives like footballs. Both the people of Bangladesh and India kicked us, we rolled from here to there and meanwhile they looted everything'.

I quote here the press release from the Ministry of External Affairs, Government of India on 20 November 2015.

> In accordance with steps agreed to between India and Bangladesh during Prime Minister Narendra Modi's visit to Bangladesh on June 6-7, 2015, as per the Land Boundary Agreement (LBA) 1974 and Protocol of 2011, 51 erstwhile Bangladeshi enclaves in India and 111 erstwhile Indian enclaves in Bangladesh were physically transferred to the other country with effect from the midnight of 31 July 2015. Based on the joint survey exercise meticulously carried in the enclaves, it was determined that 989 persons out of total 38,521 residents from erstwhile Indian enclaves in Bangladesh have opted to retain their original nationality while all 14,863 residents of the Bangladesh enclaves in India have opted for Indian nationality.
>
> Under the aegis of the India-Bangladesh Joint Boundary Working Group, modalities for the physical movement of these enclave residents were worked out. The State Government of West Bengal has put in place elaborate arrangements for their stay in temporary resettlement camps and for issue of necessary documentation to them. Facilities made available at the camps include tin houses,

> common dining hall and kitchen, community toilets, anganwadi centre, playground equipment, etc. Arrangements for bank account opening, biometric enrolment, currency exchange and relief kit for each family have been made. The first batch of 62 persons arrived through Changrabandha (India) – Burimari (Bangladesh) Immigration Check Post yesterday. They were greeted with honour in a joyous ceremony organised by the Cooch Behar district administration. The MP of Cooch Behar district, MLA of Cooch Behar district, District Magistrate of Cooch Behar, Superintendent of Police of Cooch Behar, Assistant High Commissioner of India in Rajshahi and others were present to welcome the returning Indians to India. 8 more batches will arrive in India by the stipulated deadline of November 30, 2015.
>
> New Delhi, November 20, 2015

In this chapter I will discuss about the subjectivity of the people of Chhitmahal, how that is being shaped by the modes of 'resistance', how the Chhit dwellers are constructing their notion of 'self', how the material conditions are influencing this whole process and this process is also influencing the material situations.

What is Chhitmahal? How was it formed? In 1661, a war started between Maharaja Prana Narayan, the king of Koch dynasty and the Mughals. Naturally, it was not possible for a regional king to resist the Mughals. The Mughals conquered some fragmented lands from Koch territory. These lands were known as 'Moglan'. Later, when the treaty of Allahabad was signed on 12 August 1765 between the Mughal Emperor Shah Alam II and Lord Clive of the East India Company, which marks the beginning of British rule in India, these Moglans became parts of British India, while Koch kingdom was not a part of it. In 1947, at the time of India's partition, the then king of Koch dynasty, Maharaja Jagaddipendra Narayan was taking time to decide where to go with his kingdom, India or Pakistan. But those Moglans were included within Rangpur, the then East Pakistan. On the other hand, according to popular tales, these lands were used as stakes in chess games between two regional kings of Coochbehar and Rangpur. Thus, after partition some fragmented lands in Coochbehar remained under the proprietary of East Pakistan and vice versa. When Coochbehar joined India finally, it caused the same between India and East Pakistan. The word 'Chhit' means fragment and 'Mahal' means land. In Bangla language 'Chhit' has several meanings like 'defective', 'a drop of liquid', and 'a short piece of cloth'. All of these meanings somehow denote the conditions of 'Chhitmahal'. There were 101 Indian enclaves within the mainland of Bangladesh and 51 Bangladeshi enclaves within the mainland of India. A joint census in 2010 found 37,334 people residing in Indian enclaves within Bangladesh and 14,215 people in Bangladeshi enclaves within India.

Before the exchange of enclaves on 1 August 2015, since 1947, in every sense, the enclave dwellers have been deprived of basic human rights, they have been isolated from their state. Even the state maintained a lengthy dilemma in giving them a valid identity card, that is to say, state-provided facilities to survive. The people, born and brought up in enclaves, had no official acceptance of their existence. In order to be a valid citizen, one needs an identity card, by which the state legitimizes a person's existence and includes him/her within its geopolitical borders. The enclave dwellers, born after 1947, never realized that how it feels to be included in a state without threats of being seized as trespassers or illegal immigrants before the exchange was done. Even the state, they accessed 'illegally', was not their own. They lived in a situation of statelessness, but they have always been exploited by the state machinery, they have been thrown behind the bars as 'trespassers', although there was no fencing between enclaves and mainland. The peculiar fact is, they had no state, but they had their native land. They have never moved permanently, never separated themselves from their homeland. Here, the notion of their nationality becomes complicated. The state, supposed to give them legal residence, was on the other side of the border. They have always found the state to be the 'other'. According to the given notion of nationality, a person, residing in their homeland, belongs to the nationality of their native land. However, these enclave dwellers had to be included in the nationality of that 'other'. They were conscious about the fact. But they lived their lives on the side of the border that was known to be their homeland. So, while constructing their notion of nationality, i.e. the legal relation between a state and an individual, they located themselves to the state they were surrounded by, not in which they lived. Ironically, this was supposed to be the nationality of the 'other' state. This situation gave rise to an extremely ambiguous notion of nationality in the enclaves before the exchange program. This brings to surface the increasingly complex question of how these enclave dwellers have been negotiating with an ambiguous notion of 'self'.

The people of Chhitmahal are mostly farmers. They grow mainly three types of crops in these lands in a year – Jute, rice, and tobacco – all of these money-making crops are mainly grown here, although rice doesn't have much popularity. The area is famous for its growth and quality of jute and tobacco. Accordingly, the quality of life of these people should have been much more comfortable, at least financially. However, the scenario was completely the opposite. They lived in the enclaves, but due to the absence of adequate market/buyers for their crop, they had to enter India 'illegally'. Owing to their vulnerable situation, they had to face various sorts of vandalism, perpetuated on them by the people of the mainland. Any type of protest led to threats of getting them behind the bars as trespassers. This was a regular affair and became a part of their everyday life. People of Chhitmahal have always had to accept their hapless fate. They have never had the chance of having either 'dignity' or 'identity'. People, who have been exploited since time immemorial and don't know how to claim their rights, move towards a form of acceptance as they say 'this happens, this is our fate, we can't help but accept it'. They learn to evolve their own alternative ways to survive. Denial of a state identity led to the usage of fake voter cards. For getting one's children into neighbouring Indian schools, fake Indian parents had to be presented in return of lump sum amount of money. Women had to show fake Indian husbands for getting admitted to neighbouring Indian hospitals for child delivery. Resistance does not always emerge through conscious concerted movements. This 'illegal' practice, as a survival strategy, itself was a form of resistance as it succeeded to resist their exploitation several times, allowed them to function and granted them legitimacy. It is natural for us to think that these kinds of practices have given rise to immense mental suffering for the people of Chhitmahal, as these made the families vulnerable. But according to the dwellers of Chhitmahal, feeling depressed about such practices was a luxury that these people could not afford. These 'illegal' practices were a 'normal' way of life since they witnessed these kinds of situations at birth and these were the conditions in which their children grew up. According to them these were 'normal' ways of living. Many of these enclave dwellers even voted by faking their addresses and voter cards, knowing very well how this exercise promises nothing to them. Still they hoped for some sort of security, that they or their children won't be harassed if ever they decide to come into the mainland. When state differentiates between 'legal' and 'illegal', there is always an existing way to follow the 'legality'. Rather, the state feels the necessity to mark that act as 'illegal' which transgresses its imposed notions of 'legality'. The words 'legal' and 'illegal' had completely different connotations for the people of Chhitmahal. It is quite evident that these people had to follow 'illegal' ways to sustain themselves. Even the government had full knowledge of these illegal practices but chose to remain silent to conceal their inability – not their inability to stop these 'illegal' exercises but the inability to give these people the promise of basic necessities and legal identity. 'Illegal' practices necessarily make the existing system questionable and the enclave dwellers carry the potential to drill gaps in the system through their daily 'illegal' practices.

How did the movement for claiming basic human rights and citizenship emerge in a place where the people have accepted their own exploitation for so long and adapted to illegal practices? Inscribing the word 'I' on a scarecrow is a clear mark of cultural and political resistance. Here the scarecrow is appropriated to symbolically perform resistance for specific groups of people who visit Chhitmahals from outside. It signifies that they do not blame their fate rather they blame the mainland dwellers. Borderlands of India and Bangladesh are mostly farmlands. That is why scarecrows form an indispensable part of the culture of these border areas. Do these two scarecrows from Chhitmahal and the outer border lands mean the same? No. A line of difference is drawn by the notions of identity and ownership of land. People have often compared scarecrows with evil power, but Chhitmahal provides a unique example: the dwellers draw analogies between themselves and the scarecrow. They posit as if they are not really human in spite of being one. Deprived of basic human rights, scarecrows provide a distorted picture of the enclave dwellers slowly eroded by the deadly sun, monstrous storm, and rain while holding on to their lands. Standing still in the green lands of enclaves the scarecrows are smiling sarcastically at the people of the mainland, laughing at this civilization! With an inscription on them – 'I'. Now they have found something or someone to blame for their condition. In the case of 'illegal' practices they didn't have a coherent notion of opposition. To claim basic rights, it is necessary to have an opposition, by whom one has been deprived of the rights. Following the 'illegal' way was also a form of resistance. What differentiates these two types of resistance then? In the first case, they had no one to accuse for their condition. Therefore, they learnt to make their own alternative path; they never tried to claim their rights legally; they accepted their deprivation in a certain way; they never questioned but negotiated from within the system of exploitation. But in the second case, they formed an organized movement to acquire a 'legal' life. The movement for the inclusion of 'Chits' or enclaves into the mainlands of Bangladesh and India had started mainly in the 1990s under the leadership of Dipak SenGupta, the former M.L.A. of Dinhata constituency of Coochbehar district, India. The people of the enclaves started being conscious about claiming their rights with the consolidation of this movement.

When people take part in a movement for their basic rights, they become conscious about questions of identity. So, questions like 'who am I?', 'what is my societal status?', began to surface and the answers to these questions started to be addressed from within the movement. Naturally, this yields an effect on their actions. This consciousness strengthens their basis of resistance. Chhit dwellers are no exception. Not only the scarecrows, they have used various metaphors in the 'self-making' process. It is remarkable how a particular ideology guided them to select these metaphors. Another metaphor, which plays a very interesting and important role in the self-making process of Chhit dwellers, is that of the 'hijrah' – a vernacular term to define third gender people, which is often used as a slang too. The people of Mashaldanga often compare themselves to the hijrahs. This has come up in the course of various interviews done by me. While talking to Belal from Mashaldanga, a person comes to the spot whose name is Abdul Salam. People started laughing at him and calling him 'hijrah'. When enquired about the reasons as to why they were calling him so, they explained that many people from enclaves migrate to big cities such as Delhi and Jaipur to work as carpenters and daily labourers. Nobody bothers about their identity in these big cities. When these people return home, they bring with them a bag full of stories. People tell stories of how the hijrahs begged in the trains. hijrahs have always been a less accepted class of people, people generally have a lot of apprehensions about them. Being a person from an enclave and thereby being cut off from the world outside, Abdul expressed his curiosity to know who actually a 'hijRah' is. From then on, other people tease him by calling him 'hijrah'.

After the inclusion of the enclaves, Chhit dwellers arranged a meeting to discuss which Indian political party they would now support. It was held on the same day, 8 September, 2016. I attended the meeting. Abdul said that although people tease him by calling him a hijrah, all the enclave dwellers were hijrah before the enclave exchange program was enacted. Just like nobody agrees to marry the third gender, no Indian or Bangladeshi family agrees to wed off their son or daughter to the people from Chhitmahal. The enclave exchange program was almost like a treatment offered to them for becoming a man or a woman. The Chhit dwellers are now getting their authentic Indian or Bangladeshi identity cards. Now marriage proposals are beginning to come in. Marriage is just one of the many examples of how they are kept outside of social institutions. Just as the people of the third gender are still marginalized in society, people of Chhitmahal were marginalized in the same manner. Apparently, this societal exclusion has united them with third gender people conceptually. But when they adhere their notion of 'self' to the hijrahs, they also, inadvertently, indicate that exclusion is the natural fate of the third gender, but as the Chhit dwellers are not hijrah in real, their social upliftment is important. It also indicates an inherent derogatory attitude towards the hijrah. In this way, ultimately the probability of solidarity between two different marginalized communities gets dissolved by the inherent divisive ideas that inform the way in which they use the metaphor.

Before the enclave exchange program, the state did not provide any identity card to the enclave dwellers or possible options for them to make a living. In spite of this fact, these people have existed, their spontaneous modes of living are written into their own cultural practices. The Muslims of Bangladeshi enclaves in India have been tortured not only as enclave dwellers but also by the people of mainland in the name of religion, as they are minority. So, this sense of othering on the basis of religion has shaped their consciousness and have rendered them vulnerable. This is why the cultural practices in the Muslim-dominated enclaves have been highly influenced by the institutionalized religion. But the Hindus have not been exploited in the name of religion in enclaves. They have not brought in religion consciously in their cultural practices, as in case of the Muslim-dominated enclaves.

There are folk songs, religious songs, as well as songs of movements of their own in the cultural practices of Chhitmahal, which represent their lifestyle and identities. An excerpt from one of those movement songs is:

Fire breaks into the Chits
Whenever internal quarrels take place in India.
What did they do by setting fire to the Chits?
Come here and see,
They have looted ourattles.
They have looted everything,
Nothing is left there for us.
How do we live now?
We cannot protect our lives.
Whom would we convey our sorrow?
Whom would we
convey our sorrow? ...

This song composed by Maleka Bibi, an enclave dweller, tells us about their exploitation, the story of how a movement was formed. Why are they comparing themselves with scarecrows? Why are they comparing themselves with the hijrahs? This song answers these questions.

> It was 14 April 1966. Goons looted our home. Five rounds of firing left nine people injured and three people critically injured. They were admitted to Coochbehar M. J. N. hospital to be treated to save their lives...
>
> The doctor asked for the address. My father was captured immediately under the law as his reply was Chhit Poyaturkuthi. After eighteen days of treatment, we were overwhelmingly occupied with the police station, court and judgement. Following passport law, he faced a fine of five rupees and imprisonment of seven days. He got released by paying fifteen rupees...
>
> We the people of Chitmahal want to say that there are three jails in our life, one is congenital and the other two are state-jails. The government officials are assigned for the security of prisoners and forests are under the supervision of the government. But we have no one except 'Ishwar' or 'Allah'.

The above is a part, translated from a two-page autobiography by Mansur Ali Miah, an octogenarian enclave dweller. Though he claims it to be a biography, it does not follow the standard form of the genre. He started feeling the necessity to write down this biography while the enclave exchange program started taking place. He named it 'A detailed description of Chhitmahal'. Here the politics of selecting events in biography and naming it using the term 'Chhitmahal' is notable. Here Mansur as an individual does not care to talk about all the other dimensions of his identity but tries to express himself as an oppressed enclave dweller.

While surveying the field at Chhit Balapukari, a former Bangladeshi enclave in India, I met Santoshi Adhikary, an enclave dweller. She showed me a broken temple and its yard, the set-up being called 'chandi-mandap' in vernacular. Since 1980s a Durga Puja had been organized here, an annual festival celebrating the worship of Hindu goddess Durga. Both people from the mainland and the enclave Balapukari were organizers, which was its peculiarity. However, in 2003 it was obstructed by the people of the mainland who accused the enclave dwellers of consuming electricity and other facilities from the mainland 'illegally'. Needless to say, I took that visual impression of the place as a text. This was the first thing Santoshi told me when asked to speak about themselves. It signifies how much importance she gives to this narrative while representing themselves.

There have also been musical performances, where they express the melancholia –

> One day, our home will be under the earth;
> My friend, why do you build buildings?
> One day, the bird of life will leave the cage.
> Everything will remain the same, only you will no longer be there.
> One day, all your friends, even your parents will become strangers!
> My friend, why do you build buildings?...

This is a very popular Bengali folk song performed by the enclave dwellers. I would like to mention an Islamic song here. It is a prayer to Allah, performed by them –

> If the world is so beautiful,
> I wonder, how much beautiful then you are.
> I wonder and wonder, time flies,
> The heart of the thirsty gets filled—
> I wonder, how much beautiful then you are.
> The star spreads smile in the sky
> The flower spreads fragrant in wind
> If the star and the flower are so beautiful,
> I wonder, how much beautiful then you are ...

These folk songs, at the surface, represent simple joys and spontaneity. But this practice of singing these songs expresses that even the deprived people feel the thirst for beauty – a hunger to express their existence through creating and performing. It paves the way to realize that there are other things to do beyond the peripheries of basic needs. While on one hand, the identity, thus the existence, is denied by the state, on the other hand, the people of Chhitmahal created various identities through these cultural practices. It is to clarify that this is not a conscious process. They follow these practices to maintain tradition and to get joy out of it. The 'excess' in these songs expresses the thought of going beyond the basic needs. If we follow how they are using the metaphors of scarecrows and third gender people, we will find a pattern, where the enclave dwellers are claiming their rights beyond the state-provided identities. They are consciously initiating a movement in the act of appropriating metaphors and in conflating their sense of self with these marginal representations. So, the ritualistic practices make newer meanings when they are brought into the protest movements. Therefore, the apparently innocent cultural practices are evolving as a conscious protest movement against their denial of identity. The process of protest, going on there, lacks an organized, cohesive vision since they have not stemmed from a conscious action. The processes of claiming a symbolic identity, where the state is not giving a valid one, is a pattern of protest in itself. However, these practices never become a potential threat to the state apparatus because there is a lack of a unified consciousness and of organized action in these scattered practices. If we look into their lives, we will find that these people have a thirst for beauty of a certain kind and that reflects in their daily life activities. That frames their aesthetic values. It is expressed in handloom works, decorating and cleaning huts by mud and cow dung, making seats with bamboos in the yard, decorating their ancestors' tombs in their own grounds, the urge to sing while sowing seeds, celebrating wedding ceremonies by singing in groups, the love for their lands or taking care of their children's sketchbooks, full of dreams that they learnt to carry in their minds. I am suggesting that these practices have the potential to evolve as organized resistance against the hegemonized deprivation because as long as they follow these practices, they are articulating a desire for life and for aesthetic value.

The way they are representing scarecrows, the hijrahs, the *chandimandap*,[2] or the consciousness which is provoking them into composing songs about their own situation and penning down an autobiography, has an ideological basis. This ideology started taking shape from the time, the enclave exchange movement started. This ideology marks them as distinct from the unaware, scattered practices. In this case, a conscious process is informing the practices. This ideology is helping in the development of resistance while paving the path for social upliftment. As there is a particular ideology, it is an organized process and people are conscious about its development. In the formation of this ideology, their identity as 'enclave dweller' is being highlighted and not their religious identity. Therefore, the autobiography does not represent only the individual author but the collective notion of being deprived and exploited enclave dwellers. When they are expressing that they have been deprived, they are actually expressing the resentment about the fact they were supposed to live without basic human rights, that the rights should have been restored. In this way, informed by a definite ideology, these practices take the shape of a political agitation. Now being organized, the enclave dwellers articulate resistance. Being organized is a necessary condition to ensure that what they disagree with that which should no longer take place. It has been a resistance at many levels. Through a series of organized actions, they compelled the opposition to change the ongoing process of deprivation. This resistance has been identity-based as the Chhit dwellers opposed to be identified by the term 'Chhit'. People used to call them this way to underestimate their worth. Eventually they are not Chhit dwellers anymore. This resistance also has been behavioural. While these people expressed their dissent through elements like songs and scarecrows, they chose to remain nonviolent. Above all, needless to say, it has been a material resistance, it has mostly been a subject of material security.

Are the scattered and spontaneous cultural practices, which form rituals of their daily life but do not necessarily stem from a politically motivated consciousness of being Chhit dwellers, less important than the identity-driven practices then? What is the relation between these two types of cultural practices then? The aspirations, needs, and struggles of everyday life often find expression through their creativity. This creativity flourishes in different manners in individuals at a stage when they are not roped into political movement. These types of cultural practices are therefore the pre-phase of resistance, which have been channelized into modes of resistance against the hitherto exploitation they faced. Now, since there is already an organized form of resistance, we can recognize the unorganized part as the pre-phase of resistance. This 'pre-phase' underlines the need of beauty in daily life and re-emphasizes that the inspiration of human lives is not limited to an assurance of basic needs or of survival rather there is an organic drive towards joy and harmony. This inherent need for aesthetic value also frames their resistance alongside the struggle for basic human rights. So, both forms of cultural practices are equally important to forge a voice of resistance against their deprivation.

Whenever an individual or a group of individuals become conscious of their identity, they become conscious of what their role should be and how they ought to behave and react. They also become conscious about what 'others' think of their 'propriety'. The awakening of this consciousness regarding the 'self' and the 'other' and the binary relation between these two determine the notion of identity of the 'self' of an individual or a group of individuals. This works in the case of Chhitmahal dwellers as well. These people have used the ideologically backed cultural practices as a site of memory. They want to represent themselves in a certain way to the outsiders. This is the reason for inscribing 'I' on scarecrows, to deliver a message to the outer world. The formation of this dialogue with the outer world is an outcome of resistance, as they composed the song aforesaid –

> Whom would we convey our sorrow? …

The idea of nationality is accepted as a given factor while considering the formation of their subjectivity. Nationality is related to the emotion and sentiments regarding homelands. This further consolidates the idea that a person/community, citizen of a particular country, shall represent the nationality of that country. Only when one delves into matters similar to that of Chhitmahal, does one realize that the question of 'nationality' stems differently, with a special importance, because here a situation of complex notion of nationality has been developed for a long time. A sense of 'lack of nationality' has constituted their subjectivity, and these people have fought to become a part of a particular nationality. So, once they succeed in this, the problem might be effaced. The fact is that they always used the word 'citizenship' while claiming their rights. In this particular case, claim of citizenship might be seen as a claim of nationality. But as any nationalist perspective foregrounds nationality as something sentimental and emotional, it was not the same for Chhit dwellers. Citizenship and nationality both are paths towards maintaining legal relationship with the state for the chhit dwellers. Even at the time of enclave exchange, a few hundred Hindu people migrated from Indian enclaves in Bangladesh to India, leaving their homelands permanently to avoid their religious minority identities. So, the claim of nationality is not related to emotions and sentiments here. Certainly, it is about ensuring basic securities. The subjectivity that is so profound in their resistance has no strong relation with nationality in every regard; in fact, their subjectivity traces the limitation of nationality. That particular ideology is all about ensuring basic needs whether they become a citizen of any state or not. One may thus infer that 'nationality' is only a constructed issue and clearly has no role with fulfilling the basic needs of the people living within the limits of a nation. These people are uniting not on the basis of nationality, but on the basis of acquiring their very basic needs of existence and thus on the basis of that specific ideology which leads them to stand for their rights.

Now, after four and a half years of the exchange, when they have valid documents to prove their identity, what we observe is that the people, who were at the forefront of the exchange movement are taking part in jingoistic activities. They are othering and dehumanizing the other side of the border in the name of nationalist sentiments. They are now divided into different political parties. Why? They are still affected by the trauma of the past and are thus carrying the baggage to prove themselves as 'ideal citizens' to the larger society. Here 'ideal citizen' refers to one who promises loyalty to the state. Their identities have always been questioned. Now they are trying to erase the humiliation of the past from the social memory by committing to jingoistic nationalism. Has the ideology of resistance, formulated by the enclave dwellers, being coopted into the structures of the ruling power? They have indeed achieved the legal entitlement they were fighting for. But needless to say, that is not all. They are still marginalized in this new social frame. The then enclave dwellers are now jobless citizens, who do not have much education. Therefore, they are still in a vulnerable position in the social framework marked by stratification of class. They are not yet privileged enough to adequately avail facilities like education, health, and so on. Still, they have to go to big cities to find jobs as migrant workers. So, in reality, the situations of daily struggles for sustenance are almost the same for these enclave dwellers. As entitlements related to citizenship have been granted within a particular political arrangement, the ideology embedded in their resistance has been diluted. But the source, from where the sense of resistance was evoked, the aforesaid 'pre-phase' is still active in the lives of these communities. Therefore, the probability for finding new grounds of resistance prevails. I would reiterate the aforesaid once again – that the enclave dwellers have to be conscious of what is integral to their identities and their histories of struggle. They will find agency to build resistance in the future based on this history that is connected to the present situation.

Notes

1 Toto is a four-wheeler vehicle, powered by battery. It has become very popular these days in the rural and suburb areas of Bengal for local transportation.
2 Chandi, also called Chandika, is a Hindu deity. Chandi-mandap is the set-up of the temple of the deity and the adjacent courtyard. People used to arrange meetings here. Thus, usually its cleanliness or neatness is maintained throughout the year. It serves both as a religious place of worship as well as a community space for daily use. This set-up is usually found in the rural parts.

Bibliography

Bandyopadhyay, Bhagabaticharan. *Coochbeharer Itihash*. 2nd ed. Coochbehar: Coochbehar State Press. 1884.

Chaki, Debabrata. *BratyajanerBrittanto, Prasanga: Bharat-Bangladesh Chitmahal*. Kolkata: Sopan. 2011.

Das, Raktim. *Sangbadikerkalame Chitmahalandolan*. Dhaka: Navroz Kitabistan. 2016.

Metcalf, Peter. *They Lie, We Lie: Getting on with Anthropology*. London and New York: Routledge. 2002.

Radstone, Susannah, Schwarz, Bill (ed.). *Memory: Histories, Theories, Debates*. New York: Fordham University Press. 2010.

Part V

SONGS

Transformations of Identity across Borders

9

SONGS OF CROSSINGS

Searching for Ways of Listening to Arnold Bake's 1934 Recordings of Sailors from Bengal

Moushumi Bhowmik

In April 1934, the Dutch scholar of music and Sanskrit, Arnold Bake (1899–1963) was returning home at the end of the second phase of his stay in India. The past three years Bake and his wife Cornelia, while being based in Santiniketan, had travelled in and around Bengal, including what is now Bangladesh, making recordings on wax cylinders of songs across various genres of music. Bake had also made extensive recordings of the music of Nepal in this time, besides travelling and recording music in south India, Ceylon (Sri Lanka now) and Rajputana (mainly in Gujarat).[1] He would return to all these places for songs again and again in the course of his whole life, somehow keeping a foot in Bengal throughout the journey. Anyway, in 1934, while sailing on the Streefkerk,[2] Bake was writing to the poet Rabindranath Tagore, his 'Gurudev', who was also one of the main reasons for his coming to India in the first place in 1925 and then his return in 1930,[3] about a great wealth of songs he had found on the ship.

> All the sailors and stokers come from East Bengal, and as the captain allows me to go wherever I like, I have heard quite a number of songs from their districts, mostly Sylhet and Noakhali. Some songs are really very attractive. Their dialect is not easy to understand. They pronounce a hard ch for each k, choro instead of koro, etc. They are very eager to let me hear what they know, now that they have overcome their shyness. It really is awfully nice and I enjoy my visits very much.[4]

In this chapter we will try to listen to those songs of the sailors and stokers and olimen, from Sylhet and Noakhali and Comilla that Bake had recorded in 1934, placing them alongside other songs from the region, recorded after

DOI: 10.4324/9780429356421-15

Bake's time, especially songs which have made other journeys in the bodies of other 'sailors', some willingly travelling to other lands, some displaced from home and hence forced into journeys in search of home. This chapter will also journey into the lands of that these sailors belonging to different times came from, going into those lands that they might have dispersed to. In the process, we will try to understand the many crossings, across oceans of time and space and along pathways of history that such songs have made and continue to make, especially in the context of the broken land of Bengal, marked by the seemingly endless process of border-making.

The 1934 Recordings

The Berlin Phonogramm-Archiv (BPA) lists ethnographic wax cylinders of Arnold Bake Nos. 341–355 as having been recorded between 1 and 15 April 1934. I do not know of any other archive which holds these recordings, but I could be wrong. The BPA list does not mention any detail of where these songs were recorded, but once you look at the names of the singers and who they were, the context becomes clear. Then, going through Bake's personal details, and reading his letters, you can see the exact picture. A big white man, friend of the captains, exploring the ship, meeting people, his ears keen for special sounds and songs. The man is used to recording in the field. He goes down the ladder to the belly of the ship and meets the workmen, from Noakhali, Sylhet, and Comilla in what was then East Bengal and is Bangladesh now. This man knows a thing or two about their songs, for he has travelled quite a bit, since 1925, within and around Bengal as well as elsewhere in the subcontinent, besides meeting students from many places, including Sylhet, in Santiniketan. In fact, Lakshmisvar Sinha (1905–1977), the young student Arnold Bake recorded a year ago in 1933, was also from Sylhet.[5] He listens to the sailors and knows immediately that here is something he must record. He keeps going down with his phonograph, recording song after song. For the sailors it must have been a real treat to sing their songs into the phonograph. Also, it is not hard to imagine how deeply emotional and empowering, even cathartic, the experience of singing songs from home can be for those who have left home, and do not know when they will return. The matter of voyaging with songs and crossing many a hurdle through singing is something we have seen across cultures in history, especially with the African slaves taken to America or with the indentured labour taken to the tea gardens within India or shipped from India to, say, the Caribbean islands.[6]

Bake's Bengali sailors weren't professional singers, just as Lakshmisvar Sinha in Santiniketan wasn't. Yet there is something about the land of Sylhet and the whole region surrounding it in this northeastern part of the subcontinent, which seems to make it rich with poets, song makers, and singers. As if music flows through the life-stream of the land. Interestingly, as a group, the sailors of 1934 were the only 'non-musicians' whom Bake had recorded in and around Bengal, (although we will find out that there were true 'artists' among them), apart from the occasional student or teacher of Santiniketan or some women beating a roof, singing a work song. All the other groups Bake had recorded in the region were professional or amateur musicians – be it the bauls or kirtaniyas or fakirs or Santals in a Christian mission or a jarigan troupe at a festival. Or he would record the itinerant singer or random flute player passing by his house in Santiniketan or the 'artist as a young woman' singing, among other things, songs behind some songs of Tagore.[7] The sailors were just ordinary people, with jobs on a liner, who had to perform hard labour under difficult circumstances; yet the song seemed natural to them.

The sailors' songs are listed thus in the BPA's files:

341. Sayed Ali, Sailor from Hirpur (Comilla p.o.) 1/4/'34
'Hridoy jole'
341. A a. 'amay' b. same as 341. singer Sayed Ali
342. 'prem koriye shukh hole nai' Sayed Ali.
343. 'she dukh' singer Fayazullah (stoker) from Damrasari p.o. Hirpur Bazar, district Sylhet 2/4/'34
344. 'o go namti amar' singer Tazal Ahmad (sailor), gram Ghutia, p.o. Shadar. Noakhali 8/4/'34
345. a. 'Amar mon bahulo' Sayed Ali
b. Tazal Ahmad: 'brishti pore'
346. a. 'gram upor' Tazal Ahmad
b. 'pran bondu' Sayed Ali
347. 'Shunu bondo shivsarane koi' Fayazullah 14/4/'34
347. A idem.
348. 'o pran nath' Fayaz-Ullah
348. A idem
349. 'jabe jodi mor' Fayazullah (this song compare Tag. compositions)
350. Sari gan (boatmensong) 'sarathi jibon gailo' Fayazullah 15/4/'34
351. Pir murshid-er gan 'od kore' singer Sawabali (oilman), gram Harikhailash. po. Bisvanath, Sylhet
352. 'Allah bolo naukha kholo' Lal Mian (sailor)
353. rice cutting song 'tora koile' Lal Mian & Usman Ali (sailor)
354. 'dadar boi' Sayed Ali
355. 'amar mon pagol' idem.

About two years ago, in 2016, The Travelling Archive (www.thetravellingarchive.org), which is my field recordings-based project in Bengal, in collaboration with audiographer Sukanta Majumdar, were commissioned by Berlin Phonogramm-Archive to curate an album of Arnold Bake's Bengal recordings and write the liner notes for them. We had just finished showing an exhibition titled 'Time Upon Time: Arnold Bake in Bengal', at Kala Bhavan, Visva Bharati, Santiniketan.[8] The BPA sent us their list for that purpose. The list itself was greatly exciting, because while we had seen and listened to many of the items on it at the other archives which had copies of Bake's cylinder recordings,[9] the sailors' songs was something I had only read, a mention of, in the aforementioned letter from Bake to Tagore. Once we had the recordings to listen to, the sailors' songs were enough to take one's breath away.

I kept going back to two particular songs. Cylinder no. 343 was a song titled 'Shey dukh' and Track 348 was 'O pran nath', both sung by Fayazullah of Damrasari, Hirpur Bazar, Sylhet. There was something in those songs which seemed very familiar to me. Something I could hear under the noise of the cylinder, in its skidding, and in the undecipherable words of the songs. And then as I kept listening, I knew what it was. The style of singing was so much like the maverick Ranen Roychowdhury of Ritwik Ghatak's films![10]

> **Who shall I call to take me across?**
> *Majhi tor naam jani na*
> *Ami daak dimu kare?*
> Boatman, I don't know your name.
> Who shall I call?

This is the refrain of a song from Ritwik Ghatak's film *Meghe Dhaka Tara* (The Cloud-Capped Star, 1960), on the struggles, dreams, and death of dreams of a family and people uprooted from their home in East Bengal by Partition in 1947, seeking to make a new home in Calcutta. Ghatak (1925–1976) was deeply affected by the historical event of Partition, his heart was broken, and his entire oeuvre was an attempt to ask the question of what will our lives be henceforth? What shall we do, now that the homeland like shattered glass is fallen on the ground and now that even to walk is to be wounded? Are there still dreams to dream, battles to fight, hopes to cherish, life to be born, and flowers to bloom? Or is it only a dry, lifeless riverbed staring us in our face, in an upturned time of utmost strangeness?

> Heartbroken, I weep by the shore of this life,
> Who, pray, will take me across?
> Boatman, I don't know your name.
> Who shall I call?

This song of Idom Shah holds an iconic place in the cultural history of post-Partition Bengal. Ranendra Ballav Roychowdhury (1925–1985), popularly known as Ranen Roychowdhury, brought it to life in his own inimitable way, suffusing it with the feeling of uncompensated loss and pain. The pain was the poet's, the pain was the singer's, the pain was the land's which had been mutilated. The pain was of multiple dislocation and separation – metaphorical, political, and artistic, all combined.

Who was Ranen Roychowdhury and wherefrom sprang such a sound? What was this unique way he had with the song? What was this sound he gifted to the listener; in other words, what was this sound which drew the listener in, especially the urban listener of post-1947 Calcutta? Roychowdhury was born in Tantikona village of the Chhatok region of Sylhet into a family which was involved in the arts; his elder brother was a painter. He grew up in Sylhet and came to Calcutta in 1950. Those were politically difficult and heady times for a nation newly broken up and nations newly born. His friends were the Communists, he too was a member of the Party and also active in the Indian People's Theatre Association. He had learned to sing songs in the mystic tradition of the Sufis from the itinerant and 'sadhak' singers he met at the shrine of Hazrat Shah Jalal in Sylhet, and whose close company he kept.[11] When he came to Calcutta, he carried in the vessel of his body, songs from a home he had to leave behind. But this was not just a generic body of communal music that he brought with him, this was also a music processed in the body of the artist, something of his own, something which was born of his individual experience and sensitivity.

The body as the vessel which makes possible this crossing of the song, across borders of time and space, is very important in the case of Ranen Roychowdhury. In all the fond remembrances and critical assessment of his work his friends and admirers made after his passing in 1985, from his elder brother's friend and later co-worker at the Folk Music and Folklore Research Institute, Khaled Choudhury, who was himself an artist and song collector and musicologist, to his student and the well-known folk singer Swapan Basu, to his friend, the writer Ashish Lahiri, everyone talked about the peculiarity of his gestures, his immersive manner, the deep lost look in his eyes, the pain in his voice. There was something other-worldly about him, seemed to be the general consensus.

> One day, I remember, we were in the inner chambers of Kathashilpa [publishers], raking up a storm over whether the state was semi or a quarter-feudal or whether we were living under comprador-capitalism, when Ranenda made an appearance. His voice could be heard from the distance, even before he actually arrived. *Amar kalo pakhi ure gelo bhalobashar shikol chhnire* (My black bird has flown away breaking free from its chains of love). Someone hastily got up and offered him a seat. Ranenda sang on, with his misty eyes looking into some indefinite space. He sang the whole song, stood up, then left without speaking a word. After a minute or so the spell broke and Montuda said, you know what? He had come to say something and this was his way.[12]

This intensely private artist's songs were seen to define the pain of people who had lost their homeland owing to a particular event in history, especially through the films of Ghatak, many of which were about the eastern refugees of the Partition of Bengal coming to Calcutta. Perhaps it was in that lone voice of Ranen that Ghatak heard cries of the aloneness of the refugee, plucked from their community and thrown into the deep and turbulent waters of Calcutta, with no boatman to row them across. Ghatak and Roychowdhury shared a special friendship, about which the latter wrote after Ghatak's death. It was a cold day of Kartik (which would be sometime between mid-October and November) when Ranen Roychowdhury went to meet Ghatak first time in a film studio. He was wearing a thin shirt and did not want to be late, because he had a recording for All India Radio the next day and could not risk catching a cold. But Ghatak kept him on hold and listened to song after song and with each song he sang, the impassioned director said, I want this one too.[13] What did Ghatak hear in Ranen Roychowdhury's songs? According to Khaled Choudhury,

> Ritwik Ghatak loved Ranen very much. Those who had to leave their *desh* because of Partition nurtured a sense of emptiness and intense longing for that lost homeland. Ritwik felt this way too. And it seems that he found a certain refuge in the *original and untampered* folk tunes of East Bengal of Ranen.[14]
>
> (Italics mine)

Then Khaled Choudhury goes on to elaborate on this untampered purity of Ranen Roychowdhury: how he was the real and true voice of rural East Bengal, how definitive his 'Marifati' (Sufi spiritual) songs were. He also writes about the wealth of songs Ranen Roychowdhury had brought with him from Sylhet – songs representative of communal life, such as women's songs, ritual songs, work songs, and so on. Ranen, therefore, becomes both the generic and the particular in these assessments.

Interestingly, there were three prominent and very distinct voices which came out of Sylhet and burst upon the cultural scene of Calcutta in the 1950s, quite soon after the violent breakup of Bengal. One was of Hemango Biswas, the pronounced Leftist activist-artist; the second was Nirmalendu Chowdhury, the mellifluous voice of radio and gramophone records, whose sound and style were accessible, hence popular and even commercially successful; and the third was Ranen Roychowdhury, also part of Left cultural movement, but an essentially private artist, who seemed to sing only for himself. Ritwik Ghatak's films carried both Ranen Roychowdhury and Hemango Biswas' songs, to his own particular audience and they were also marked by those voices, as the voice of Dhiraj Uddin Fakir literally set his late film *Titas Ekti Nodir Naam* in motion.[15]

Dehotori dilam chhari
I sail my boat in your name, o guru,
Should I sink, the blame is all yours.[16]

In the course of my work in the field, especially in the Sylhet and Cachar regions, I have often wondered, why is it that we never find a voice and style such as Ranen Roychowdhury's? We have heard echoes of Hemango Biswas sometimes in our own field recordings, even if differently presented. Take Barindra Das of Silchar, for example, and the song 'Shomoy thakle doyal guru go', which he sang for us in 2005. The resemblances with Hemango Biswas' 'Dehotori' are quite obvious.[17] There were also the Mass Singers, a cultural troupe Hemango Biswas had formed, who sang his own protest and folk songs, in his style. But Ranen Roychowdhury has always seemed far too unique and inimitable. Did his songs purely from his artistic self, without any communal antecedent? Was he not part of any continuity? Are we all not part of some continuity? Ranen Roychowdhury did not like to teach, as the folk singer Swapan Basu writes, and he did not like much to perform either.[18] In fact, although Swapan Basu learned many songs from him, he came out with quite a distinct style of his own, marked by his own place and time and also the demands of the media and for which he was mostly performing, namely popular television and the cassette industry. Roychowdhury's daughter, Sanchita, a singer in her own right, is probably the only person who sings somewhat like him, holding on to the song which filled up the space of her home in Calcutta. She did not learn that many songs from her father, but the music was there in the air. In an interview given to The Travelling Archive in 2009, she described how he woke up every morning at 4 am and made a flask of tea and smoked endless bidis and sang song after song.[19] After his death in 1985, she gradually began to get into the songs of Sylhet, but through the sound she had inherited from her father. For Sanchita, therefore, it is important to sing the way she does, because in so doing, she can protect her father's song. She is insistent on her father's 'purity' almost to the point of obsession. The story of the popular song 'Bhromor koiyo giya', is an interesting case in point.

Go, Tell Him How She Burns in His Absence

The voice that purists such as Khaled Choudhury considered to be truly representative of place was Ranen Roychowdhury's, because it had never tried to be anything other than what it was. Representative of what place is, however, a question. It was as if a lost song of a lost home was somehow preserved and archived in Ranen's voice. As if in its body the land still remained unbordered, although the song had made its own physical crossing across the border. As if the song had not left the land, for it had nowhere to go.

In the 1960s, some Leftist artists and intellectuals of Calcutta started the Folk Music and Folklore Research Institute: Khaled Choudhury, Hemango Biswas, the anthropologist Ranajit Sinha, ethnomusicologist Nihar Barua, her son, psychiatrist and musician Mrinal Barua, and others were its members. The young Soumya Chakravarti, who would later become a prominent field recordist, apprenticed at the institute. They were trying to make recordings on a reel-to-reel recorder and on audio cassettes, of folk artists and forms they considered important for posterity and their list included such names as Anantabala Baishnabi and Sanatan Das Baul.[20] They also recorded Ranen Roychowdhury, who was in their circle of friends. One of the songs he recorded was the Radharaman composition 'Bhromor koiyo giya'.[21] I had heard this song before, on an audio cassette of a Bangladeshi rock band in the mid-1990s. Sadly, I cannot remember the name of the band. '*Bhromor koiyo giya*. Go, Bumble Bee, go and tell how Radha's body burns in Sri Krishna's absence'. This was an upbeat number played to heavy orchestration, including guitars and drums; it had something catchy about it. It was on this trip that I learned about another version of the song sung by the Bangladeshi pop singer, Dilruba. This version had instant appeal, the clear voice of Dilruba with heavy reverb, soaring above the instruments, which would be a combination of folk dhol and violins and guitars and keyboards and percussion. Over the years, as I was collecting and listening to more and more cassettes of recorded music from Bangladesh, between the mid- to late 1990s, I learned to identify the folk form 'bichchhed' or song of separation and longing, behind Dilruba's 'Bhromor koiyo giya'. She makes a form traditionally intense with emotional expression sound kind of cheesy though.

This is how I knew this particular song till I heard Ranen Roychowdhury's 1960s recording, a capella, and in a totally different form. There was no rise and fall of the melody and the voice, no excess of emotion, as there was in Dilruba's, and the rhythm was a steady 3/4, compared to the waves of Dilruba's 4/4, accentuated by roll of the dhol. Ranen Roychowdhury was also using the word *ago*, very typically Sylheti as I would later learn, which was working as a conjunct between the lines. I sang to Sanchita, Ranen Roychowdhury's daughter, the Dilruba version and she was instantly dismissive of it. 'This is not right, period'. She would not discuss the matter anymore.

In 2006, on our field recording trip to Bangladesh, I crossed the border with two versions of 'Bhromor koiyo giya' in my voice, and went to the land that Ranen and others had left/had to leave some 60 years ago. As I interacted with artists and informed listeners, the story of 'Bhromor koiyo giya' began to take new meaning. Some heard the Ranen version and said, this was how they used to hear the song in their childhood. Ranen's form was the 'dhamail', a song to which women danced holding hands and forming a circle. Others talked about how the more 'dressy' version of Dilruba had originated, crediting it to the famous folk singer and composer of Sylhet, Biditlal Das, but the truth of this contention is hard to verify. In fact, I do not believe that such changes are enacted by any individual composer, but they come about in a particular time, as a need of the time.[22] Anyway, however, this might have happened, when we were recording Ruhi Thakur, a renowned singer of folk songs, on that very trip, he too talked about his childhood memory of the song which was like Ranen Roychowdhury's. He sang the song for us, but while singing, his version became a medley of the later popular bichchhed version and the earlier dhamail. And Ruhi da said that it was hard to go back to the past.

I believe that the many versions of 'Bhromor koiyo giya' bear witness to our reality of multiple voices, which we often fail to hear. They also signify the layers of time which exist within any given time, sometimes separable but oftentimes hopelessly tangled up. And Time here should perhaps be written in the upper case, for it is many things and in many ways. Time here is historical, personal, and political on the one hand; it is also mythical and imagined. Few sing 'Bhromor koiyo giya' as a dhamail now; the more popular version is the bichchhed, and any other later version, fusion or rock, is based on the bichchhed. But the dhamail is held in people's memories and perhaps it is also tucked in some corner where our listening has not yet reached. Moreover, it exists as the recording in Ranen Roychowdhury's voice. His daughter too will only sing this song as a dhamail and she will not entertain any idea of the validity of the other versions. For her the song is the memory of a land her father lived in and left, and from which he had carried many songs across the border and to which he never returned and where she has never been. The 60 years in between do not hold meaning for her, she does not want to know. Not only does she not want to know, she also has no need to know about what happened to the land in those six decades. I also believe that so it *should* be for her, if this is what she needs to live (so long as she does not impose her image upon others). She should be entitled to believe that the land is still unbroken, the trees still bow to the wind just as her father had described to her, fakirs share songs in great communion at the mazar of Hazrat Shah Jalal, and when the light shines on the ripened crops, alchemy still happens!

Perhaps those who leave/have to leave/lose a land (or someone) they dearly love often need to live in some kind of amnesia, even denial or they need to imagine a different reality for themselves. Or, perhaps they know the reality only too well, but also do not want to know it. For them the land's body is scorched in *Sri Krishna-bichchhed*, in the absence of the lover, Krishna, and Radha lies eternally waiting in hunger, hair untied, like a mad woman. 'Go, Bumble Bee, tell him how she burns in his absence – *koiyo koiyo koiyo Bhromor, Krishnere bujhaiya...*' It does not matter that the land has changed in the meantime, and that in place of that ripened crop, perhaps a new brick kiln has sprouted from the ground. In *Point of Return*, the novelist Siddhartha Deb wrote,

> My grandfather's references to the home left behind as East Pakistan, decades after East Pakistan had seceded from Pakistan to become the independent nation of Bangladesh, revealed something more than a grasp of geopolitical shifts. It showed that the landscape of his past would forever be permanent and unchanging, not something that was historical and therefore open to perpetual revision, but a place beyond the vagaries of time.[23]

Thinking again about Ranen Roychowdhury, I not only wonder why we do not hear anyone like him in the field anymore, but also what the sound at his source might have been. Then around the same time we come across two different sets of recordings. One made by Arnold Bake in 1934, of songs sung by Fayazullah (stoker) from Damrasari, Hirpur Bazar, Sylhet, on the ethnographic wax cylinders kept at the Berlin Phonogramm-Archiv. The second is a set of recordings from Kishoreganj made in 2017 by sound recordist Ali Ahsan, shared privately with me. In these two sets perhaps lay the answer to my questions about where Ranen Roychowdhury's sound came from and where it went after he crossed the border in 1950. If he was carrying a sound of a place, then surely, he could not be its sole keeper. This is what my common sense told me. Here I shall not be able to go into much depth with the Kishoreganj recordings, because I am not yet ready for it, but suffice here to say that I heard echoes of Ranen in Ali Ahsan's voices. Let us go instead on a journey on the trail of Fayazullah (stoker) from Damrasari, Hirpur Bazar, Sylhet. Ah! So, this was perhaps what Ranen used to hear! This was perhaps the kind of person whose company he used to keep in the shrine of Shah Jalal, and from whom he learned many songs!

Changed Place-Name, Unchanged Song

A long time ago, when I had barely conceived the idea of travelling across Bengal and listening to music, I had encountered in the sound archives of the British Library in London, a recording of a 'baulgan' from Kenduli in Birbhum, dated January 1932, sung by 'Acintadashi, sevadashi of Murali Das', the recording being credited to Arnold Adriaan Bake.[24] That wax cylinder recording had so aroused my curiosity that once Sukanta and I settled into our work in field recording for our collaborative project The Travelling Archive, we also began to explore the life and work of Arnold Bake. Our main interest has been in trying to make sense of the sounds contained in Bake's recordings from Bengal. We began to find our own inheritance in his sounds, we found overlaps between his field and ours. Over the years we have travelled to many places in and around Bengal where Arnold Bake had been, looking for his sonic traces. With each of his set of recordings – kirtan, Santal music, Fokiri songs, Rabindrasangit, etc. – we have had a different set of experiences. In some places such as in Mainadal in Birbhum or Santiniketan, Bake's sounds are still a live presence; in some places such as Naogaon in Rajshahi district of present Bangladesh, the presence of the sound Arnold Bake had recorded is marked by its total absence.[25] With the 1934 Streefkerk sailors' songs, the story of our exploration has taken a very different turn. I am currently writing my doctoral thesis on the politics of archiving, with Arnold Bake's archival recordings from and from around Bengal at the centre of my research.

Here is an unfinished story about a perhaps-unfinishable thread in this research. In November 2016, I went to Noakhali, on the trail of a particular recording of Arnold Bake's. The singer I was searching for was a sailor by the name of Tazal Ahmed, who had recorded two songs on Bake's wax cylinders, numbered 344 and 345b, now archived at Berlin Phonogramm-Archiv. He came from a village called Ghutia in Noakhali Sadar, according to the accompanying note. Following these leads, I wondered if some family of Tazal Ahmed could still be found in his village? The recording was more than 80 years old, so there was of course no chance of finding the singer. But perhaps someone with some connection would tell us something. Perhaps he had settled in London or somewhere else in the UK, as many sailors did. Perhaps someone would be able to say something about the song. So, I went to Noakhali in Bangladesh, with sound recordist Ali Ahsan. However, I could not find any village by the name of Ghutia. What I learned instead was the story of a river named Bhulua, which had changed its course in the last 40 years, washing away places which would have existed in the 1930s. Sadar now is not how Sadar was then, I was told. Most people said that there was no place called Ghutia, but some talked about Sholla Ghutia. So that is where we went but realized that it was a fairly new place, formed with the rise of a *char* (silt island), once the river had shifted course over the last 40 years or so. Could it then be that the river had washed away Tazal Ahmed's Ghutia village while changing its course? Where should we look for old records of place-names?

There was another possibility. Could it be that Bake had heard the name of the place wrong, or he had misspelt it? Perhaps the archivist had wrongly deciphered Bake's handwriting. Someone told us about a man of about 90 years who could know about those olden times; so we went to meet him. The man was very keen to go on this place-hunt with us. 'We will go to the river with a picnic, light a fire, cook a duck …' he began to dream. His family members joined in the game. People started to make phone calls to various people. Someone suggested we go to Batoiya, since there seemed to be no place called Ghutia, and since these were similar sounding names (if you think of 'Ghut' being pronounced at 'hut'). Perhaps it was Batoiya then, an older village, from where it seems that people went to work on ships. Could it be that someone who has worked on ships in the last 50 years or so might have heard the name of Tazal Ahmed? So, the next day we went to Batoiya and that is the closest we could get to Tazal Ahmed's village, which is not saying much at all.

I found nothing which could conclusively tell me whether or not I was on the right trail. There was another seaman I met in Batoiya, someone who would be far younger than Bake's Tazal Ahmed. He had his own stories from post-Partition times to tell; about people from his region who went to work on ships, about names of vessels and ports and about the War of 1971. I came home with recordings of all these voices.

Working with Bake has become for us a game in map-making with sound. Playing with changing place-names and landscapes and names of people who might have lived in these places – a game in toponymy.

But, if Tazal Ahmed's story did not go from anywhere to anywhere, other than leaving me with a string of perhapses, Fayazullah (stoker) from Damrasari, Hirpur Bazar, Sylhet became a story about a lost place and a found song. In January 2018, I went with my long-time friend and guide in Sylhet, Ambarish Dutta, to meet the 90-year-old Sushoma Das, whom we first met in 2006 and have been recording since. Sushoma 'Mashima' as we call her, Mashima meaning aunt, holds a very special place in the life of The Travelling Archive and I personally see her as a mother and a teacher. Even at this advanced age, she has the strongest voice and phenomenal memory, standing like an old banyan tree in our present time of feeble voices and callous forgetfulnesss. Mashima sits there in her room, frailer and thinner since the last time I saw her in 2015, with her daughter Bashona, son Prashanta, and a neighbour, while other family members walk in and out of the room with water, tea, and sweets. I sit in the chair next to her and play her Bake's sailors' songs from my laptop. The noise on the surface of the cylinder envelops the voice, it is not easy to listen to the song, especially from the speakers of the laptop, what with outside noises of people talking, work in the kitchen, and vehicles on the streets below and beyond. Yet Mashima is immediately alert. And in fact, it is not just Mashima, but everyone present in the room seems to be able to listen to something.

Out of the 15 cylinders on which Arnold Bake recorded the sailors on board, five (nos. 343, 347, 348, 349, and 350) were of Fayazullah of Damrasari. Before getting to Fayazullah, I played for Sushoma Mashima a song sung by Sayed Ali from Hirpur in Comilla, recorded on 1 April 1934. Mashima said, people have different styles of singing in different places, I don't know this song, but it is a 'biraho', meaning it is a song expressing longing while in the state of separation. Then I moved to Cylinder 348, recorded on 14 April 1934, titled 'O pran nath', and Sushoma Das was in her element. '*Shakkhater gaan, shakkhater pod. Radha Krishner milon hoise, miloner pore ei gaanta*' (This is a song of meeting, Radha and Krishna have met and this is song which comes after the meeting).[26] And then the words began to flow out of her. Mashima recites:

Pranonath bondhu re, bohu dine paiasi tumare.
Kato batshar hoilo gato, ore bondhu
Tilek na herilam tumare, bohu dine paiasi tumare.
Bondhu re, amar moto katoi nari
Ase tumar aggakari
Sheba kore tumake paia, o bondhu re.
Ore, ami noi tor shebar jugyo,
Kun gune paibo tumare, bohu dine paiasi tumare.
O bondhu re, adhore adhoro diya
Srubone srubon mishaiya
Noyone noyon rakaiya
Sudhamrito borishone, o bondhu shushitol koro amare.

Friend, lord of my heart, I have you to me after ages.
Many years have passed, O friend
I have not had even a glimpse of you.
I have you to me after ages.
O friend, so many women like me
Are happy to obey your orders
They serve when they have you for them.
Am I even worthy of serving you?
What gift do I have to ask you for me?
I have you to me after ages.
O friend, touching with lip on lip
Listening from ear to ear
Holding your eyes in mine
Showering me with your nectar of life,
Make me quiet and calm.

These are not the exact words that Fayazullah sang, but it is a variation on the same song. Such is the nature of songs in this oral tradition. Some lines are different, some lines are missing while there are some additional lines between the two versions. Fayazullah's line about the 'chatok', the bird of unquenchable thirst, is missing in Sushoma Mashima's song. Her lines about women in love are not in Fayazullah's. Then there is in Fayazullah's version the verse with the signature of the poet, whose name I still cannot understand after many a repeated listening; perhaps I will get it at some point, because these cylinders are difficult to listen to and it is really a matter of acquiring the skill and tuning the ears, such as one learns to read the lines behind the lines of an old damaged painting. And that is why it has struck me how keen Sushoma Mashima's listening still is. And in this context, let me make one particular point about the two versions of the song we have between us now. It concerns Mashima's listening.

After she recites the lines, I say, 'Why don't you sing, Mashima? Please sing the lines'. And she says, 'You know what, love, my voice makes such a rattling sound now!' But I keep asking for the song. Then she starts to sing (and of course her voice is still stunningly strong!). Her pace and rhythm are different, again it is a difference between Fayazullah singing in the 4/4 dhamail meter and Mashima singing a more sprawling 3/4 bichchhed. She comes to the lines '*O bondhu re, adhore adhoro diya*, touching lip on lip'. Then she stops and starts to correct herself. '*O bondhu re, srobone srobon diya/ Noyone noyon rakhiya/Hridoye hridoy mishaiya…*' The lines with the *adhor* are not in the final version that she sings. Later I wonder why this had happened. And then I listen back to the Bake recording. It strikes me that Fayazullah's song had a line which went '*Haay re bondhu adhore adhoro diye*'. Perhaps Mashima was influenced by her listening to the recording just before singing the song? (I can only speculate, because there is no way to know what exactly might have happened; even Sushoma Mashima will probably not be able to tell.). And, thus, that phrase about the lip on lip had entered her song when she spoke out the lines. Then when she started to sing, she sang the line about the *adhor*, but could not go on because that was not how she actually knew the song. So, she had to remind herself of her own old version. What a natural crossing from one text to another! Only in the oral tradition can such a thing happen, I think. And then when we debate on questions of authenticity, I ask myself, are not all these half-heard, half-sung versions all authentic in the moment when they are being sung?

On 2 April 1934, his second day of recording the sailors, Arnold Bake had Fayazullah singing a song which began with the words '*She dukh*'. This is the song which had made me think of Ranen Roychowdhury. As the song plays, Mashima and her son and daughter all listen with rapt attention and then she starts to speak out the words.

Shey dukh koibar katha noy go bolibo kare?
Jar antore jwalapuray, shokhi,
Shey bine ki onyo jane?
Shey dukh koibar katha noy go bolibo kare?

It is such an unspeakable pain, who can I tell?
She whose heart is scorched and scathed, my friend
Can anyone but her know?
It is such an unspeakable pain, who can I tell?

Everyone in the room puts in a word. '*Keu ba parobashi*', one says. 'No no, it was *bonobashi*', says another. '*Keu hoitechhe shmashanbashi*, or was it *deshantori*?' 'There is also *keu ba bhikharini*'. They hear different things, but basically variations on the idea of the dejected, almost destroyed lover, who is either leaving home, or is beggared or is choosing to stay in the *smashan* or crematorium or is going on exile. Finally, we come to the word *Deenoheen*. Is it a song of Deenoheen, Deenoheen, the folk poet? Or is the poet describing himself as *deenoheen*, one stripped of all riches, ready for total submission? Prashanta Das, Sushoma Mashima's son, recalls songs in which poets use the word *deenoheen* to describe their state of ultimate devotion. He starts to sing. From Fayazullah's song we move into a song about Chaitanya, the 16th century Bhakti saint of Bengal, who renounced home to reach his God, and sang the Name (of God) as his way of devotion and love. From Arnold Bake's ship, through the temperature-controlled space of the archives in Berlin, to Mashima listening to Fayazullah's song, to her son singing songs learned from the mother – we have crossed many borders of time and space, backwards and forwards, in the course of that one evening.

When we were leaving, Mashima customarily came to the door and as I touched her feet she said, 'Will I see you again?' The time of Sushoma Mashima's final departure is closing in on us and each time I meet her, I feel the urge to keep as much of her as I can. But keep what? And how much? Sushoma Das embodies a vast archive, as did their father Rasiklal before her, and her younger brother Ramkanai Das did too; he has gone before her.[27] How much of this wealth can be kept in an archive? How much can be recorded? The human body as the archive is essentially ephemeral and perhaps therein lies its true beauty. For, because it is fragile, its presence can be celebrated and its absence missed.

Fayazullah, sailor from Damrasari in Hirpur Bazar, Sylhet, must have been a man who knew many songs and he certainly sang beautifully. How much of that beauty can we hear in these recordings anyway? All we have is a faint shadow of the song. All we can do is to make guesses, imagine what the sound at the time of singing might have been like, what it was that Arnold Bake had heard. He clearly liked Fayazullah, and maybe he liked him more than he liked the others, along with also Sayed Ali of Comilla? This is only my guess, based on the number of songs recorded and also on my own personal preference for Fayazullah. Maybe I want to think that Bake too liked Fayazullah more. We do not have any writing from Bake to prove this. But in Naogaon, for example, he surely liked Jaura Khatun best.[28] I think that the personal choices that go into the making of an archive actually humanize it. Such as the gaps and flaws in the recording and documentation also do.

Where was Fayazullah from? What is this village which he noted down next to his name? No one in Sylhet could place it. Damrasari? It must have been Dharmapasha. There is a Hirpur Bazar on the way to the Tamabil border with Meghalaya in India. You reach there, go further down the road, go through Sarighat in Jayantapur, reach a village named Doudik where a band of jolly women with children, belonging to a minority community of

Hindus, sing Surjyobroto songs (ritual songs to the Sun god) to my recorder, just for fun…

'Is there a place here named Damrasari?'

'Is there a house here from where sailors went to sea?'

A man by the name of Azad joins Ambarishda and me on this search. Days after I have left Sylhet and am still in Dhaka, he calls on my Bangladesh number and says, 'Apa (meaning elder sister), I am still looking for Fayazullah!' Again, the whole game is similar to our search for Ghutia village in Noakhali Sadar from where Tazal Ahmed supposedly came. But there is a marked difference between these two searches.

Did we not find Fayazullah in spite of not finding his village or his family? I don't think that we didn't. This is contrary to what happened with Tazal Ahmed of Noakhali, whom we did not find at all (we found other stories and histories, but that is a separate matter). Who then is this Fayazullah whom we found? And how and where did we find him? Finally, why is it that in spite of not finding the villages or families of both Fayazullah and Tazal Ahmed, I am saying that we found the former and did not find the latter?

Perhaps we had started to find Fayazullah even before we went looking for him. We first found him in the voice of Ranen Roychowdhury. Later we found some more of him in the songs that Sushoma Mashima and her son spoke and sang. Bake's notes were clearly flawed in many places, or at least in the way the notes have come down to us, there appear to be many errors. So, for both Ghutia in Noakhali Sadar and Damrasari in Hirpur Bazar, Sylhet, it is likely that he had got the names wrong. Perhaps they told him something in their Sylheti or Noakhailya way, and he wrote down what he heard. The sailors were in all likelihood unlettered and so they would not be able to spell the names or the names of their villages for Bake. Again, this is only a speculation based on thin evidence or plain common sense. But, as evidence, let us take the example of Cylinder No. 347 from the sailors' songs. According to the documentation we have from Bake, the song Fayazullah had recorded was 'Shunu bondo shivsarane koi'. Now, that line makes no sense whatsoever. I played the song and Sushoma Mashima and everyone else in the room listened. Then Mashima began to speak the words, and out flowed a whole song.

Shuno bondhu tumar sricharane koi
Mor ki loy re bondhu, tumay chara roi
Bondhu re, jothay tothay jao tumi, ami chaiya roi
Koite na'ri shoite na'ri, kuno jwala shoi.

Bondhu re, tumar monete mon mishaiya moner dukkho koi
Amar mone shadh re bondhu, tumar dashi hoiya roi
Shuno bondhu tumar sricharane koi

Bondhu re, tumi na korile doya ami jabo koi?
Tumi bine Radharaman parobashe roi.

Friend, see, I beg at your feet.
How, my dear, can I stay without you?
Wherever you go, Friend, I look your way
It is hard to say and hard to bear, the suffering this brings.

My Friend, I meld my heart with yours and tell you my pain
I wish in my heart to serve you all life long
Friend, see, I beg at your feet.

O Friend, if you do not care, then where shall I go?
Without you, Radharaman feels banished from his land.

'That's how the Radharaman song goes, but this singer has mixed up the verses (*ultafalta korse*) and has also not signed off with Radharaman's name as the *rosit* [রচিত, which is a very Sylheti way of saying writer/composer and it is utterly untranslatable]', Sushoma Mashima said. Then a lot of discussion followed on the question of the *rosit*, and how people sing without the name of the *rosit* or when they mix up texts and from that it went to a song of a rare woman composer of Sylhet, Rupmanjari, which Mashima had heard as being wrongly credited to Radharaman. Then she sang Rupmanjari's song with her *bhonita* or signature. Later Prashanta sang a song of his grandfather Rasiklal, and finally the session with endless possibilities had to come to a close, as the evening had slowly darkened into night and it was time for rest and sleep.

It was in that whole exchange at Sushoma Das' house that the singer Fayazullah began to take further shape and his song acquired new meaning, surpassing the limits of Arnold Bake's recording and the cryptic note we had from the archives. It does not matter that we could not find his home, because we found his trace in all the other songs we heard and thus he became part of an ancestry. Tazal Ahmed's story could also have ended up similarly, but it didn't and the reasons are many. Firstly, Bake's recording of Tazal Ahmed did not resonate with us in the same way as Fayazullah's songs did. At the very first instance of listening to his song, Fayazullah had awakened memories of past listenings, namely to the voice and style of Ranen Roychowdhury, and had, thus, established an organic connect with a whole complex story of crossings of songs over physical and metaphysical borders. Secondly, my relationship with the particular land Fayazullah came from, to its songs and stories, is deep and goes back many years. So, I could take his song to those who would understand him and see him through their eyes and hear him in their songs. Noakhali is still an unfamiliar landscape for me and therefore its roads will not take me to Tazal Ahmed, at least not yet.

Crossing from One Home to Another: of *Bari*, *Basha*, *Ghar*, and *Astana*

Among the sailors' songs of Arnold Bake, there was another song, a 'Pir murshid-er gan "od kore"', sung by one 'Sawabali (oilman)', from 'gram Harikhailash. po. Bisvanath, Sylhet'. All these details are picked from Bake's notes accompanying the cylinders, kept at the Berlin Phonogramm-Archiv.

When I had sent these details to my long-time friends and fellow listeners of the music of Sylhet, Ambarish Dutta, a retired banker and cultural activist, and Suman Kumar Dash, journalist, music researcher, and writer, they said there wasn't a Harikhailash in Bisvanath but a village by the name of Harikalash in Bishwanath thana area. (As an aside, I have mulled over Bake's spelling of the names Harikhailash and Bisvanath. In his letter to Tagore he had written about the 'kh' sound in place of 'k', which he had heard the sailors speak. Hence, he phonetically wrote the name of the village as Harikhailash, although he wrote khailash for kalash. At same time, he wrote Bisvanath for what would probably be written as Bishwanath or Bishvanath, if he was writing phonetically. And here is the Sanskritist Arnold Bake writing a familiar name in a way familiar to him. Hence, the archivist is not only noting down details of the field, but he is also bringing his personal preconditioning into the field).

On 16 January 2018, with Ambarish Dutta and Tushar Kar, another old friend, I went to Harikalash village in Bishwanath police station area of Sylhet district in Bangladesh to see if we might find anyone or anything there to connect with Bake's sailor song recording on Cylinder No. 351. Ambarishda had a contact for Harikalash, so we had one first place to stop and ask. The people in this house weren't very friendly, but a young man started walking with us as we were leaving and he said he would take us to an old man of about 80 or 90 years, in their same neighbourhood, who might know something. Our next stop was at 83-year-old Pachon Malakar's house. And it was from here that the story of Sawabali began to slowly reveal itself. I am consciously using the word reveal here, because that afternoon, after a point, it seemed that we were no longer in control of the story, but something was happening before our eyes and all we could do was to submit ourselves to this revelation. From Pachon Malakar we walked through this typical "Londoni" (used in colloqial Bengali. Means "like London") village of massive empty houses, the kind of place that Katy Gardner writes about,[29] to an old house which was Sawabali's. He sold it later and went off elsewhere, but people remembered him and his family. Everyone, including Pachon Malakar, remembered that he smoked *ganja* (marijuana). There were many *aashors* in the house, when Sawabali and his friends smoked and played music. This was a prominent family, a *piraki* household, for Sawabali's father, Romdi, was a *pir* – a seer, interpreter, and healer. With the pirs, the interpreting and healing is often done through the means of music. People come to them seeking help. People came to this house in Harikalash too.

The older men and women knew about Sawabali and his brothers, about their London episodes and how they came back. They remembered his daughter from his first marriage, Mala, who had died, and his first son from his second marriage, Alfu, who had also died as a child. They talked about how he sold off the property and moved to Alapur, not far from Harikalash, they said. Then he left that place too and went to somewhere in the hills and died there. We were told that there might be some family in Alapur, his sons should be there, though they didnt know their names. We were told to go and ask Moin Daktar at Kaliganja Bazar where Sawabali's house is and he will show the way. That is the route we took to go to Kaliganja first and then to Alapur. The doctor asked us to walk down that road and ask anyone where Anfur Ali's house is.

A beautiful man with the kindest eyes and a greying beard and the softest voice met us in front of his humble house. The man could be a poet. Or a *pir* (saint). This was Anfur Ali, the second son of Sawabali, whose actual name was Sawabullah we learned, from his second wife, whom he had married late in life. That explained Anfur Ali's age of 53 years and his younger brother's, who was just a year-old baby when their father passed away around 1983.

In my many years of experience in the field, such blessed moments have come only rarely. We have taken Arnold Bake's recordings to many places, often to the families of Bake's musicians, such as to the Mitra Thakurs', the kirtan singers, of Mainadal in Birbhum, West Bengal. They were no doubt moved to listen to the sounds of their ancestors' voices and *miridangadhwani*, but they were not entirely surprised, because they are a family of music practitioners and their practice goes back more than 500 years, from the time of Chaitanya Mahaprabhu, and they have had star performers in their midst too. In anything, the Mitra Thakurs have since become more aware of their heritage and their rightly deserved place in the archives of the world. Or say the case of the Tagore singer Chitralekha Chowdhury. When we took to her a recording from her school days, she was delighted, while wanting to know if there were more songs in the archives, for she clearly remembered singing several songs for 'Bake Shaheb'. The Santals in Kairabani wanted to talk and sing together when they heard their ancestors' voices on Bake's wax cylinders. They did not seem to have any special feeling for the past, because all that the recordings did was to arouse the song in them. Their attitude was a bit like, 83 years or 100 years – well, how does it even matter? After all, the tradition of song and dance that Bake had recorded is still very much alive for them and quite unchanged too, and they were still as marginally placed in society as almost a hundred years ago.

Anfur Ali, a friend Batir Ali, his younger brother Asar Ali (who was first named Asman), the women of the house, children, us who had gone from outside, the young man who showed us the way – we all sat in their courtyard in the fading winter light, and I played the song of Sawabali from my laptop. When we had gone, Anfur Ali was thinking what he could offer to his guests. He had said to the women, 'Make some tea'. We had said, 'Please don't bother, we have just had tea'. So he had asked, '*Paan* then?' As the song was playing, Anfur Ali said, to whom I do not know, but I hear in my recording of that day, his voice above his father's. 'Make some tea, make it strong'.

The song was over. Everyone was silent. '*Dhoinyobad*, thank you', Anfur Ali whispered. The song had opened old wounds, while also taking him to memories of a time of beautiful loving. 'My father loved me very much, he used to call me Afu'. He spoke a little, then stopped. Then someone else spoke, maybe his much younger brother, who was sleeping inside the house when we had gone. He drives long-distance trucks through the night. Anfur Ali works as an electrician, he works when he is hired; they struggle to make ends meet. There was grief in his eyes, but no grievance about anything. It was probably a sense of grief that ran in the blood of this *piraki* family, a line of seers, poets, and healers. Music was a part of their being. 'I don't usually sing', Anfur Ali said. Besides, it is expensive to hold *aashors* at home, where musicians gather and smoke and have tea and sing, such as used to happen in his father's time. 'I go to different shrines and some nights when the song rises in me, I sing song after song, sometimes all through the night, sometimes all alone'.

Several times in the course of that evening, while sitting in their courtyard or while walking us to the road, he said, '*Abbay koita*, Abba used to say...', and then maybe just recited few lines of a song. 'Will you sing for us please?' I asked. He said,

> It is hard you know, when the air is so heavy with remembrance. Who would have thought a voice from so long ago, Abba's voice... this really is *jotheshto paona* for us, more than what we could have ever imagined, we shall never forget this day.

I said, it was actually *jotheshto paona* on both sides, far greater than what a researcher or field recordist can ever ask for. This is a blessed moment in anyone's life.

Bake's Sawabali or Sawabullah was an other-worldly man, his son said. He knew 12 languages, sheltered Hindus and Muslims in his home at the time of the *Shongram*, meaning the 1971 War of Liberation, went out and spoke to the Pakistani soldiers in Urdu or Hindi or whatever language it was, till they were gone. 'Just today Nripendrababu had come and he sat here and was talking about Abba and was weeping', he said. Nripendrababu,

Umeshbabu, Ashwini Nath – all the Hindu families who were given shelter in their house in 1971. He had brought back some money from his job as a sailor, and also from his stay in London, but he also gave it all away. Gave food to so many. Gave home to all sorts of fringe people, the blessed and the mad ones. Abba had brought with him one Koilkattai Pir. He could bite into hard iron and bamboo. Then there was one Hoq Bhandari, who went round and round crying Hoq Bhadari Hoq Bhandari! They lived for 12 years in this house. Called our Amma Ma. They were like children. When people teased them, they went to Amma and cried.'

As Anfur Ali remembered things, others around him also started to remember. A collective memory of joy and pain began to rise and fill up the space of the courtyard of that humblest house, as the *azaan* of *Maghreb* (call to evening prayer), was heard from the mosque nearby. Then from another mosque in the distance, then from another further away. It was so beautiful. I folded up my laptop, packed my things, and rose to leave.

'Where is your *bari*, your home?' Anfur Ali's friend Batir Ali asked me.
'I've come from Kolkata.'
'Kolkata? And your *basha*? Your nest?'

I laughed and explained that I had lived between so many places that my home and nest had all become one, especially for us whose parents' original home was on one side of Bengal border and then once Partition happened, they lost that home and had to go to the other side. Since then, all we have is a search for home.

'So your *astana* then, your shelter for tonight?' Batir Ali seemed worried for me.
'That is going to be at Ambarishda's house in Sylhet.'
'Make this *ghar*, this home, your *astana* tonight,' he said, welcoming me to stay in their home. Anfur Ali and Batir Ali were brothers in their shared devotion to a very humane god, I could see that.
'Did your father treat the sick, since he was a pir?'
'No, that was my grandfather, Romdi Pir. Abba could only heal mute animals.'

'*Abbay koita*, Abba used to say…'
Anfur Ali broke into a song and Batir Ali joined him.

Uchana dolane boshi, ki koro mon parobashi re
Amar parobashi, oshar ei jibon re
Gour tore gharer bar ke korlo re
Aij amar moner banchha purilo re.

Chiripurer disha dhori nao bhashailam bhab sagare re
Amar nouka jaito Chiripurer ghate re
Gour tore gharer bar ke korlo re
Aij amar moner banchha purilo re.

Deeno Bhabanande koy amar noukar khobor ke ba loyo re
Amar noukar khobor loiba niranjan re
Gour tore gharer bar ke korlo re
Aij amar moner banchha purilo re.

Sitting in that lofty house, what to do, O exiled mind?
This exile life has no meaning at all.
Gour, who has got you out of home?[30]
Today my heart's desire is fulfilled.

I set sail on the river of life, Chiripur is where I must go[31]
My boat will go sailing to that blessed Chiripur
Gour, who has got you out of home?
Today my heart's desire is fulfilled.

Deeno Bhabananda says, who will ask about the boat I row?[32]
The Saviour of my Soul will know about my boat
Gour, who has got you out of home?
Today my heart's desire is fulfilled.

'Abba used to sing this song. After he lost everything and went to Companyganj in search of work, he would sit and sing this song. He badly missed his close ones whom he had left behind'.

All Singers Are Sailors

This paper has not been about the individual sailor. All singers in this story are sailors, carrying the song from one shore to another. So, it is not about Tazal Ahmed or Fayazullah or Sawabali or Ranen Roychowdhury or Hemango Biswas. But it has tried to talk about the flow of the song and about the many crossings the songs have made to make the archive into something unfixed but moving and changing all the time. So far Arnold Bake's recordings are concerned, between the kirtaniyas of Mainadal and these sailors' songs, the difference to my mind is this: in Mainadal, there is the exact family to take the songs back to, to 'repatriate' the recordings made in 1933. The song is still sung as it used to be sung over 80 years ago. Yet the archive is frozen in time. And you know that the end has come. Perhaps the song will be gone after one more generation. With the sailors, there might be nowhere to go, none to take the songs back to. But there is no need for that either. There is no need for a forceful revival of this music. Because it is there, already. The archive is alive. Dispersed like seeds. Scattered, as the people of a land have scattered, over many lands. Grown, as the people have grown. And changed too.

I have listened again and again to my recording of Sawabali's son, Anfur Ali. It is such an amazing thing which happened that day. So much of it was about the ancestor's voice, about sound triggering memory.[33] The words *bari, basha, ghar*, and *astana* were used in our conversation that day. We tried to play with the different meanings of the word home and our different experiences and perceptions of it. Such a range of experiences can only come out of a broken land holding a displaced people. The song flows through the *bari* to the *ghar* to the *astana* to the *basha* and flies out like a bird. This *basha* is ever impermanent; it is the nest which holds the fledgling till it grows wings to fly to its own open sky. The song is that fledgling – the promise of new life.

Notes

1 For studies on the work on Arnold Bake, see Nazir Ali Jairazbhoy, *The Bake Restudy in India, 1938–1984: The Preservation and Transformation of Performance in Tamilnadu, Kerala and Karnataka*, (Van Nuys, CA: Apsara Media, 1990, video monograph; Carol Tingey, 'The Nepalese Field Work of Dr. Arnold A. Bake: A Guide to the Sound Recordings', M. Mus. thesis, London: Goldsmiths College, 1985, Vol. 1, 21, and Vol. 2, 40; Christian Friedrich Poske, *Continuity and Change: A Restudy of Arnold Adriaan Bake's Research on the Devotional and Folk Music and Dance of Bengal 1925–1956*, PhD thesis. SOAS University of London (2020) and Bob van der Linden, *Arnold Bake: A Life with South Asian Music*, (London: Routledge, 2018).

2 For the Streefkerk, visit www.rdm-archief.nl/RDM-NB/RDM-077.html. Accessed 3 January 2022.

3 Arnold Bake had heard Rabindranath Tagore speak in Leiden University as a student in 1920 and like many of his generation in post WWI-Europe, he was drawn to the poet and his ideas. He had also had a taste of Tagore's music and loved it, and so when the time came for him to decide what he would do after university in the Netherlands, with encouragement from his teachers Professors Wilhelm Caland and John Phillipe Vogel, he had decided to come to Santiniketan. For further details, see Linden, *Arnold Bake: A Life with South Asian Music*, op. cit, pp.1–4 and Bob van der Linden, *Music and Empire in Britain and India: Identity, Internationalism and Cross-Cultural Communication* (New York: Palgrave Macmillan, 2013), pp.107–128.

4 Letter held at Rabindra Bhavana archives, Visva Bharati, Santiniketan. Written on 1 April 1934, while 'Sailing on the Red Sea'.

5 Lakshmisvar Sinha (1905–1977) came from a family of landlords of Rarishal village in Habiganj district of Sylhet region. The family had a strong connection with Rabindranath Tagore and Santiniketan, while Sinha himself was extremely multifaceted and an explorer at heart, who travelled to many countries, wrote books on a wide range of subjects ranging from carpentry to cotton cultivation to travels in Lapland to an anthology of kirtans sung in Sylhet. He was also a pioneer Indian Esperantist during his time.

6 There is vast literature on the subject of course, a whole and diverse field of study in its own right. We can look at works such as W.E.B. Du Bois, *The Souls of Black Folk* (New York and London: W.W. Norton & Company, 1999), Marcus Rediker, *The Slave Ship: A Human History* (New York: Penquin, 2007), Sowande Mustakeem, *Slavery at Sea Terror, Sex and Sickness in the Middle Passage* (Illinois: University of Illinois Press, 2016), Stan Hugill, *Shanties from the Seven Seas: Shipboard Work-songs and Songs Used as Work-songs from the Great Days of Sail*, (London: Routledge & Kegan Paul 1961), and many others. There are 'recordings' of various kinds of songs that people carried with them when they made their journeys across lands and oceans, not necessarily as audio recordings or song texts, but as songs they knew or had heard, memories of songs. Such songs got written in the new songs which were born in their new lands (see, for example, works of Tejaswini Niranjana, Surabhi Sharma or Meghnath, and Biju Toppo). A very interesting collection of songs/poetry that an indentured labourer wrote, based on songs he had carried with him in his body to the Caribbean was what has later been translated as *I Even Regret Night*. Lalbihari Sharma, *I Even Regret Night: Holi Songs of Demerara*, translated by Rajiv Mohabir (Los Angeles: Kaya Press, 2019). In 2004 I recorded labourers in a tea garden in Srimangal, Sylhet, where the singers were singing songs from a past land where they had never been, in a language they did not fully speak any longer; they did not even know what place their ancestors came from. The song in the body not only gave comfort during the journey but became a relic of a lost land for generations to come. www.thetravellingarchive.org/record-session/srimangal-sylhet-27-december-2004-tea-garden-singers/, accessed 3 January 2022.

7 For example, Bake's recordings of Savitri Govind singing Meenakshi, from which Tagore composed his 'Basanti he bhubanomohini'; wax cylinders numbered Bake India I/9-10, British Library Sound and Audiovisual Archive (BLSA) catalogue number C52/1649-50.

8 See www.thetravellingarchive.org/exhibition/time-upon-time-arnold-bake-in-bengal-2016/, accessed 3 January 2022.

9 Mainly the British Library and the Archives and Research Centre for Ethnomusicology of the American Institute of Indian Studies, Gurgaon, India.

10 For Ranen Roychowdhury, see www.thetravellingarchive.org/tribute/a-boatman-named-ranen-roychowdhury/, accessed 3 January 2022.

11 Khaled Chowdhury's memoir and the YouTube link to 'Nishithe jaiyo phulobone', can be accessed from the link given in Note 10 above.

12 Lahiri, Ashish, *Sanskritir Bangla Bazar* (Bengali), (Calcutta: Ritakshar, 2012), p. 88. (transl. mine).

13 See Note 10 above.

14 Ibid.

15 Dhirajuddin sings Lalon Fakir's 'Ajob Lile', a song about a strange upturned world, in the opening scene of the Ghatak's *Titas Ekti Nodir Naam* (A River Named Titas), 1973.

16 Hemango Biswas sings this song in Ritwik Ghatak's 1965 film *Subarnarekha*.

17 Listen to Barindra Das here www.thetravellingarchive.org/record-session/silchar-25-august-2005-barindra-das/, accessed 3 January 2022, and he is also on this podcast, www.thetravellingarchive.org/exhibition/baba-betar-at-chobi-mela-shunyo-2021/, accessed 3 January 2022.

18 See Note 10 above.

19 Listen to Sanchita Roychowdhury's interview here, www.thetravellingarchive.org/record-session/jadavpur-12-december-2009-sanchita-roychowdhury/, accessed 3 January 2022.
20 Soumya Chakravarti writes about his experience of going on a recording trip to Anantabala Baishnabi's house in 1968. See www.thetravellingarchive.org/related-research/soumya-chakravarti-account-of-recording-folk-singer-anantabala-baishnabi-in-1968/, accessed 3 January 2022.
21 Radharaman Dutta (1833–1915) was a mystic poet of the Jagannathpur region of Sylhet.
22 In an interview given to The Travelling Archive in 2006, Biditlal Das had talked about the importance of 'ornamentation' in folk music and described how he tries to 'beautify' an otherwise plain song. See here www.thetravellingarchive.org/record-session/sylhet-21-april-2006-biditlal-das/, accessed 3 January 2022.
23 Deb, Siddhartha, *The Point of Return*, Basingstoke and Oxford: Picador, 2002, p. 26.
24 BLSA shelf mark C52/1761, Bake India II, cylinder 109.
25 Bake recorded kirtan of the Mitra Thakur family in Mainadal, and when we went, we found the 500-year-old musical tradition to be still part of the family's living history. Listen to Bake's Mainadal recordings made between 12 and 14 August 1933 here https://sounds.bl.uk/World-and-traditional-music/Arnold-Adriaan-Bake-South-Asian-Music-Collection. The Naogaon recordings can be listened to at the same site, under the date 28 February 1932.
26 In the divine love story of Radha and Krishna, love moves through various stages, from seeing, appreciating, desiring, seeking, meeting, playing, parting, and finally to union. However, union does not occur in consummation, but it finds sublimation in surrender and the surrender is of both the worshipper and the worshipped, unto one another.
27 For Rasiklal Das, his singer and songwriter wife Dibyamoyi, read the autobiography of Ramkanai Das, *Sangit O Amar Jiban* (Music and My Life) (Dhaka: Nabajug Prakashona, 2011).
28 In his letter home after the Naogaon recordings made on 28 February 1932, Arnold Bake wrote, 'Early the next morning a Mohammedan baul woman showed up; she played some interesting music'. He recorded more songs by her than of any of the other fakirs he also met on that trip.
29 Katy Gardner and Zahir Ahmed, 'Place Social Protection and Migration in Bangladesh: A Londoni Village in Biswanath', Working Paper 118 (Sussex: Development Research Centre on Migration, Globalisation and Poverty, 2006)
30 Gour is Gouranga, the Golden One. The 16th century Bhakti saint of Bengal, Sri Chaitanya, was also called Gour for his ever-radiant colour.
31 Chiripur would be a colloquial way of saying Sripur, the place to reach at the end of the spiritual quest.
32 Bhabananda was a folk poet of the early 19th century from Moulavibazar, Sylhet, who wrote devotional songs in the fluid Bhakti-Sufi syncretic tradition of Bengal. Deen or Deeno is an epithet used to describe the state of total humility required for ultimate surrender.
33 See Erika Brady, *A Spiral Way: How the Phonograph Changed Ethnography* (Jackson: University Press of Mississippi, 1999), pp. 118–125.

10

SURMOUNTING BORDERS

The Corridos of Jenni Rivera

Minni Sawhney

Corridos are popular narratives in the folk music north and south of the Mexican–U.S. border and wherever sizable pockets of Mexicans live.[1] The genre includes rags to riches stories, heroic tales of narcotraffickers portrayed as social bandits, paeans to northern Mexican states associated with drugs, and diverse class and gender solidarities, all sung with a decidedly masculine perspective. Narcocorridos have been described as oral histories that provide information unavailable from other sources, microhistories of events often misrepresented and sensationalized in official media. They are presently a response to the war on drugs which found its latest avatar in President Felipe Calderón who in 2006 pitted the federal Mexican state against provinces like Sinaloa. This crusade was a continuation of the war originally launched by Richard Nixon and intensified by Ronald Reagan, and since the production of narcocorridos has been in tandem with this history, a brief explanation is necessary. The cultivation of poppy and marijuana goes back to the 19th century and was endorsed by Presidents Roosevelt and Ávila Camacho after Hitler prohibited its cultivation in Turkey during the Second World War. The climate of Sinaloa was ideal for this crop needed for the manufacture of morphine needed in hospitals. But overnight this scenario changed when the cultivation of marijuana was declared a crime against health and 2000 arrests were made in Culiacán with the persecution and torture of planters. These facts and the history of the rebellion of Sinaloa have given rise to sympathy amongst the locals for the narcotraffickers who are looked upon as heroes who fight against the federal army and the United States.[2]

The growing legalization of marijuana in a few Latin American countries and in the United States has led to a wider understanding about these songs and their consumption. These narratives of resistance, however, have steadily acquired a commodified image due to the huge profits which accrue for the producers, clubs, and radio stations in areas with a majority Latino

 DOI: 10.4324/9780429356421-16

population in the United States. Their anti-establishment, contrarian flavour has also led to their prohibition in parts of Mexico and the United States.

Imbued with symbols of popular cachet they touch on themes of likely interest for their generally subaltern audience and since the 1990s corridos have been constantly identified with migration and narcotrafficking. The immigrant as well as the narcotrafficker, subjects created by globalization, are scapegoats on both sides of the border and find ample resonance in the corridos.[3] One of my intentions in this paper is to deconstruct the cultural configuration of narcotrafficking/narcocorridista and show how the latter responds pragmatically to the vicissitudes in their lives. The vast weight of media output and attestations on figures associated with drugs makes this necessary in order to cut through bias when analysing a figure like Jenni Rivera, a female narcocorridista. I will touch upon her life and the layered psychology that emerges when we discuss her *habitus*, the songs that are closely intertwined with her own personal and family history, and the critiques her music has been subjected to over the years.

Death as 'a Completion of the Persona'.[4]

According to observers, Jenni Rivera's fame exceeded that of any Latino politician at the time of her death in a plane crash in December 2012.[5] Since then, her myth and legend continue unabated. After the appearance of her posthumous album, 'Aparentemente bien' (Apparently Well) in 2020, Jenni Rivera, '*the first lady of the narcocorrido*' became the only regional Mexican music star to appear on the billboard in Times Square. The vocals of this song had been earlier recorded in different studios of the United States before she died and the album saw four million subscribers in a single day. This rapturous reception outpaced narcocorridista legends such as Los Tigres del Norte. She is still known as *La Diva de la Banda* as no female ranchera singer has been able to replace her.

Rivera was always something of an anomaly in the regional Mexican music scene amongst the predominantly male *Banda* or *ranchera*[6] musicians and singers. In a genre known for its patriarchal ideology, she infused a refreshing note of independence and nonconformity and the candid lyrics were far from being paeans to victimhood. Her first song was recorded in 1992 in the family album *Somos Rivera*. Over the years she had developed a business empire, television and radio channels, and had her name endorse beauty products. Despite the rumours surrounding her narcocorridos, she reiterated that all she had achieved was due to her own efforts and within the confines of the law.

Jenni Rivera, who had written songs that alluded to the beauty and her love of Mexican provinces like Jalisco, saw herself as a native of both countries and completely identified with the Mexican diaspora in the United

States. As revealed in her autobiography, *Inquebrantable*, her songs were a reflection of her life. Leila Cobo, her biographer, also gives us vignettes about the strong identification of the Latina residents of West Side Long Beach, California with Jenni Rivera whose lives mirrored that of the singer. In spite of being an excellent student, she left school at age 18 when she got pregnant with her first child. The problems she subsequently encountered like her marriage to an abusive and violent man did not kill her spirit and her drive to move on. Her main support was her family, her brothers who stood by her during all the turbulence in her life. In spite of the alleged rivalries as some reports claim with her brother Lupillo Rivera, there was always an unshakeable bond of solidarity amongst the parents and siblings. In difficult moments, as for example, when there erupted the sexual scandal surrounding a video produced by a member of her music group, her brothers defended her in public.

Jenni had her share of profound grief during her short life. She was raped by three men after singing in a bar in the early years, she made the traumatic discovery that her first husband and father of her three children had repeatedly raped her sister and sexually molested his own daughter. She was also thrice divorced and had to constantly negotiate a media that seemed to delight in her misery. These biographical anecdotes about Jenni Rivera, gleaned from her biography *Inquebrantable* (Translation mine: 'Unbreakable: My History, My Way') undoubtedly shore up the image of a tough woman who had risen from the ranks and who tries to be 'indestructible'.

The veracity of these anecdotes has never been questioned but Elijah Wald has described her as an unlikely 'hard bitten narco star'.[7] Instead, Jenni imaged herself as an empathetic Latino woman and someone who had pulled herself up by her bootstraps, her misfortunes cast a glittering light on the rest of her life.

In an interview to Elijah Wald, her father Pedro Rivera had described Mexican Americans like himself as the 'neediest people' in the United States. To maintain the family's Mexican singularity in the larger Anglo world, he insisted that Spanish be spoken inside the home. In this way the Rivera family with five artists became a force to reckon with in the music industry. The narcocorridos that his family wrote reflected the lives of Mexicans in the United States who were often outlaws in their own country. The outlaw charisma of the narcocorrido that had now begun to take roots in Los Angeles paved the way to their success. The pre-Trump era in the United States afforded them another chance and a new lease on life.[8] A song that Jenni's father Pedro wrote on Brian Barker, (a deputy sheriff who had shot himself and whose death was attributed to Latinos), reflects the socio-cultural framework of contemporary America:

> The world does not have an owner, we can go wherever we want,
> When God made people, he did not just make white people.

He made them of all colors, nor did he choose flags...
What do you think of those whites, with their discrimination
Toward the Latino people who enrich the nation?
If it were not for us, they would not even have underwear.

Fiction and Autobiography

The themes of Jenni's corridos were not radically different from that of *corridos* sung by men or the few women corridistas before her. Her songs were for and about those like herself who were low in the pecking order. She sang of love and the family and even touched the vexed subject of honour. She insisted on her Mexicanness and the Mexican American population in the South was her ally in an industry where she did not have the conventional symbolic capital to become famous. Her life and work help us understand the evolution of the Mexican diaspora in the United States.

Narcocorridos are a kind of oral history as Maria Herrera-Sobek has emphasized in *The Mexican Corrido, A Feminist Analysis*. Herrera-Sobek explains the historical cultural archetypes in corridos that date from the 19th century: the good/terrible mother, the *soldadera*/lover.[9] These categories were given a twist by Jenni Rivera in keeping with the neoliberal times. A caveat is necessary here to explain the nuances that differentiate her protagonists (in a song like *La chacalosa* loosely translated as Party Girl) from the numerous *buchonas* or lovers of drug dealers exemplified by Teresa Mendoza in *La reina del sur* or more recently in its American remake *The Queen of the South*. In the songs analysed below, the protagonists of Jenni's lyrics (*La Maestra del contrabando*) are often driven to drug dealing by desperate circumstance just like Teresa Mendoza, the Queen of the South. But unlike them, Pérez Reverte's Mendoza revels in what Sayak Valencia has described as *gore* capitalism where the woman becomes an object of consumption though she believes herself a subject in a predatory capitalist society based on necropolitics and death as an industry where the State has delegated its rights and duties to narco lords who accrue benefits and pose as the new *caudillos* or strong men offering protection. Women protagonists of the narco novel/corrido are enmeshed in *gore* capitalism, they attune their desires and bodies to the exigencies of the narcoculture. But as Sayak explains, there are also those who resist the glaring patriarchy of this culture, the so called 'mad women' or *locas*.

> Son verdaderamente locas para la cultura patriarcal aquellas mujeres que por imposibilidad, desobediencia o rebeldía, transgreden las cualidades de la feminidad (....) (The women who transgress feminine norms either because of the impossibility (of abiding by them) or out of disobedience or rebellion. are considered really mad in patriarchal culture.
>
> (Sayak Valencia 257)

These 'mad women' are the protagonists in Jenni Rivera's songs and the progeny of the original narcocorrido heroine Camelia the Texan, who kills her lover when he decides to leave her for another woman after they have successfully smuggled drugs across the border. If Camelia was from a rural background with revenge and passion as her calling card, today's 'mad women' of the narco world, the 'post Camelias' construct their subjectivity with capitalist consumption patterns. These patterns preclude them from seeing themselves as victims and their 'emancipation' is based on the libertinage and hedonism they flaunt. However, in Valencia's analysis, despite the promising signs, the moment of triumph of the *locas* is an illusion because they are now in the grip of capitalism.

Though Jenni's protagonists were the 'mad women' or *locas* of the narco patriarchal system who had even acquired agency and did not shy away from narcoculture, they sided with the underdog amongst their diasporic compatriots and did not get subsumed into North American culture. While some of Jenni's protagonists (*Las Malandrinas* and *La chacalosa*) discover agency through capitalism, others like the *Novia del plebe* privilege the backwoods life of Sinaloa and Durango underlining the beauty of Mexican provinces that threatens to be overshadowed by association with the narco.

The *Habitus* of Jenni Rivera: 'Chicago lindo y querido'

In an emblematic article written in 2010, Juan Carlos Ramírez-Pimienta has argued how the idea of Mexicanism is not anymore inscribed in central Mexico or the Bajío region nor in the *charro* and *mariachi* but in the cultural production of the border and in the cities of the United States which have an overwhelming Latino population. Jenni Rivera's fan following comprised the great Latino community, the progeny of the wetbacks immortalized by Octavio Paz in the 1950's in *The Labyrinth of Solitude* who intuited that Jenni was one of them. This was her *habitus*, a public who shared her concerns: the world of the diaspora Mexicans who were always surmounting physical and/or emotional borders. Narcocorridos were their soul food, their existence proved that one of their kind was making good in America. Jenni Rivera's ethnic songs added to their sense of self and responded to their hopes and aspirations. According to Pierre Bourdieu, the *habitus* is a product of history and produces collective and individual traits. In his words:

> The structures constitutive of a particular type of environment (e.g. the material conditions of existence characteristic of a class condition) produce habitus, systems of durable, transposable dispositions…(…) Thus, for example, in the interaction between two agents

> or groups of agents endowed with the same habitus (say A and B), everything takes place as if the actions of each of them were organized in relation to the reactions they call forth from any agent possessing the same habitus so that they objectively imply anticipation of the reaction which these reactions in turn call forth...
>
> (Bourdieu 72)

Jenni's *habitus* inclined her towards *ranchera* and *banda* music. Like her followers, she too had lived through times of abuse and trauma and had survived. Jenni put her life in her art. In the song *Mariposa de barrio*, she reiterated her modest upbringing and compared her life to that of a caterpillar who becomes a butterfly. 'Aquí estoy, vengo desde muy lejos./ El camino fue negro./ Pero al fin ya triunfé!/ Me arrastré..viví todos los cambios/ y aunque venía llorando,/ mis alas levanté'. (Trans: 'Here I am, I have come from afar./ The journey was bleak/ But I have finally triumphed./ I dragged myself up.. I lived through it all/ and although I cried/ I lifted my wings'.

Rivera attributed her success to her fans. As the song goes: 'Me quieren porque quieren quererme y uds. me han levantado,/ me aceptan tal como soy/ con mis defectos y mis virtudes'. (Trans: 'You love me because you want to love me and you have lifted me up/You accept me as I am/with my virtues and defects'.) Jenni was commercially savvy and knew that her fans were unsophisticated hicks, the kind of person she had been before she channelized her talent in her father's record company and she gave them the credit for being who she was.

But her fame and money came from beyond the pale of what was considered socially acceptable and signified a challenge to what was considered good taste by the elite. In the words of Mark Cameron Edberg

> The narcotrafficker then represents a certain, culturally shaped, individual route to power for those who feel powerless, a challenge to the customary 'rules' for how one achieves status and influence, and a route to status for those usually shut out.
>
> (Edberg 121)

An analysis of the criticism she faced reveals the divide between the legitimate world of conventional music, *highbrow* art, and the subaltern world of folk music which had given birth to the narcocorrido. The music industry can be likened to the field of cultural production as described by Pierre Bourdieu – the site of encounters where each artist wages a battle in order to impose his definition on what it means to be an artist. Conscious of the struggles on the road to success, the narcocorridistas as well as the narco industry on both sides of the border elaborated new yardsticks with which to measure success.

In *Narcocorrido, A Journey into the Music of Drugs, Guns and Guerrillas*, Elijah Wald laid bare the prejudices that these artists have had to face

> One does not even have to be a corrido fan to feel that Mexicans are getting a raw deal from the US entertainment media. (…) Even in Los Angeles, where Mexicans, Guatemalans, and Salvadorans (all of whom tend to listen to Mexican music) are the overwhelming majority of the Latino population, it is common to find commentators writing as if 'Latin' music were all salsa and merengue, or possibly rock en español. (…) California, once a part of Mexico and becoming re-mexicanised at an impressive clip, seems to be full of Anglos in denial. Some are shouting for immigration restrictions, cutting off aid to immigrant families, and trashing bilingual education. Others are celebrating multiculturalism, but now use 'Latin' as they once used 'Spanish', as a way of separating the romantic stereotypes they like from the ordinary, poor population growing all around them.
>
> (Wald 120–121)

Jenni Rivera's songs began to be heard over the radio. Pepe Garza, the jockey of the radio channel *La Q Buena* (KBUE), one of the biggest Spanish radio stations based in Los Angeles founded in 1995, began to pay attention to narcocorridos and the Rivera family. Jenni's father had introduced her to Pepe Garza. In his words,

> In the beginning I had my doubts because women are usually not very successful at regional Mexican music. But her public soon became convinced.
>
> Yo en un principio dudaba porque las mujeres no tienen mucha suerte en el regional mexicano. Pero empezó a convencer a su público.
>
> (Cobo 50)

A special prize was created for the narcocorridos category; this measure facilitated the dissemination of a marginalized and yet very popular music. Los Angeles, the city where the Rivera dynasty had first become famous, had the largest number of Mexicans outside Mexico City. By 2010 her album La Gran Señora had made her the biggest selling regional Mexican artist.

The Ethical Conundrums of Jenni Rivera's Narcocorridos

Often Jenni Rivera's spectacular rise hides the many barriers on the road to fame and the obstacles she had to overcome. With the success of groups like Los Tigres del Norte, Los Tucanes de Tijuana, and Jenni Rivera, the criticism against them has had to be articulated from other vantage points. Like the narco novelist writers of the U.S.–Mexican border, the narcocorridistas have had to face accusations that they celebrate violence and are the allies of the narcotraffickers. Jenni knew how to make of her aspirations a weapon to counter the strategies used by her rivals. She admitted this in the context of the composition of the song 'La chacalosa',

> Its real hard to enter the market right now. In the first place, a lot of us sing the same, the tone of our voice and everything sounds the same, (..) I mean, if you sing nice ballads like Mariah Carey and Celine Dion, you're just another artist out there, but if you sing about how you are a drug dealer and how you can kill somebody if he'll mess with you, people are like, 'Oh she's very different'.
>
> (Wald 142)

Jenni defended her decision to sing narcocorridos in front of those who raised ethical questions about songs that neutralized the terrible effects of drug overdose. Elijah Wald writes that although the Mexicans of Sinaloa could say that drugs were a problem for drug consumers in the United States and that cultivation depended on consumption, the Rivera family could not take recourse to this argument because West Side Long Beach was lush with crack addicts and traffickers. When *Narcocorrido*... was published in 2001, she defended herself saying that the Rivera family, in spite of living in the colony where *crack* was found in abundance, was not mixed up in drugs and parents should protect their children. In various studies on the narcocorrido it has been reiterated that drugs are available but a certain kind of proclivity or inclination towards them has to be controlled.

> I would argue that narcocorridos – and other music or media of the same type in other cultural situations – do not have a determining effect on behavior, though they can have a shaping effect. Media such as this provide a culturally resonant shape and coherence for certain patterns of action that are already under way to one degree or another or if not already underway, highly imminent) for other, more proximate, reasons. These reasons include personal circumstances.
>
> (Edberg 120)

Jenni's fans were with her even if the mainstream might have disdained her. They identified with her songs that reflected their immigrant lives and privileged the Latino individual and the Spanish language. Her followers had little symbolic capital and agency, led humble lives in an Anglo society that subtly rejected them. But the narcocorridos with which they could identify increased their consciousness of who they were, their history and their beliefs. As Jenni said about her 'bad' songs:

> It gives people an adrenaline rush, they get hyped up and it makes them happy. It makes them feel tough and it makes them feel, like, really Mexican. And I think we all like to feel that.[10]

The songs were not just love songs in which women enjoyed agency. Jenni also sang deeply political songs with her brother Lupillo Rivera like 'Sangre de Indio' (Indian Blood) that had the lines: 'Por las venas de mi padre / le corre la sangre también como a mi/ sangre del indio que cae, que llora/ que ama, que sabe sufrir'. (The blood that flows through my father's veins and mine is Indian blood. It cries and loves and knows how to suffer). In the song, '*Novia del Plebe*' (The girlfriend of the plebeians) she privileges northern Mexican provinces that constitute the periphery for a centralized Mexican state and also the lowly cantina where *aguardiente*, the drink of the campesino is served. Far from being a toast to consumerist binge spending, the song wants to give the pleasures of the humble an airing and spark interest in Mexico. Yo soy la novia del plebe/ de aquel plebe sinaloense/ que en la cantina de Dos de Oros/ siempre se encuentra presente/ con su compa de Durango/toman copas de aguardiente (...) Pero sigo siendo plebe/y no me avergüenzo de nada (...) que nos toquen los corridos/con la rebelión norteña/y que brinden con nosotros/las amigas parranderas. (Translation: I am the girlfriend of the plebeians/the plebeians of Sinaloa / who is always found/in the Dos de Oros canteen/with her companion from Durango/who drink *aguardiente* (...)/I continue to be a plebeian/and I am not ashamed of anything/they should play corridos for us/as a sign of Northern rebellion/ and the party girls should toast with us.)

Jenni saw herself as a social agent, as someone who had the power of her habitus to modify the ideas of her compatriots abroad. In 'Chicana Jalisciense' she talked about her origins and life choices.

> Yo soy chicana californiana (I am a Californian chicana)
> y de Jalisco mis padres son (My parents are from Jalisco)
> y mis costumbres son mexicanas. (My customs are Mexican)
> Mi sangre es brava y le canto al amor. (...) (My blood is brave and I sing to love)
> Viva Jalisco y los sonorenses, (Viva Jalisco and the Sonorans)
> es gente alegre que sabe gozar (They are happy people who know how to enjoy themselves)
> porque de ahí viene esta hembra valiente (from whence comes this brave woman)
> que estos corridos se atreve a cantar. (who dares to sing these corridos)

Always positioning herself on the side of the people, in her second song 'Las Malandrinas', Rivera privileges spontaneous unsnobbish girls who like corridos and beer as opposed to the 'popis', or rich girls.

> Nos dicen las Malandrinas (They call us the Malandrinas)
> porque hacemos mucho ruido (Because we make a lot of noise)
> porque tomamos cerveza (Because we drink a lot of beer)
> y nos gusta el mejor vino. (And we drink the best wine)
> En los salones de baile (In the dance halls)
> siempre pedimos corridos (We always ask for corridos)
> No somos como las popis (We are not like the popis)
> que se paran mucho el cuello (who are stiff necked)
> nos gusta la rancherada (we like rancheras)
> de nada tenemos miedo (and we are afraid of nothing)
> y le damos gusto al gusto (and we match pleasure with pleasure)
> aunque otras no estén de acuerdo. (although others might not agree)

In her biography by Leila Cobo, Jenni refers to this song and reiterates her commitment with the Mexican American women of Los Angeles who found no role models in the public sphere. The stars of those times were Thalía, Paulina Rubio, J-Lo, and Shakira and their sexuality was celebrated by the media. Jenni did not fit in this scenario and yet she had numerous fans. But there were also many narcocorrido critics who excoriated the entry of women into this world. In northern Mexico, the major political parties like the PRI, PAN, and PRD[11] and the chambers of commerce of the radio and television industry vied with each other in restricting the dissemination of narcocorrido music.[12] In 2012, Erika L. Sánchez wrote an article in the *Huffington Post* denigrating the genre and singers who she termed unlawful and thus not worthy of being listened to.

> Though corridos have now dramatically changed in content, they continue to be characteristic of the lower classes and are often considered 'música naca,' rural or 'hick' music. (...) The genre has become a tool for the drug cartels. Any narcotraficante with enough money can commission a song for himself. The transmission of history is being dictated by the wealthy. Narcocorridistas can't be the voices of the poor and voiceless when by 'representing' them, they are reaping the benefits of capitalism. They're now active participants in the structures that they so boldly defy. The narcotraficante is not 'la voz del pueblo;' he is a very specific figure who has attained social mobility and is no longer in need of representation. (...)
>
> (Sánchez)

Sánchez' objectivity becomes a little questionable when we consider how many mainstream artists like Michael Jackson and Britney Spears have broken the law or been imprisoned for various reasons. Moreover, the allegations that narcotraffickers get songs written in their honour is only partly true. There are also sociological studies that show that the tentacles of narcotrafficking and money laundering are difficult to restrict in the parallel economy. They have also spread to the entertainment industry.

Sánchez reserves her strongest criticism for the women of this musical genre.

> It's ironic that women are now more visible in the hypermasculine narcocorrido genre. This visibility, however, comes at a cost because their identities are inextricably bound to macho culture. Female norteña singers have also become more prevalent, but in their case, their popularity relies heavily on their bodies and clothes to accentuate their sexuality. Though it may seem progressive and feminist that the women in corridos are now active agents, these songs are still participating in consumerism and patriarchy. (…) It appears that the attempt may be feminist, but really, these women simply perpetuate patriarchy and capitalism.
>
> (Sánchez)

Women had always played a marginal role in the narcocorrido; however, as Juan Carlos Ramírez-Pimienta pointed out, the music from the north always represented the woman as strong in comparison to those from the centre and south. But Sanchez describes it as 'música naca' and first reprimands the group Los Tigres del Norte for their enormous profits when they are actually the 'voice of the people'. Then she launches a critique against Jenni Rivera. According to Sánchez, she sings the narcocorrido for money, and uses her sexuality for business motives.

> 'La Chacalosa,' for example, has inherited her career from her father and she immediately takes on masculine characteristics. In an interview Rivera said that she writes corridos because she's trying to make a living. While corridos were once a means to transmit history, now they have become a means to make money. (..)I think that we need a thorough understanding of the source of the narcocorrido rather than simply blaming the genre for propagating violence. The tension between defiance and contribution to capitalism will remain until either the narcocorridistas decide to radically change their content or until there is no need to traffic drugs. It's obvious that both are unlikely to happen anytime soon.
>
> (Sánchez)

The 'masculine characteristics' inherent to their art might advance machismo and patriarchy, but these affirmations are relevant for many artists/singers and many genres of music. The narcocorrido is an easy target because it is still not a reference point for those who the industry has consecrated. Sánchez also repudiates the male narcocorridistas who aspire to be the voice of the people, because according to her, they have accumulated too much wealth. Herein lies a contradiction: if millions listen to this music and the money earned by the Tigres del Norte evidence this, how can this group not be representative of the people?[13] Sanchez disdains the narcocorrido. Her analysis of Rivera's music is premised on a division of labour based on genre and social class, a distribution of roles according to these parameters. So according to this reasoning, if there are women like La Chacalosa who compete with men in capitalism, they play dirty and don't deserve accolades because with their masculine characteristics they glamorize patriarchy, but this point of view forgets the obvious: that all big business is capitalist and aggressive.

Some years ago, Susan Faludi warned against a critique apparently based on equality of opportunity for all social classes and genres but which disapproves the entry of women in the work force. The attacks against the free circulation of women in the work force were based on a disinterested preoccupation with the common good but in reality, they came from elitist and conservative sections. Faludi describes the reaction of those who demean the success and work of women.

> Although the backlash is not an organized movement, that doesn't make it any less destructive. (...) In the last decade the backlash has moved through the culture's secret chambers, travelling through passageways of flattery and fear. Along the way, it has adopted disguises: a mask of mild derision or the painted face of deep 'concern'. Its lips profess pity for any woman who won't fit the mould...
>
> (Faludi 16)

Though Sanchez' criticism laments the excessive capitalism and patriarchy that Rivera is supposed to represent, her criticism is tendentious. She considers this music as inferior and she agrees with the conservative viewpoint of the readers of the *Huffington Post*. Commenting on the song 'La Chacalosa', Sánchez says:

> The protagonist of this song is perpetuating the notion that woman can only attain power through masculinity and exploitation. This is evident when 'La Chacalosa' boasts about her gun adorned with gold. The gun is a symbol of both masculinity and capital. The fact that men can't tolerate/tame her is likely because they are intimidated by her masculine traits and her success. She has been able to

> attain farms and laboratories and we see that she's ruthless in her dealings because of the 'scraps' she leaves her enemies. Like other narcocorridos, this song isn't the voice of the poor. The woman in this corrido is incredibly wealthy and doesn't at all represent the average disenfranchised Mexican woman. (…)
>
> (Sánchez)

'La Chacalosa' is the daughter of a drug trafficker and unashamed to be one. She works hard and knows the business well. The masculine characteristics of the song must be these:

> Soy hija de un traficante, (I am the daughter of a trafficker)
> Conozco bien las movidas, (I know the moves well)
> Me crié entre la mafia grande (I grew up amongst the mafia)
> De la mejor mercancía (May father showed me how)
> Me enseñó a vender mi padre.(…) (to sell the best product)
> Los amigos de mi padre (My father's friends)
> Me enseñaron a tirar. (Taught me how to shoot)
> Me querían bien preparada (They wanted me to be well prepared)
> Soy primera al disparar. (I am the first to shoot)

In any other business – these characteristics denoting energy and motivation would be positive. But though Sánchez might rile against Rivera and yet bemoan the degeneration of the contemporary narcocorrido because it is a tool in the hands of capitalists, she is on weak and erroneous ground. The image of the narcotrafficker is entwined with money as are narcocorridos with the market. Though this song has violence, Rivera's other music covers a wide variety of themes and situations: sentimentality, the home, love.

Jenni Rivera often refers to her family, her own and that of other Latinos joined by affective bonds. We might be surprised at the contradiction between the sentimentality in her songs dedicated to her family and the violence associated with narcotrafficking that destroys communities and countries. A song like 'La Maestra del Contrabando' (The maestra of contraband) is significant in this context. This theme describes the life and character of a woman trafficker.

> Ya descubrieron que soy una dama traficante (They have found out that I am a woman trafficker)
> que entró al negocio prohibido para salir
> adelante y todo porque sus hijos se estaban
> muriendo de hambre. (…) (who entered the business to get ahead because her children were dying of hunger)

> Cuando andas en malos pasos, la sociedad te desprecia
> (when you are in an unfortunate period, society despises you)

Critics often describe the work of narcocorridistas/narco novelists as filled with a stark realism where the author has abdicated from his/her responsibility of invention and sublimation because reality should be invented not portrayed. In *Violence Without Guilt*, Hermann Herlinghaus assesses the spirit of the narcocorridos and ponders the role of women in these songs who apparently eulogize violence and revenge, 'the masculine characteristics' that Sánchez mentions. For them, according to Herlinghaus, the home is not anymore an arena where universal norms hold sway instead class differences determine the kind of rules that are relevant at home.

> The tendency of either exhaustion or marginalization of formerly secure sectors carries a disturbing effect, for it threatens to hollow out the features on which a late liberalist image of the cosmopolitan citizen has been built. On the other hand, the onslaught of neoliberalism has provoked a recent reevaluation of the practices of primitive or original accumulation. (..) The assumption that predation, fraud, and violence belonged to an early phase of capitalism that is no longer relevant has proven false.
>
> (Herlinghaus 9)

In a neoliberal world of exclusions, survival means ferocious resistance to save the home. In these circumstances, it is the mother who takes the lead to protect her own at any cost. Mothers like Jenni Rivera, with apparent power, are 'the profane actors in sacred territories', exceptional figures who have acquired power in neoliberal times, when scarcity and need have propelled them to play roles that are far from being that of soft passive spirits unable to change their circumstances. They now assume proactive roles that can become violent if need be. The description given by Herlinghaus of a mother in the Colombian novel *No nacimos para semilla* is relevant for our analysis of Jenni Rivera's place in the neoliberal world.

> Regarding the phenomenon of matriarchs, we must repeat that the mothers of sicarios do not primarily consecrate their sons to killing but to vigorously and aggressively defending life at its limit. These women can be considered the secret administrators of the threshold. Above all, and regarding the roving criminality, they relieve their sons of the burden of guilt. Who other than mothers could perform such a gigantic deed? Who other than mothers could provide the unconditional affective support that can turn labour into (power over) life itself? And who other than mothers could generate the immanent forces of 'legitimacy' in favor of those living on the

> abandoned side of the social edifice and the legal apparatus? Herein lies one explanation for the fact that the word crime does not exist in the language of Medellin's hit boys. They think of themselves not as evildoers, but as outcasts in a universe in which the distribution of money, order, and rule are wrong anyway.
>
> (Herlinghaus 121)

Rivera's songs validate these assertions. In '*También las mujeres pueden*' ('Women also can'), two women from Sinaloa assassinate three Colombian women after an argument over false bank notes This kind of violence gives us an insight into society in the north of Mexico that has been devastated by narcotrafficking caused, in turn, by the prohibition of the product. In the song '*Los Traficantes*' (The Traffickers) one of the heroin transporters is Yolanda, who together with her three companions dies while trying to cross the Río Bravo on the way to Texas. The sympathy in these songs is undoubtedly for the desperate border crossers and the women are portrayed as ravaged individuals who do not shy away from taking risks like the men. The contextualization of Jenni Rivera's songs yields a richer meaning surely than that attributed to them by Erika Sánchez.

The Legacy

Jenni Rivera had a chequered life and career. Her success lay in her championing of woman as she herself affirmed. In 2010, she was named the spokesperson of the prestigious organization National Coalition Against Domestic Violence. Her candid attitude when talking about her own experiences, her efforts in creating the Jenni Rivera Love Foundation for the victims of abuse demonstrate her commitment to the above theme. In her activism as well as in her musical career she was not hypocritical. Neither was she politically an ingenue, she was committed to her Mexican American people. She marched in Arizona to protest against the anti-immigrant laws and made public appearances denouncing discriminatory laws. Urging on her fans to vote, she said in a conference,

> It is very important to have political influence. (…) Our vote, our yes or no is important (..) We are important, we are more important than we think, not just in politics, but in television, in everything. There are many of us. We are the largest minority in the country.
>
> (Cobo 116)

Despite the negative criticism about the narcocorrido, its internationalization by Jenni Rivera and others gave results. Her life and work inspired many desolate and abandoned Hispanic women. Although she called herself a diva, her *habitus* was always accessible and devoid of super star airs associated with a Michael Jackson or a Britney Spears. For these reasons, Hispanics felt represented and included in her extended family. Jenni's corridos have evolved since the days of 'La Chacalosa'. Towards the end of her life, she sang less about violence and more about daily events in the lives of Latinos and above all the Latinas in the United States. Hopefully, the new policy of the legalization of marijuana in some U.S. states will also influence the evolution of the narcocorrido genre.

Notes

1 Their origins have been traced to the Aztecs as well as to the conquistadors but they have, of course, become more popular since the Mexican Revolution. The dismantling of the social fabric of Mexico from the 1960s and the dashing of hopes in the Mexican economic miracle made these songs that praised outlaws who refused to participate in the system more popular. At the same time, the massive diaspora of Mexicans to the United States at the end of the 20th century provided an audience for narcocorridistas. See Juan Carlos Ramírez-Pimienta *Cantar a los narcos* (18) and 'Narcocultura temprana: El consumo de drogas en la corridística de la primera mitad del siglo XX' (201–216).

2 See Arias Montoya L.O. 'El narcocorrido, Culiacán a través de su historia' (46–66).

3 Explaining the popularity of the Tigres del Norte band, Juan Carlos Ramírez-Pimienta observes: 'This public, that had been forced to move to a foreign land often illegally, would view other transgressors with less severity especially if the songs they sang emphasized poverty as a factor that had made them migrate'.

> (Este público, obligado a desplazarse por necesidad a un país extranjero y muchas veces en calidad de ilegal, va a ser más proclive a mirar con menos severidad a otros transgresores sobre todo si las canciones que les rinden homenaje a éstos frecuentemente enfatizan la pobreza como un factor que los empujó a delinquir.)
>
> (Ramírez-Pimienta 18)

4

> …death seems to *complete* the persona, such that death is not the ending, but the 'launching' of an individual into a timeless existence as an iteration of the persona whose life will float in the popular imaginary: reputation cemented and memorialized forever, free from the barriers that prevented attainment of full status in this world.
>
> (Edberg 117)

5 'Jenni was heading toward something big and people wanted more', says Gonzalez, whom Rivera often called for advice. 'We realized that no (Latin) celebrity in recent times, not even a politician, has received that kind of coverage.' Victor Gonzalez quoted in Justino Águila, 'The Second Life of Jenni Rivera' in *Billboard*. 12 October 2013: 22.

6 Banda is a style of music played with wind instruments typically brass and percussion. Rancheras are rural folk songs.

7 (Wald 141).

8

> Here in the United States, we are the neediest people, we are the most – how should I say it? – not to put us down or anything, but we are the people who have the most problems in our country. If we are here, it's because we needed to leave our own country, because we couldn't support ourselves, or some people are here because they killed so and so, other people because they robbed..
>
> (Wald 137)

9 Juan Carlos Ramírez-Pimienta also makes a similar classification of the women in narcocorridos from the north of Mexico where he writes on the portrayal of stronger women (327).

10 Qtd. in Wald (145).

11 PRI (Partido Revolucionario Institucional) is centrist and had been in power in Mexico from 1929 to 2000. It was succeeded by the PAN (Partido de Accion Nacional), a centre right wing conservative Catholic party that has a stronghold in the northern Mexican states. The PRD (Partido Revolucionario Democrático) is a centre left party with a strong base in Mexico City and presently rules Mexico.

12 At times rival bands like Los Tucanes de Tijuana in 2002 allied with the authorities in banning songs by the Tigres del Norte because they came out against the policies of Felipe Calderón. Although solitary voices were raised questioning the viability of banning freedom of expression, the mainstream media marked a distance from this kind of music.

13 Narcocorridos could not exert the popular pull that they do unless they touched on sentiments that are widespread, and touched these sentiments via a cultural form that is marked for such sentiments. It is here that, in my view, the narcocorridos do draw from, and intermingle with, commonly shared understandings about oppositions of social position: Mexicans versus Anglos, Mexico versus the United States, Mexicans of a rural or poor background versus Mexicans of elite background, and, in general, northern/border Mexican peoples versus the central Mexican government and those who represent them (police, government officials, etc.). (Edberg 127).

References

Águila, Justino. "The Second Life of Jenni Rivera" in *Billboard*. 12 October 2013. 20–23.

Asmann, Parker. "Mexico's Narcocorridos: A Case of Misunderstanding" https://insightcrime.org/news/analysis/mexicos-narcocorridos-case-of-misunderstanding/. 24 April 2019. Accessed 30 August 2021.

Bourdieu, Pierre. *Outline of a Theory of Practice*. Cambridge: Cambridge University Press, 1977.

Cameron Edberg, Mark. *El Narcotraficante Narcocorridos and the Construction of a Cultural Persona on the U.S. – Mexico Border*. Austin, TX: University of Texas Press, 2004.

Cobo, Leila, *Jenni Rivera, La increíble vida de una mariposa guerrera*. New York, NY: C.A Press, Penguin, 2013.

Faludi, Susan. *Backlash, The Undeclared War against Women.* London: Chatto & Windus, 1992.

Herlinghaus, Hermann. *Violence without Guilt, Ethical Narratives from the Global South.* New York, NY: Palgrave Macmillan, 2008.

Herrera-Sobek, María. *The Mexican Corrido, A Feminist Analysis.* Bloomington, IN: Indiana University Press, 1990.

Montoya Arias, L.O. El narcocorrido, Culiacán a través de su historia. ARENAS *Revista Sinaloense de Ciencias Sociales*, (17), Sinaloa: Universidad Autónoma de Sinaloa (2008).

Paz, Octavio. *El laberinto de la soledad.* México: Cuadernos Americanos, 1950.

Ramírez-Pimienta, Juan Carlos. *Cantar a los narcos, Voces y versos del narcocorrido.* México: Planeta, 2011.

Ramírez-Pimienta, Juan Carlos. "*Chicago lindo y querido si muero lejos de ti*: el pasito duranguense, la onda grupera y las nuevas geografías de la identidad popular mexicana". *Mexican Studies/Estudios Mexicanos*, Vol. 26, Issue 1 (Winter 2010): 31–45.

Ramírez-Pimienta, Juan Carlos. "El consumo de drogas en la corridística de la primera mitad del siglo XX". *Studies in Latin American Popular Culture*, Vol. 37, (2019): 201–216.

Ramírez-Pimienta, Juan Carlos. "Sicarias, buchonas y jefas: perfiles de la mujer en el narcocorrido". *The Colorado Review of Hispanic Studies*, Vol. 8–9, (Fall 2010–2011): 327–352.

Raygoza, Isabela. "Years after Her Death, Jenni Rivera Is Still a Hard Act to Follow" in *Rolling Stone.* August 6, 2019. www.rollingstone.com/music/music-latin/jenni-rivera-aparentemente-bien-video-858087/. Accessed 30 August 2021.

Rivera, Jenni. "Aparentemente Bien". (Versión Banda: Vídeo Oficial) www.youtube.com/watch?v=tq9mgTRQM8k 2020. Accessed 30 August 2021.

Rivera, Jenni. "Chicana Jalisciense" in *Se las voy a dar a otro.* Woodland Hills, CA: Fonovisa Records, 2001. Compact Disk.

Rivera, Jenni. *Inquebrantable Mi historia a mi manera.* New York, NY: Atria, 2013.

Rivera, Jenni. "La Chacalosa" in *Jenni Rivera y sus mejores 17 éxitos.* Long Beach, CA: Cintas Acuario, 1995. Compact Disk.

Rivera, Jenni. "La maestra del contrabando" in *Reina de reinas.* Long Beach, CA: Cintas Acuario, 1999. Compact Disk.

Rivera, Jenni. "Las Malandrinas" in *Que me entierren con la banda.* Woodland Hills, CA: Fonovisa Records, 2000. Compact Disk.

Rivera, Jenni. "Los Traficantes" in *Dinastía Rivera.* Vol. 3. Miami, FL: Sony Discos, 2001.

Rivera, Jenni. "Mariposa del barrio" in *Mi vida loca.* Woodland Hills, CA: Fonovisa Records, 2007. Compact Disk.

Rivera, Jenni. "Novia del plebe" in *La Diva de la Banda, éxitos con bando norteño y mariachi.* Long Beach, CA: Cintas Acuario, 1995. Compact Disk.

Rivera, Jenni. "Sinaloa princesa norteña" in *Que me entierren con la banda.* Woodland Hills, CA: Fonovisa Records, 2000.

Rivera, Jenni. "También las mujeres pueden" in *20 exitazos con la Dinastía Rivera.* Miami, FL: Sony International, 2001.

Rivera, Jenni. Rivera, Lupillo. "Sangre de indio" in *Mi vida loca*. Woodland Hills, CA: Fonovisa Records, 2007.

Sanchez, E.L. "What Has Happened to the Mexican Corrido?" in *Huffington Post*. 31 May 2012.

Valencia, Sayak. "Género(s) y narcocultura" in *Camelia la texanay otras mujeres de la narcocultura* eds. Juan Carlos Ramírez-Pimienta, María Socorro Tabuenca Córdoba, Culiacán, Sinaloa, 2016.

Wald, Elijah. *Narcocorrido: A Journey into the Music of Drugs, Guns and Guerrillas*. New York, NY: Rayo, 2001.

Part VI

PERFORMANCE

Challenging Rationalities of Mass Killings

11

WHAT IS LOST AND REGAINED IN STAGING VIOLENT REALITIES

Thinking of *Dear Earth…Hope You Are Keeping Well!*

Kavita Panjabi, Debaroti Chakraborty, and Debasish Sen Sharma

This chapter is written in two parts – the first part by Kavita Panjabi and the second part by Debaroti Chakraborty and Debasish Sen Sharma. The first part offers a cross-cultural reading of Rabindranath Tagore's short story Kabuliwalah, Zaheda Hina's fictitious letter 'Kumkum Theek Theek Hain' within a comparative framework to question deeply embedded borders of narrow nationalisms in South Asia, of cultural xenophobia, of religious fundamentalism through an understanding of shared history and cultural traditions of the subcontinent. The second part examines the aesthetic choices and challenges of making a performance based on these narratives to forge an emotional and affective bonding in the face of contemporary narratives of political and cultural violence.

Part I

Kavita Panjabi

In the last decade of the 20th century, thousands of Afghan refugees fled to India to escape the war and persecution by the Taliban in Afghanistan. The story that forms the basis of the performance we discuss here, however, starts much earlier, in the theatre of international trade routes in the 19th century when the Kabuliwalas – the men of Kabul – began coming to Calcutta to sell dry fruits and asafoetida, and often stayed on to become moneylenders too. The foreignness of the Kabuliwala in Calcutta was sealed securely for decades in the ominous stereotype of a ruthless Shylock demanding his interest, and even more pervasively, of a large, bearded alien who kidnapped children. These stereotypes were often evoked to frighten children too, to

DOI: 10.4324/9780429356421-18

keep them away from these outsiders to the city. This was till 1892, when Rabindranath Tagore published 'Kabuliwala', a story, about the Afghan Rehmat befriending the five-year-old Bengali girl Mini who reminded him of his own daughter Amina left behind in Afghanistan. 'Kabuliwala' has probably become the most dearly loved narrative of Bengali literature not just in Bengal, but, translated as well as performed in several languages, right across the Indian subcontinent. It transformed the perception of the Kabuliwala in the Indian psyche from the menacing other into an exiled man pining for his faraway land, a father yearning for his daughter. Made into a film in Bangla by Tapan Sinha in 1957 with Chhabi Biswas playing the benign Afghan, and in Hindi in 1961 by Hemen Gupta, with Balraj Sahni becoming the poignant face of the Kabuliwala, the monster was fully humanized, the alien became beloved.

The event that became the founding moment of our play was the Pakistani writer and peace activist Zaheda Hina's reading of her story '*Kumkum Theek Theek Hai*' ('Kumkum Is Doing Fine'), an Urdu sequel to 'Kabuliwala', at the 2011 conference of the Indian Association of Women's Studies in Wardha, India. Born in Bihar the year before the Partition of 1947, Zaheda Hina moved from India to Pakistan as an infant when her father migrated to Karachi. Talking of the outsider's experience she says: "I know well what it is to be an outsider. I struggled to make my identity in the new land as circumstances had greatly changed for our family with the migration" (Dutt). Introducing the story at Wardha, she recounted that 'Kabuliwala' found place in her heart in early childhood when her grandmother used to read out Tagore's 'Kabuliwala' to her. After the Talibanization of Afghanistan, and the U.S. counter-attack on Afghanistan following the 9/11 tragedy, Tagore's story came back to haunt her and '*Kumkum Theek Theek Hai*' materialized out of that experience. She had chosen to read it to us, at the South Asia Panel of the Women's Studies conference in India, in a gesture of cross-border solidarity and as a tribute to Tagore. That the impact of 'Kabuliwala' had lasted well over a century, and that it had become even more relevant in her story in the cross-border cultural identification and political solidarities of South Asia, was evident in the passion with which Hina read her story, and in the profoundly emotional reception of it at Wardha too.

Hina says of 'Kumkum Theek Theek Hai' that:

> In this story, time has moved forward and Mini of Kabuliwala fame is a granny. Her granddaughter Kumkum, a doctor, volunteers to go to Afghanistan after the US attack on the country. There she forms a fond bond with an injured Afghan militant.
>
> (Dutt)

The story takes the form of a letter from Kumkum to her grandmother, and I quote at length from it to share what we came to experience as the humanizing power of a literary text across the political borders of India, Pakistan, and Afghanistan, across the linguistic barriers between Bangla and Urdu, and across more than a century:

> And then there was a real life story, from your own childhood, in this very life time about Rehmat, the hawker from Kabul. When you first saw him, you were frightened and thought that his bag was full of little children. Then you became friends, you would talk together, he would listen to you and fill your aanchal with almonds, raisins and walnuts. Once he told you that he had a huge elephant in his small bag. You told me that the day Rehmat Baba was released after eight years in prison, was the day of your marriage. He borrowed dry fruits from another hawker and gave it to you as your wedding gift. When you told me this story for the first time, your eyes were full of tears, and then I knew that even adults can cry like children. You told me that Rehmat Baba had also a daughter of your age who lived in Kabul. He didn't have the money to get her photographed or perhaps in those days, there were no photographers in Kabul, so he had a print of her hand on a piece of paper, and used to keep it in his pocket, near his heart, just like Papa used to keep my photo in his wallet. Your father, I mean my Great-grandfather, had given some money to Rehmat Baba so that he could go back to Kabul and see his daughter which made the Great-grandmother very angry. Rehmat Baba never came back after that.
>
> Nowadays when I receive wounded, bleeding patients, shouting with pain or breathing their last, I sometimes ask myself, had you not eaten those almonds and pistachios from Rehmat Baba's bag seventy years ago, had my Great-grandfather not written his story, would I still be here in Kabul, in Kandahar, in Herat, in Helmand? Perhaps not. Most certainly not. I still remember well those days of last October when American warplanes started bombing Kabul and we watched those scenes on TV, you got your rocking chair shifted to TV lounge and would sit glued to the TV all the time.... The whole world loves the story of Rehmat Kabuliwala written by Great-grandfather. [1]

Mini's granddaughter Kumkum grows up to become a doctor who chooses to take a posting in wartime Afghanistan and nurse the wounded there – and she attributes this move to the power of her grandmother and great-grandfather's stories of the Kabuliwala Rehmat. Mini's personal engagement and her friendship with the Kabuliwala had not just demolished the threatening stereotype of the Kabuliwala, but had actually become the basis for deep bonding; and the emotional power of this bonding had, in turn, catalysed Kumkum's need to reach out to the Kabuliwala's people in their times of trouble. It becomes evident from Hina's reception of 'Kabuliwala' that the humanizing force of Tagore's story rests in the affective power of intersubjective acts – of friendship and a profound language of gifting. After our first exhilarating cross-border peace visit to Pakistan, a friend had said thoughtfully: "When you engage with people in flesh and blood you cannot continue to think of them as the enemy any more".[2] Mini had become friends with the Kabuliwala on the basis of her understanding of his lived experience of exile and his longing for his daughter, and understood his deep affection for her when he borrowed dry fruits to gift to her on her wedding day; and Kumkum learnt to value such friendship as part of a cultural legacy handed down from grandmother to granddaughter.

This world of imagination, of stories and child's play, revels in human relationships that transcend 'othering' and religious borders too, and find validation in scientific evidence, in Kumkum's medical practice:

> You have told me that you had made the daughter of Rehmat Baba an unseen friend of yours. In your imagination, you would marry your boy doll with her girl doll. Since the boy doll was yours, the girl doll would leave Kabul and come to Calcutta. Great-grandfather wrote stories and you were his only darling daughter. So who could blame you if you decorated your lonely childhood with these stories. But when Great-grandmother heard it from you she was angry, how could a Hindu doll be married to a Muslim one! And the wedding ceremony, according to which rites would it be held, pherey rounds around the sacred fire to the chanting of mantras by a Hindu priest or Nikah sermon recited by a Muslim priest? When Great-grandfather heard all about it, he was not happy at all: 'At least don't turn a marriage of dolls into a conflict of religions!' He said that, frowning, and Great-grandmother left the room, grumbling. You were laughing when you narrated all that to me. 'My father's heart was very big, it could accommodate all: Ishwar, Allah, Hindus and Muslims.' You said fondly, remembering Great-grandfather. And when I performed the heart dissection for the first time in the medical college, at once I started looking for Allah, Ishwar, Hindus and Muslims, but there were only muscles, veins and arteries.

Cultural wisdom finds confirmation in scientific evidence. What is also significant then in these relationships between Mini and the Kabuliwala and Kumkum and a war-torn Afghan people is that they take shape not just across the borders of India, Pakistan, and Afghanistan, with the author Zaheda Hina posited in Pakistan between India and Afghanistan, they also take shape across religious barriers – Mini is a Hindu, and the Kabuliwala and his people Muslim.

The affective power of Tagore's story is such that it is capable of challenging the jingoism of politicized religious boundaries and militarized political borders, and that of Hina's story, in turn, is that it enables us to look beyond the demonization of Afghanistan as the land of the Taliban to the human beings – such as the grandchildren of the beloved Kabuliwala – and the processes by which some of them may have been Talibanized. Affective bonding, these stories tell us, have the power to mobilize alterative perceptions and new histories.

Kumkum sees the war-torn Afghanistan through her own personalized prism, lit by the memory of Rehmat Baba and the imprint of his daughter's hands that he carried close to his heart:

> Here, there are shadows of death on the walls of each house, and lines of blood in each street and bazaar. Rehmat Baba left ages ago, his daughter must have perished too. And who knows her children got killed by the Soviet gunfire or by American bombing, or perhaps they died of starvation. Here devastation stalks everywhere, each city of this country is in ruins. When I left home, you kissed my hands and told me 'Stitch all their wounds with these hands.' But Dadima, here I am, all exhausted, stitching the wounds but the wounded, they still keep on coming…
>
> Did I come across your childhood hero in the streets of Kabul! I didn't meet even his daughter, his granddaughters. And how could I have met them when they must have perished in the cellars of their homes. Probably his great-granddaughters don't even have palms for their fathers to carry their coloured prints. I have stitched the wounds of those girls who no more have hands, who would no more put henna on their palms on Eid, would never put bangles on their wrists.
>
> Now when I see here the wrists with no hands and stitch their wounds, I cry in secret. We had finally got the English out of our country, but from where have their kinsmen come and settled in our neighbourhood? And until when shall we keep on sacrificing our thumbs, palms, feet and heads at their altar?

Given its South Asian perspective, it is of course no surprise that Hina's story is as much a critique of Islamic fundamentalism as it is of U.S. imperialism. Kumkum does not mince words in her letter to her grandmother – she writes:

> Nowadays where I am living, is the war theatre of USA. Genghis Khan's army annihilated the population of Bamiyan and left. But today's Genghis do not leave. Like Dracula, they stick their teeth in the necks of nations and keep on sucking their blood. Their

> warplanes drop death with butter packets, and biscuits with land mines.

In this theatre of war Kumkum writes about the cycle of inhuman savagery:

> Then Dadima, I had a strange night. We had journeyed through Bamiyan and Shabarghan and were camping in Dasht-e-Leili where the whole flock of media people had come, in search of the news and pictures of the mass graves of those Taliban who were being brought from Mazar-i-Sharif to Shabarghan in cargo containers. When all of them died of suffocation, trenches were dug in Dasht-e-Leili and all of them were buried in them. Years ago when Taliban conquered this region, they massacred the people and, to hide them, buried them in mass graves. Now Time has turned full circle for Taliban and they are resting in the trenches of Dasht-e-Leili.

The savage irony is that 150–200 prisoners would be packed tight into such containers that were meant for 'aid'. On one hand, as Kumkum writes, the warplanes bringing butter and biscuits dropped death on the people; on the other, the cargo containers that brought 'aid' became, verily, the death chambers of the people. A detailed expose of the 2001 massacre, of those who were brought in cargo containers to Shabarghan, and the fact of time having turned 'full-circle' that Kumkum writes about above, was published by John Barry in the Newsweek in August 2002. He reports that:

> 'Death by container' has been a cheap means of mass murder used by both the Taliban and the Northern Alliance for at least five years. Abandoned freight containers – international standard size, 40 feet by 8 feet by 8 feet – litter the roads of Afghanistan, rusting reminders of the many tons of aid that have poured into the country over the past 20 years. It was reputedly a savage Uzbek general named Malik Pahlawan who first saw the container's potential as a killing machine in 1997. After a Taliban assault on Mazar-e Sharif had been repulsed, Pahlawan – according to a subsequent U.N. report – killed some 1,250 Taliban by leaving them in containers in the desert sun. When the containers were opened, it was found the inmates had been grilled black. When the Taliban took Mazar-e Sharif in 1998, they in turn killed several hundred enemies in the same fashion.

Irish filmmaker and former BBC producer Jamie Doran's documentary *Afghan Massacre: The Convoy of Death*, according to the website on which the film is available, 'tells the story of thousands of prisoners who surrendered to the US military's Afghan allies after the siege of Kunduz' in late

November 2001. Doran reports that mass graves of thousands of victims were found by United Nations investigators.

> According to the film, some three thousand of the prisoners were forced into sealed containers and loaded onto trucks for transport to Sheberghan prison. When the prisoners began shouting for air, U.S.-allied Afghan soldiers fired directly into the truck, killing many of them. The rest suffered through an appalling road trip lasting up to four days, so thirsty they clawed at the skin of their fellow prisoners as they licked perspiration and even drank blood from open wounds.

Kumkum writes about an encounter with a young Taliban boy in the middle of a night in the little bombed out hamlet of Dasht-e-Leili – and of her conflict between the impulse to report him or heal him.

> All of a sudden some sound woke me up. It was dark in the tent. It seemed as if an animal is scratching the tent with its nails. Without thinking, I came out bewildered. The greenish yellow moon of January on the dark sky, the sands of Dasht-e-Leili on all sides, mass graves at some distance, and before my eyes a young boy, reclining by my tent. Fresh, dry stains of blood on his shirt, fear and terror in his eyes, his whole body trembling. He was shot at by some American bullet, and falling and faltering, hiding and stopping, had crept up to our camp. I couldn't guess how long ago he was wounded. When I thought that maybe he was still armed, my nerves got strung. My first thought was of calling a camp guard. Then Dadima, something unexpected happened, it still gives me goose-pimples when I write about it. In a flash, the boy's face transformed, he took something out of the sack lying near his feet and extended it towards me. I looked at his hand, it was full of almonds, raisins and walnuts. He was calling you. Nervously, I looked at him. I swear by God, that was Rehmat Baba in the light of January moon, and his shirt was stained with blood. Great-grandfather had written that every January, he used to go back to his home, beyond the Hindukush Mountains. Tears came to my eyes. How could I get him arrested! He was your childhood, my Great-grandfather's story. I brought him to my tent. Dadima, that night, I witnessed death with my own eyes, touched it with my own hands. That night I learnt that whether the bullet hits the ribcage of a friend or of an enemy, I am destined to take it out. That night, when I was stitching his wounds, neither could I say anything to him nor could I listen to his story. Dadima, we didn't know each other's language. Then I was constantly thinking of you and of the stories of those heroes

> of our past which you used to narrate to me: Tipu, Sirajuddowlah, Babu Kanwar Singh, Lakhshmi Bai, Hazrat Mahal.

The motifs of demonized Muslim versus medical evidence intensify in Hina's story, for Kumkum's engagement with the young Afghan boy is situated at the radical intersection of an encounter between an Indian woman of Hindu origin and a Taliban footsoldier of Islamic fundamentalism and, equally, at the juncture of medical ethics between a doctor and a wounded patient. In the conflictual stalemate between the rational forces of these two locations, it is the humanizing power of affect, of the haunting memory of Rehmat Baba's love, that becomes a mobilizing force, cutting through fear and dominant political narratives to lead to another human engagement, and, eventually, to a political stand that is as rational as it is radical:

> That night, when dawn was about to break, I gave him some medicines and food packets in a bag and a blanket, and then signaled him to leave. He kept on looking at me, then stood up faltering. As he was putting the bag and the blanket on his shoulder, I thought of something, I took some money from my purse lying on the bed, he shook his head refusing, his eyes were full of tears. Then Dadima, I put the money in his hand and closed his fist around it. He took the same hand to his forehead and saluted me, threw his bag and blanket on his shoulder and went out of the tent. I kept on staring at his receding form. A lone soul, enveloped in fog and moon dust. After a few steps, he stopped and turned and looked towards me. Those were the eyes of a defeated tribe. Then those eyes turned away from me and headed towards the blind caves of isolation and history, towards the dark forests of Tarai and unnamed graves of Dasht-e-Leili. In that moment, time rushed past me, my age fast forwarded. And now I am a thousand years old, perhaps two thousand years. You are lucky Dadima, that you have only read the story of the defeated of the History, and not seen the miasma of isolation in their eyes.

The young footsoldier of Hina's story is, we realize by the end of the narrative, as much a victim of the Taliban as he is of the U.S.-led forces ravaging his land – and the desolation in his eyes is of a helpless animal fatally trapped between a savage present and a blank future. It was this story that we initially set out to script and perform, introducing another cross-border perspective from the U.S. military outpost of Guantánamo Bay, in the form of poems written there by political prisoners, some of whom would have been Afghan prisoners too. Our play was thus posited between and beyond the fundamentalist politics of South Asia and the political power of the United States reaching out across the Islamic world, with a critical base in the Latin American island of Cuba. The aim was to recreate in performance the power of human engagement that is capable of challenging the imperatives of both Islamic fundamentalism and U.S. imperialism, and to confront the desolation of the future, of defeated youth as victim of both. At one point in her letter Kumkum writes to her grandmother: 'Perhaps I have taken after you and Great-grandfather, that's why I dream with open eyes'. The idea for us too was to learn to dream with open eyes, to dare to envision other worlds with feet planted firmly in reality, in full knowledge of the realpolitik destroying this world.

Then, on 16 December 2014, the very day we had finalized the outlines of our script, the unthinkable happened. The Taliban launched its deadliest attack ever, killing 132 Pakistani schoolchildren, at the Army Public School in Peshawar, Khyber Pakhtunkhwa. How could any vision hold in the face of this latest wave of deep hatred, how could the affective power of our play even have a chance, far less succeed?

References

Afghan Massacre: The Convoy of Death documentary by Jamie Doran. https://topdocumentaryfilms.com/afghan-massacre/ accessed on 23 March 2017.

Barry, John. 2002. "The Death Convoy of Afghanistan." *Newsweek*, 8/25/02 www.newsweek.com/death-convoy-afghanistan-144273 accessed on 23 March 2017.

Dutt, Nirupama. 2008. "Women Writers for Peace" in *Half the Sky*. http://nirupamad.blogspot.in/2008/10/ accessed on 23 March 2017.

Hina, Zaheda. 2008. "Kumkum Theek Theek Hai." Translated by Yousuf Shahid as "Kumkum Is Doing Fine." http://aud.ac.in/upload/Kumkum%20is%20doing%20fine.pdf accessed on 23 March 2017.

Tagore, Rabindranath. 1892. "Kabuliwala." Translated by Mohammad A. Quayum. *Transnational Literature* Volume 1 No 2 May 2009.

Further Reading

Nasir, Jibran FB Video/Press Release 19 December 2014. www.facebook.com/video.php?v=1599682126922353&set=vb.1534354373455129&type=2&theater

Notezai, Muhammad Akbar, 2015. "Remembering the Peshawar Attack", The Diplomat, December 15, 2015. Accessed on https://thediplomat.com/2015/12/remembering-the-peshawar-attack/ on 22.10.17.

Part II

Debaroti Chakraborty and Debasish Sen Sharma

As performance makers, we wanted to communicate the philosophical and political scope of the alternative worldview of humanism as embedded in Tagore's story 'Kabuliwala' and in Zaheda Hina's fictitious letter 'Kumkum

Theek Theek Hain'. So we had decided to explore a theatrical language that is based on an auto-ethnographical lens to weave together the voices of Mini, Kumkum, our grandmothers, and other women from whom we have inherited telling and re-telling of stories of displacement, violence, and empathy. Our attempt was to amplify the rationale of an alternative world-view using the medium of theatre, focusing on organic storytelling, cultural connections, intuition, and collaboration. We hoped that our presentation *Dear Earth…Hope You are Keeping Well!* would set up a space for an immersive engagement in narratives of compassion and emotional bonding, which may otherwise be lost in a critical academic pursuit.

On 16 December 2014, when we met for the first workshop, we received the shocking news about the Taliban's brutal attack on schoolchildren in Peshawar, Pakistan. As artists, we struggled to pull ourselves out of this shock and find motivation to stage our performance based on a literary text that also empathizes with a young Taliban boy who has been a victim of political and religious fundamentalism. The political climate became so sensitive and vulnerable that we did not know how to communicate a story that would help look beyond the waves of palpable shock and devastation and critique the deep-seated structures of fundamentalism. At this juncture, we came across an evocative official video release (a 'special message' as it was called), circulated on social media, from protestors who stood in front of Lal Masjid representing citizens of Peshawar. They reclaimed the mosque, their religion, their community as spaces that are integral to the living traditions and identities of people who belong to the country. They demanded that the mosque should represent their voices, stories of their grief and loss rather than be appropriated to propagate the fundamentalist ideology of the Taliban. While the protestors, very firmly, condemned the brutality of the Taliban forces and spoke about the grief of many who had lost their children, they asserted that they do not want any counter-violence or bloodshed. Amidst this incident of unbearable shock, the innate sense of compassion in the message of the protestors inspired us to find home in narratives that speak of forging human connections in a world that is torn by forces of hatred. Their message critiqued Islamic fundamentalism from within the state and upheld humanism and solidarity in the face of state-sponsored religious fundamentalism as well as extremism. It brought home the necessity of seeing a child, whether he/she be a suicide bomber or a victim of suicide bombing as vulnerable and in need of empathy within a true 'civil' society. This response brought to surface the necessity of finding alternative means of revisiting education policies, statist and extremist discourses so that fundamentalist ideologies may be attacked at the core. It inspired us as a group of theatre makers to use this performance piece as creative means to launch a critique of fundamentalism and to register solidarity with nonviolent protest movements against political atrocity across borders. However, we were cautious to not get wrapped up in visions of idealism, but wanted to foreground a rational political perspective that can confront strategic discourses of fundamentalism.

In our workshops that followed, we immersed ourselves in reading different texts from across cultures and historical time that resist violent statist discourses with a universal philosophy of humanism steeped in an idiom of love and solidarity. Some poems of resistance penned by prisoners detained in Guantánamo Bay provided us with a crucial window for understanding the situations of oppression created by the U.S. imperialist forces. Guantánamo is caught up in a perennial geopolitical quagmire such that hills surrounding the bay make it a natural enclave; United States used it primarily as a coaling stop, and more recently, as a military base. United States retained 'perpetual lease' by treaty after independence in 1903 by means of which United States retains 'complete jurisdiction and control' and Cuba retains ultimate sovereignty (Cuba disputes treaty). 'Jurisdiction' versus 'sovereignty' creates legal loophole allowing United States to use it as 'black site' prison post 9/11. Marc Falkoff and a few volunteer lawyers visited the prisons in 2004 after receiving secret level security clearances from FBI.[3] It was revealed that the prisoners, mostly Muslim and Afghan militants, have been thrown into gruelling experiences, severe isolation and detention without charge or trial. They are subjected to mental stress, sleep deprivation, extremes of heat and cold and other forms of harrowing sexual abuse. The prisoners wrote poems to surface their voices of resistance against the unfathomable tyranny that they are subjected to in Guantánamo Bay. These voices drove home a critique of U.S. imperialism as much as of Islamic fundamentalism bringing to light, a despair around how global politics of hatred is gaining consensus using different forms of cultural tokens.

We embraced these cultural resources to touch upon the politics that lie at the core of this philosophy and to find inspiration for ways to creatively express the affective power of these texts which can catalyse human engagement and yet not communicate any sort of support for or validation towards the dominant political narratives. Tagore celebrated the 'higher moral power' in the face of narrow fundamentalism.[4] In 1916, Tagore rang a prophetic alarm in his critique of a particular brand of nationalism that sought to follow the western principle of governmentality that was hinged upon territorial power. He signalled a conflagration of violence in the ways the borders were manipulated by the structures of uneven economy while they obstructed human traffic. Tagore foregrounded the domain of Indian spiritual thought, human love, and inclusion as an organic basis of unity in situations when different cultural resources and origins coagulate. ('Rabindranath Tagore – Essays – Nationalism – Nationalism in India ()') Tagore has always dealt with the nuanced idea of waiting for the inside to meet the outside, for the inner self to embrace the other, the passage between the 'home' and the 'world'. His fictional works are connected by the same philosophy of universal humanism in the depiction of how the inner worlds of Amal in *Dakghaar*, Bimala in *Ghare Baire*, or Raja in *Raktakarabi* strives to expand. In our dramatization that we had titled *Dear Earth…Hope You are Keeping Well!*, we used window frames as a theatrical tool which evolves as a metaphor that indicates how each character is confined within borders – geopolitical, social, and internal, yet trying to reach out to the outer world – be it the world of Kabuliwala, the world of Mini's childhood or Kumkum in her inherited world of idealism. This theatrical language also speaks of how each character relates with the world through her own prism shaped by lived experiences, memory, and imagination. In our dramatization of this letter, little Mini, older Mini/*Dadima* and Kumkum converse across all these barriers in space and time.

Zaheda Hina's fictitious letter 'Kumkum Theek Theek Hain' builds on the premise of conversations, intergenerational memory, and dreams shared between 80-year-old Mini and her granddaughter Kumkum. The stage space is zonally designed with a spot created for Kumkum in audience left down stage (geographically located in Kabul but also in a shared space of idealism with her grandmother) while *Dadima*, Mini, read the letters from the audience right down stage corner. The light falls on them simultaneously to designate the 'here and now'-ness of their emotional bonding as well as the distinctly different geographical and temporal spaces that they were situated in. The play begins with the following conversation that articulated the opening of Zaheda Hina's letter:

> **Kumkum(writing):** My darling Dadima, today when after weeks I came back to Kabul, the post was waiting for me. Besides yours, I have received other letters from home: Mom's, Brother's, Uma Didi's and Sushmita's. But sweetest letter is yours
>
> **Dadima(reading):** In which you threaten me with making me stand in a corner with my nose to the wall, and boxing my ears as a punishment for not writing home for such a long time
>
> **Kumkum(writing):** All this scolding of yours makes me feel as if I have again become a little girl, sitting in your lap, swaying to and fro with you in your rocking chair. You are telling me stories…
>
> **Dadima(reading):** The big white porcelain bowl on the nearby teapoy has the same blue border as your white sari of 'aab-i-rawan'.
>
> **Kumkum(writing):** You pick a walnut or a raisin or an almond from the bowl. I set my teeth onto your fingers. You glare at me and then start telling me stories, from your own childhood, about Rehmat, the hawker from Kabul.

At this very juncture of the play, we reveal a third space on the stage – the space of Mini's memory – her childhood. Zaheda Hina's letter delves into this space of intergenerational memory that translates into a specific spatial design on stage. We, theatrically, recreated child Mini's interaction with her father, based on Tagore's story 'Kabuliwala'. The sequence ends with Mini calling her friend 'Kabuliwala' from her window. Immediately the zonal lights fade out and we are introduced to a fourth space on stage – the digital screen. We see a clip from the film 'Kabuliwala' based on the original story by Tagore, where we see a moment of joyous interaction between Mini and Kabuliwala, sharing stories. So we come to terms with a kind of simultaneity, marked by parallels and conflicts, between the spaces of old Mini, of young Kumkum (both these spaces *are happening* here and now), and the memory – space of Mini's childhood as depicted in Tagore's text and that of Rehmat (on digital screen). In keeping with the Brechtian theory of estrangement, we sought to re-create the relationship between the actor and audience as a dialectical one. By using this theatrical devise, we intended to disrupt the linear narrative pattern of causal relationships and of our sense of space and time and to introduce the responses of our emotional faculty and compassionate bonding. The performance script engages with fragmented reality as an aesthetic principle wherein memory, space, objects, non-linear events become essential narrative tools. We enact frequent alterations between the voices of the characters and that of the actors/co-creators of the play, such that the creators are present in the performance to evoke interaction with the audience. The performance on stage is intercepted by clippings of protest messages and resistant movements which, on one hand, assigns the performance with the nature of documentary-theatre and on the other hand aligns our play with ideologies, political movements, and creative responses that resist fundamentalism at large, across borders.

One of the scenes in our play was constructed to situate the two selves of Mini – old Mini and young Mini on the day of their marriage – theatrically located in the centre stage. This imaginary interaction does not exist in the literary texts but was created to forge an affective connection. Both the characters hold a window frame through which they try to reach out to each other but fail to do so. It hints towards a rupture, a disillusionment that stands like an iron wall between the two selves of Mini. The world of idealism that belonged to the child has been punctured by a sense of despair that wraps up old Mini. Little Mini, while listening to the stories of Rehmat had built a world of fantasy within her mind. She has told stories to her granddaughter Kumkum, about this world of Rehmat which in many ways have transpired into Kumkum's worldview. In a monologue from the play script Mini says:

> Kumkum will go to the land of my dreams… the land of my kabuliwalah… the land of tall, rugged mountains on two sides, red-hot with torrid heat, magnanimous caravans bobbing up and down through the narrow, dusty passage way in-between, turbaned

> traders and travelers passing by, some on camel back, others on foot; a land where the night keeps awake to the tinkling of gypsy dance and the thumping of drums…all joining processions of a carnival…it was a land of magic, a land of dreams.

The tales of this dreamland as well as her awareness about contemporary global politics have driven Kumkum to move to Kabul as a voluntary doctor. But the plight, the deprivation of today's devastated Afghanistan shatters her fantasy and leaves her in deep pain as she writes to her grandmother, her only confidante. Agonized, Kumkum utters:

> Dadima, had you seen this city even once in a dream once, you would never have let me come here. Here, there are shadows of death on the walls of each house, and lines of blood in each street and bazaar. Rehmat Baba left ages ago, his daughter must have perished too. And who knows her children got killed by the Soviet gunfire or by American bombing, or perhaps they died of starvation. Here devastation stalks everywhere, each city of this country is in ruins. When I left home, you kissed my hands and told me 'Stitch all their wounds with these hands.' But Dadima, here I am, all exhausted, stitching the wounds but the wounded, they still keep on coming.

At this critical juncture, we meet a young boy on stage representing the teenage Taliban boy in Zaheda Hina's story. In our workshops, we discussed the humanizing narratives that we have come across to imagine the possibilities of what the life of this young boy could have been. So in our play script – this teenage boy also has a story to tell – he waits with handful of almonds and nuts for his father to return from a faraway land. This character slowly emerges, theatrically, from being an individual to a voice, a voice of resilience and humanity.

In a monologue he says:

> Brown used to be my favourite colour. While my friends loved the warmth of red, green and yellow, for me brown meant raisins, almonds and pistachios. Abbu used to come home once every two years and I waited for him with all the almonds and raisins that I had collected. We used to sit on the rock up there and share stories. Now I have no one to wait for with raisins and almonds. Now when I see brown, I think of the colour of a bullet. Whenever I feel sad, a numbing cold spreads inside of me.

The play foregrounds a helpless miscarriage of dreams at the personal as well as at the political levels. The worlds of little Mini, of old Mini, of

Kumkum, and of this teenage Taliban boy meet through windows of conflicts and resolution. Each of these worlds is represented as a bordered space on the stage, which the characters cannot cross or make transit, yet there is a traffic of shared emotions and history between these worlds. We always find Little Mini, in the centre stage, always at an equal distance from the space of old Mini and that of young Kumkum. She is trapped in her own time. Old Mini and Kumkum are at two ends of stage spectrum, while little Mini is wrapped up in the world of Kabuliwala, in her fantasy. Kumkum, on the other hand, encounters the reality of contemporary Kabul that constantly collides with the stories from her grandmother which she has grown up with. Kumkum witnesses the devastation of Afghanistan through her own personalized prism, layered by her grandmother's memory of an unusual friendship with Rehmat Baba as a child, by her own connection with her grandmother through stories, habits, and morality that defied stereotypes, by the lingering shadow of the imprint of Rehmat's daughter's hands as well as her awareness of contemporary cultural politics and the mass destruction that she witnesses in war-ridden Afghanistan. In this context, her subjectivity as a woman, who has grown up in a quasi-liberal Bengali household in Calcutta, leaves her severely affected by the suffering of women in Talibanized Kabul. This drills a deeper contradiction because she is also able to perceive how young boys in Kabul are made victims of politics of hatred towards women. They grow up in a land where women are systematically disrespected, violated, killed, or made invisible. In a particular scene, we find Kumkum, old Mini, and the child Mini on stage trying to reach out to each other while a stark visual of this mass destruction and global displacement is projected on their bodies. They try to reach out towards each other but are stuck in their own limited space and historical time. The play draws upon a famous song by Lhasa de Sala, an American-born singer-songwriter raised in Mexico.[5] The performance echoes the same question that song 'My Name' asks.

The narrative of the Taliban boy adds a complex layer to the nuanced notion of home, loss of home, and that of faith in situations of geographical displacement, dispossession, or religious bigotry. While the other characters like Mini (old and young) and Kumkum are forcibly displaced (though Kumkum away from home based on her choice), this teenage boy comes across as the most vulnerable one. He lives in his own land, yet does not have a 'home'. Thus, in the performance, he is first made to appear outside of space where the rest of the play is enacted. Again, when he appears for the second time, his space is bracketed out (with lights) as an isolated zone. The visuality of this spatial design repeats itself throughout the play to emphasize that the Taliban boy is socially positioned at the margin. This space is represented as ambiguous, always at a distance from the 'centre', focusing on his marginal identity in the global capitalist world. His character resonates with that of Jagannath (from the play *Jagannath* directed by Arun Mukhopadhyay in 1977), of Bagharu in *Teesta Parer Brittanto* (a novel written by Debesh Roy in 1990), or Herbert in *Herbert* (a novel written by Nabarun Bhattacharyya in 1994) to underline how the capitalist system and structures of oppression exploit the insecurities, the vulnerabilities, and the deprivation of many teenagers like him to propagate a culture of terror. This character is thus made to intervene in the narrative of the letter at several junctures to raise a few pertinent questions related to identitarian thinking in the grid of global politics tied to situations of homelessness and mass displacement.

British Somali poet Warsan Shire's 'Home' has become the rallying call for the refugees and people fighting for them. Among the other cultural resources that shaped our theatrical adaption, this poem served as a crucial pivot. Her piece, 'Conversations about home (at a deportation centre)', drafted after a 2009 visit with refugees from Somalia, Sudan, and Congo also has echoes of her famous poem.[6] Shire writes

> They ask me how did you get here? Can't you see it on my body? The Libyan desert was red with immigrant bodies, the Gulf of Aden bloated, the city of Rome with no jacket. I hope the journey meant more than miles because all of my children are in water. I thought the sea was safer than the land.

In this play, the crisis that has rendered this teenage Afghan boy vulnerable speaks to the continuous process of mass displacement that started with the emergence of the modern nation, legitimized by straitjacketed categories of disposability and non-disposability. We journey across deeply embedded borders – of narrow nationalisms in South Asia, of cultural xenophobia, of religious fundamentalism, of terrorism through bridges of shared history and cultural traditions of the subcontinent. The play looks at how the narrow political divides that we erect in the name of security, in the name of territory, in the name of governance, translate into psychological borders that lead to one of the most harrowing human disasters of mass displacements and homelessness. Warsan Shire's lines are staged through vignettes of interactive multimedia presentation in our play. On the one hand, when this poem talks about violence, loss, homelessness, statelessness, and the unspeakability of the trauma, the character theatrically responds to the song Zombie (sung live on stage), which in itself is a protest song by the famous Irish band The Cranberries. Historically, the song was written as a visceral response to condemn an IRA (Irish Republican Army) bombing in 1993 that caused the death of two children in the Cheshire town in Warrington.[7] In the context of this play, it also speaks to the sense of helplessness and dislocation that Kumkum is witnessing in Kabul, which parallels the narrative of the young Taliban boy. The state of indiscriminate victimhood unleashed by fundamentalist regimes in different contexts across the globe is made to surface through an inter-textual nature of the play script. The poignant lyrics of this song carries as much the pain of devastation of the mothers who lost their children in the March 1993 bombing as much as it tells the stories of the losses of our time. This tragic act was carried out in the name of jingoistic nationalism in Ireland which points at how narrow nationalisms thrive on divisive politics and a culture of fear. Kumkum writes of how the innocent joys of childhood, like that of enjoying the rain, could be life threatening for children growing up in a war-ridden place like Kabul. She writes that she has been afraid of the rain ever since she has been in Kabul:

> Here children can't risk getting into rain showers, can't make paper boats and sail them in water streams, for the fast current during rains shifts the land mines. What was a safe place to play, becomes dangerous with dynamite everywhere. When it rains here in Kabul, children hide in the shelter of their homes, their school.
>
> Schools?

The use of projection and digital image becomes a very important fulcrum of storytelling in the play. In the performance space the documentary elements used in digital projection help create an *alienation* effect such that the audience is encouraged to move beyond the framework of Zahedi Hina's letter and think about issues of mass displacements and extermination wrecked in the name of narrow nationalism and border security across the globe. The play tries to underline the ways in which media reports, video footage, newspaper clippings, blogs, and other digital portals sensationalize as well as normalize violence and tragedy often inducing anger, hatred, or unaffectedness as immediate responses. The bombardment of information, images, and news feeds over media often familiarizes violence. So we had to make difficult creative choices around how and what to integrate from resources available on media as 'objects/images' that would interact with our live performance. While we acknowledge the democracy that is espoused by digital media, we were cautious so as to not represent images of violence in ways that can evoke hatred or inadvertently normalize them. So we decided to project the still images from the Peshawar bomb blast, the Syrian refugees, the iconic image of Aylan Kurdi on our performing bodies. This design, through which the images visibly merge with the characters on stage, hints towards a theatrical act of relating with the horrors; it articulates a mode of solidarity and encourages subjective responses to the violence. The images spill out of the borders of the performing bodies to give a different identity to the actors – who eventually, from being characters of the play script, become co-participants of the performance, sharing voices of solidarity and resistance with the audience. It tries to evoke an immersive experience for the audience and the actors by allowing the performance to become more fluid in terms of the experiences shared and the form in which they are shared. The actors are encouraged to viscerally respond to these images, communicate with them (physically and emotionally), and create another layer of realism that is informed by the actors' subjectivity.

The play ends at the poignant fictitious moment from Hina's story when Kumkum meets the young Taliban boy, the frequent marginal, the intruder in the play. Following the description of the story, he appears on stage with dry stains of blood on his shirt, fear and terror in his eyes, his whole body trembling.

> In a flash, the boy's face transformed, he took something out of the sack lying near his feet and extended it towards me. I looked at his hand, it was full of almonds, raisins and walnuts. I swear by God, that was Rehmat Baba in the light of January moon. But it was pure pain that he gifted your Kumkum.

That night, Kumkum witnessed death with her own eyes, touched it with her own hands. It was the death of a dream of a world nourished by compassion – a shared world of Kumkum, of young Mini and old Mini. All the characters had to encounter this tragedy together on stage – each becoming an extension of the other. So to translate the nuance of this story on stage, we create three separate zones on stage with spotlights on three different positions. In the separated zone, each of these three characters meets the boy in a designed choreographic movement. The boy shifts from one zone to the other and finally leaves the stage, journeying towards a path of despair. We find these three characters (Kumkum, old Mini, and young Mini) in own spaces of solitude, of despair, and of contemplation. Kumkum breaks the silence as she reads from the letter:

> The winter is harsh here, a cold is spreading inside me. What more is there to write? I have written all to you. Don't tell Mom or anybody else in the house anything. Just tell them that Kumkum is doing fine in Kabul. Kumkum theek theek hain!

Zahedi Hina's letter began to evoke a polyphony of voices and literary texts, all of which have consolidated into a deep philosophical insight and a moment of inspiration for the multiple renditions. Since 2014, as political and cultural contexts shifted, new waves of political violence, dispossession, and religious bigotry afflicted masses of people we have returned to this multi-toned narration with a deep-seated dilemma about our subjective position as witnesses to/victims of abrasive political apparatus and as conscientious artists attempting to talk about universal humanism in staging these violent realities. In 2020, after six years, I (Debaroti) hopelessly added a few more lines to the performance script with the hope of 'no more'!

Mercy!

A 19 –year old, a 19 year old girl, a 19 year old dalit girl, a 19 year old dalit girl from a distant village is gang raped. She dies. Her body is burnt in the break of dawn. Her family pleads to see her for the last time. They are shoved aside. She burns.

We rub our faces, brew our coffee, spew our anger through our windows

A 12 year old, a 12 year old boy, a 12 year old hungry boy, a 12 year old hungry boy laid off from a spice grinding factory in the city. Hangs from the back of a truck. He wants to never be poor. Holds on to a rim of a truck. Starved, in the pandemic. He wants to go home. He never wants to be poor.

We scratch our tails, clean our nails, spew our anger through our windows

Bills are passed.

A farmer burns.

Bills are passed.

A faith is burnt.

Bills are passed. Freedom burns

We stick our tongue into the pyre of the sovereign, secular, socialist, democratic republic

Manto's powerful dedication in his prolific work *Siyah Hashiye – A Black Margin* when he says 'to the man who, when recounting his many bloody deeds, said when I killed that old woman I suddenly felt as if I had committed a murder' (Hasan and Manto). Manto recounts one of the most horrific human tragedies with a moment of faith in humanity. We believe that it is this epiphanic moment, nourished by a deeper philosophy and cultural wisdom as is embedded in these literary texts, that has the potential to mobilize an alternative history.

Notes

1 Zaheda Hina, 'Kumkum Theek Theek Hai' ('Kumkum Is Doing Fine'), Accessed from https://aud.ac.in/uploads/1/admission/admissions2014/Kumkum%20is%20doing%20fine.pdf. All extracts from the piece reproduced in this chapter are from this open-source document.
2 Rajashri Dasgupta, journalist and feminist peace activist, Kolkata, India.
3 www.fairfield.edu/news/press-releases/2008/april/guantanamo-bay-attorney-to-speak-at-fairfield-university.html.
4 https://tagoreweb.in/Essays/nationalism-216/nationalism-in-india-2626.
5 www.youtube.com/watch?v=Vwyhb8Il5TI.
6 www.poetryinternational.org/pi/atpoem/22840/auto/0/28794/Warsan-Shire/CONVERSATIONS-ABOUT-HOME-AT-THE-DEPORTATION-CENTRE/en/tile.
7 www.bbc.com/news/entertainment-arts-42702781.

References

Hasan, Saadat, and Rakhshanda Jalil Manto. *Black Borders*. Rupa, 2003.

Poem Hunter. "Warsan Shire." Poem Hunter, 2010, www.poemhunter.com/warsan-shire.

"Rabindranath Tagore – Essays – Nationalism – Nationalism in India ()." Tagoreweb, 2012, tagoreweb.in/Essays/nationalism-216/nationalism-in-india-2626.

Reporter, Guardian Staff. "Guantánamo Prisoners' Poems Published." *The Guardian*, 20 September 2017, www.theguardian.com/books/2007/dec/13/news.

Further Reading

Eco, Umberto. "Semiotics of Theatrical Performance." *The Drama Review*, vol. 21, no. 1, 1977, pp. 107–117.

Sircar, Badal. "Badal Sircar: Scripting a Moment." *The Drama Review*, vol. 48, no. 3, 2004, pp. 59–78. https://aud.ac.in/uploads/1/admission/admissions2014/Kumkum%20is%20doing%20fine.pdf accessed on 20 November 2021.

12

TEATRO TRAVIESO AND THE PERFORMANCE OF FEMINICIDE IN *WOMEN OF CIUDAD JUÁREZ*

Jimmy A. Noriega

Ciudad Juárez lies on the U.S.–Mexico border just south of El Paso, Texas. Home to hundreds of *maquiladoras* (factories), the city represents the oppressive and exploitative side of neoliberal reform and free market trade. Often cited as one of the most dangerous cities in the world, Juárez attracts impoverished individuals in search of work. Within this system of capitalist primacy, vulnerable people – including women, children, and members of Mexico's indigenous populations – become objects of corporate exploitation and greed. Many find work in the *maquiladoras*, where they are paid low wages for long hours and are denied basic safety and health protections by the companies that employ them. Others turn to less desirable sources of income – including drug cartels, gangs, and sex work – in order to survive. In addition to economic uncertainty, these individuals migrate to the border city without a system of social or civil support: they often arrive alone and live in shantytowns with inadequate electricity, plumbing, and security (including streetlights). It is within this dangerous border zone that these individuals must learn to navigate numerous obstacles in an effort to survive.

In addition to poverty, gender is another category that precariously affects life in this border city. Ciudad Juárez has become synonymous with woman killing. Sergio González Rodríguez calls the city a 'femicide machine', which he describes as, 'an apparatus that didn't just create the conditions for the murders of dozens of women and little girls, but developed the institutions that guaranteed impunity for those crimes and even legalized them'.[1] Since 1993, hundreds of women and girls have been brutally raped, tortured, and murdered in the industrial city. Many of these female bodies have been dismembered, burned, and left unmarked in the desert in an attempt to evade police and ensure that the victims cannot be identified. A system of corruption and impunity permeates the city, making it difficult to hold anyone accountable for these crimes. Reports and statistics of the number of murdered women differ depending on the sources: government agencies downplay the numbers, while families and human rights organizations fight to

DOI: 10.4324/9780429356421-19

bring attention to their own figures. Journalist Diana Washington Valdez, who investigated and reported on the murders, calls them a 'harvest of death' (3). In an appendix to her groundbreaking book *The Killing Fields*, she lists 475 feminicide victims from 1993 to 2006. Others argue that over 1,000 women have been murdered over the past two decades. The number of missing and disappeared women is unknown.

This chapter discusses the work of Teatro Travieso/Troublemaker Theatre, a U.S.-based theatre company that I founded in 2012, and its touring production *Women of Ciudad Juárez* by Cristina Michaus.[2] Teatro Travieso operates on the premise that theatre can create positive change in the world. At its core, the group seeks to cause the best kind of trouble – the type that tells untold stories, creates witnesses, and fights for those who seek justice in our society. As of August 2021, the company has produced 11 plays, which have been seen by more than 30,000 people in ten countries.[3]

Women of Ciudad Juárez is the group's second production and debuted in January 2014. The play uses the theatre as a space to examine, reflect on, and call attention to the feminicides taking place alongside the U.S.–Mexico border. The production offers a space to draw attention to and memorialize the countless female victims whose murders have been reduced to contested numbers and a gross display of injustice. It presents multiple female perspectives of life in Juárez and speaks out against all forms of violence against the female body and psyche. Teatro Travieso's journey with this production has spanned more than eight years and three continents, with over 25,000 audience members witnessing the story we tell on the stage (including a performance in Pune, India in November 2019). The members of the company and Michaus worked closely on the social and political messages that we carry while on tour throughout the United States and world; we see our work with this production as a form of transnational artistic activism. Through *Women of Ciudad Juárez*, Teatro Travieso seeks to keep female and minoritarian memory alive, honour those lost, create allies against feminicide, promote activist spaces in the theatres and campuses we visit, and offer a voice to those silenced and erased through a dominant culture of misogyny, exploitation, and violence.

Background History

When Michaus first saw our production in April 2014, she said, 'When I stopped performing *Mujeres de Ciudad Juárez* years ago, I never imagined that any other actress, let alone young people from the U.S., would take on the grave responsibility of acting out these women's stories again'.[4] Michaus is a Mexican stage, film, and television star whose work has received international acclaim and a number of accolades, including the prestigious Ariel Award from the Mexican Academy of Motion Picture Arts and Sciences. She first wrote and performed *Mujeres de Ciudad Juárez* in 2001: her one-woman show ran for over six months in Mexico City and was followed by a decade-long tour throughout the nation. Her performances sought to educate the citizens of Mexico about the horrific crimes and injustices taking place in the border city. Michaus recalls,

> I performed the show in large and small theatres, community centers, auditoriums, schools, plazas, streets, and parks. Sometimes my audience was more than five hundred, eight hundred, one thousand people. Men and women, families, and children all came to watch me perform the stories of the women of Juárez.

While on tour she also circulated a petition that asked the United Nations to formally issue a declaration against the feminicides; she gathered 2,600 signatures which she personally delivered to the Committee on the Elimination of All Forms of Discrimination against Women at the UN in New York City. For Michaus, her body, voice, and celebrity became the weapons that she could employ to hold the Mexican state and its citizens accountable for the feminicides committed in Juárez. Her performance used the stage as a site of dissent to denounce the state of impunity that surrounded the murders and disappearances.

I first encountered Michaus's text in 2008. I was immediately struck by the brutal honesty with which she addresses the audience in her writing and her unusual approach to telling the stories of the many different types of women in Juárez. In her note to the script she says, 'If the play does not touch, make contact with, and disturb the public, then the production has failed'. Michaus wants the audience to feel the pain, shame, and grief of witnessing these women tell their stories on the stage. For her, this is not supposed to be typical theatre; the performance is meant to be an organism of change.

I directed *Mujeres de Ciudad Juárez* in 2011 – in the original Spanish – at Cornell University. That production was subsequently invited to an international theatre festival in Quito, Ecuador, where it was presented to a large audience gathered to celebrate the power of theatre. The reactions ranged from sadness and sympathy to shock, pain, and disbelief. Time and time again, the response I heard most often was, 'I did not know this was happening'.

In 2013, I returned to the play with an invigorated sense of urgency. While in New York City, I attended the screening of a new documentary called *Narco Cultura*. The audience was packed and afterwards everyone praised the film and the ways it spoke to the violence of Juárez. I, however, was angered and shocked to see that nowhere in the entire documentary was there mention of the feminicides. I thought to myself: Was 20 years enough to forget these crimes? Did people not realize that women were still being raped and murdered in the city? Were people tired of hearing about the feminicides and seeing the same pictures of deceased young women and pink crosses? Or was this a cultural issue? Did English-speaking audiences not know enough to care about the women of Juárez? The next day I started to translate Michaus's text. It was my hope that an English-language script would help to educate people about what is taking place south of the U.S. border and offer a form of theatrical activism that could instigate further discussion of these crimes.

By the fall, Teatro Travieso was looking to solidify its mission and structure and I wanted our next project to have a greater social and artistic impact. After discussions with Michaus, the plan was to stage the translated version of her play and to take it on a small tour: our goal was to promote it as a binational effort to refocus attention on the feminicides. Although there was the option to use professional actresses over the age of 30, I decided that I wanted to cast the play using young women between the ages of 19 and 24, whose bodies more closely resembled the majority of those raped and killed in Juárez. I also thought that the use of young women would make this play more relatable to college students, who would be our first audiences.

Staging the Show

I did not provide anyone a script before casting; rather, the actresses were asked to research the Juárez murders as preparation for the audition process. At auditions, I asked the women to recount what they had learned and to share what their research had done to them in three different ways: intellectually, emotionally, and physically. For callbacks, the actresses were brought together and asked again to discuss their research – this time as a group – and to teach each other about their discoveries. Callbacks then involved a series of exercises that utilized forms of Augusto Boal's image theatre and Michael Chekhov's psychological gesture. These techniques would appear again in the rehearsal process.

Rehearsals began in October 2013. On the first day, the actresses were finally able to see the script. Other than the occasional reading and discussion of the text, the first two weeks of rehearsals consisted entirely of group research, including discussions of documentary films such as Lourdes Portillo's *Señorita Extraviada* and Michaus's *Juárez: Desierto de Esperanza*. Additionally, the cast and production team read five full-length books and 14 articles on the Juárez murders, as well as watched countless videos and interviews on YouTube. Stage manager Ben Pfister recalls:

> The rehearsals were incredibly research-based and as a member of the company I was responsible for sharing in all of the research for this performance alongside the actresses. This decision was beneficial in many ways. For one, I was able to grow a strong and

> unbreakable bond with the cast members. This was important because we are separate in the performances, them onstage, me off, but connected through our research and commitment to the message of the play. Second, as a man, I became a strong advocate and scholar on the feminicides of Juárez, which made me feel like I was doing important work just like the women onstage.[5]

Janna Haywood, one of the actresses, recalls,

> Without any of the research, I would not be doing justice to the women who have died in Juárez. I can't just approach my monologues as characters in a play. They were and are real people and I have to do as much as I can to learn about them in order to feel like I am helping to create justice.[6]

In this regard, the first part of the rehearsal process was more than just focusing on the theatrical aspects of the show. It was about forging an emotional and intellectual community capable of engaging in the dialogues and debates surrounding the feminicides.

As we began to work on characterization and physicality, we made a conscious effort to follow the playwright's instructions, which read: 'The best method of acting should resemble the work of a medium: truly quieting the ego in an effort to represent the women'.[7] With this in mind, the women approached the play with a different mentality than they had previous roles. They were a collective on stage, working together to present a unified narrative that supported the political and social agenda of the play. To help aid in the process, I asked the four actresses to play different roles on different days. This allowed them to explore and create the parts with an additional level of freedom. They didn't have to get it 'right' or think too much about how audiences would view their work early in the rehearsals. Instead, they were playing all the roles and learning firsthand about all the women presented in the play. I feel this helped them to understand more fully the other women they were sharing the stage with and their own process of development in the character work. One month into the rehearsal process I began to assign the roles, though a couple of swaps would take place later. The women's openness to perform all the roles in the play, and not a specific part, allowed the show to develop more organically and contributed to the shared effort in creating the women's stories onstage.

My own work as a translator was also aided in this process of discovery. As the actresses learned their parts and worked on character development and choices, I was able to play with the language of the text. At times, the movement helped to clarify the different words that I would use in each moment; at others, transitional phrases became necessary as I provided context for a non-Mexican audience. Silence became an important tool for me as I transitioned into the role of director. I wanted to ground the show in stage images that would help to push the action of the play forward, while also enhancing the different levels of interpretation and symbolism offered to the audience. Some of the main directing choices I made in this show included: the use of a giant plastic sheet as the background behind which the shadows of the actresses first appear, as well as the moment when they cut through it and emerge as monster and victims; acts of transfer and touch between the women that operated as scene shifts and psychological connection; object work that became central to each monologue; and the mess created on the stage as the play progressed, which was meant to represent the remaining traces of the (disembodied) women.

The rehearsal room was always treated as a sacred space because we knew that this was based on real events and lives. Stephanie Castrejón notes,

> From very early on, it became apparent that we could not approach these women as 'characters,' but rather as people who had actually lived and died. As such, more importance was placed on discovering who they were outside of the contexts of their deaths and to making sure we respected them at all times in our work.[8]

We made a commitment to avoid negative energy and disagreements while in the room. The primary role for the director and stage manager was to create a safe space where the actresses could develop their roles. Though I followed a traditional directing model, which included fairly strict blocking and staging of pictures, as well as work with the technical elements, the women were always free to voice concerns or ask questions. One major change to the typical rehearsal structure included the opportunity to stop rehearsal entirely if the material or work became too emotional or psychologically draining. This occurred on several occasions: the four women would stop, separate, and then regroup to follow it with a discussion and plan on how to move forward and provide the best support for each other. The psychological and physical well-being of the women was a priority and they turned to each other for support and comfort whenever it was needed.

The Play

The text consists of an opening scene, ten monologues, and two ending scenes that represent different types of women – mothers, daughters, government officials, sex workers, factory workers – that either died or are living within the context of the feminicides. Apart from the beginning and ending of the show, each actress performs an individual character as the others watch them on the stage. The play opens with a prayer as one actress kneels before a cross:

'I want to ask you for your forgiveness.'
'Forgiveness? For what?'
'For all the failures. You see, in the end we woman are always alone.'

With these words, the ghosts of the murdered women rise from the four crosses to circle the stage. From this point forward, a different woman – uninterrupted – will get the chance to tell her story. As the play continues, the actresses move about the stage, transforming the space and their bodies into new images and characters. In one monologue, a forensics expert conducts an autopsy on a body that was found inside of a plastic bag in a deserted lot. After cataloguing all the cuts and puncture wounds covering the deceased body, she reveals that, 'She was an indigenous Mazahua, only 10 years old'. In another scene, a grieving mother tells the audience about her young daughter who was murdered. She recalls, 'My daughter was very kind. Studious, tidy, very cautious'. Through these monologues the audience gets to see and hear aspects of the murdered women of Juárez that are not often presented in official documents or the press. As the actresses perform their roles, the audience gets to witness a live woman before them – a striking and sobering juxtaposition to the fact that the women being spoken about are dead.

Two monologues in the play, performed by the same actress, belong to government officials. The first woman, Deputy Hortensia, speaks before the Congress of the Union in Mexico City. In her speech, she implores the government officials present – including deputies, representatives, senators, and the President of Mexico – to do something about the crimes:

> I would like to request, given the disposition that has grown around these cases and since Mexico is a democracy, for you to organize a committee, suitable and worthy, to take urgent action against this genocide. Or better yet… this FEMICIDE, a crime against humanity.

She then calls attention to report 44/98 from the National Human Rights Commission regarding the Juárez case. As she concludes her monologue, in a symbolic gesture indicative of the impunity that permeates the Juárez crisis, she tears and throws the official documents as she screams at those present. In her final plea for justice, she says,

> Sir, if in fact you are truly the President of all Mexicans, I ask you not to act with the same indifference of your predecessors. In the administration of justice, failure to act is a crime. We won't be accomplices to inaction!

Later in the play, the same actress portrays another government official: a special prosecutor for the Juárez case. The monologue begins in a similar tone as the previous one, with the prosecutor seeming to speak before an audience of government officials. She wields a gun, which she aims menacingly at her public, as she demands that something be done about the feminicides. Her aggressive, yet effective, speech is cut short as a phone rings and we see that the woman is actually in the privacy of her office. She takes the telephone call of one of the mothers of the deceased. Pressed for answers, all she can say is, 'You just don't know how it works… here, downtown, everything moves very slowly. Law enforcement and the government, in general, move so slowly… so slowly… so slowly'. At the end of the monologue the woman lifts the gun to her head, ready to pull the trigger. Her act of desperation highlights the fact that she is unable to enact change within the government or create accountability for the crimes. Her final image – gun at the temple – speaks to the sense of desperation that surrounds not only the murdered women of Juárez, but also those who have worked to seek justice on their behalf. Both government officials in the play are performed by the same actress as a way of demonstrating the difficulty and repeated barriers that they must face as they navigate the complexities of these crimes, investigations, and public discourse.

Two monologues, in particular, stand out as aggressive and harsh in their depiction of life in Juárez. They also portray sides of the Juárez cases that often remain invisible in the public sphere: the perspective of the killers and a call for justice for the murdered sex workers of the city. In the first, in what becomes the turning point of our production, an actress takes on the role of a 'man' as she presents a number of hypotheses for the identities of the murderers. She recites her lines in an almost poetic form, as she contorts her body in a grotesque and exaggerated manner:

> We have a thousand hypotheses:
> Of the friend that's a fiend.
> Of the snuff films that are… roughhh!
> Of the Egyptian: innocent, but definitely indecent.
> The captured travelers
> almost… almost charged.
> We have the serial killer
> as well as the copy cat.
> Didactic narcos and congressional politicos,
> who through revenge and orgies,
> perfected their marksmanship and shootings.
> Perverse gringos.
> Spring breakers.
> Human smugglers and coyotes.
> Assembly plant foremen.
> Pimps, stepfathers, and bosses.
> We have the jealous husband,

> the unruly yuppie,
> and the privileged and spoiled sons of money.
> All of them, very very manly.

Halfway through the monologue, the other actresses strap a large dildo onto her body. She has become 'a sexual Frankenstein and modern Igor'. At this moment, the actress's body represents a conglomeration of all the men responsible for murdering the women and girls of Juárez. She performs this monster as she kills the three other women on the stage, leaving their bodies motionless on the ground. Up until now, the bodies of the murdered women have only been spoken about or represented by the pink crosses in the space (or in a plastic bag). In this monologue, which is performed in an eerily dim, red light with a yellow glow in the background, the act of feminicide becomes even more real. As the actress tosses the women's bodies across the stage and describes the vulgar and gruesome details of their deaths, the audience becomes almost paralyzed. It is, indeed, a heavy scene. It ends, however, with the actress removing the phallus and turning to the audience as the bright lights come up on her. She is now testifying about the facts of the murder: 'Any questions, Mr. Attorney General? Cause of death? Unknown. Certainly, that slimy liquid deposited in the Victim's orifices ... has not yet been identified. We have more than a dozen cases like this one'.

Another scene, titled '*El Azufre*' ('Fire and Brimstone'), begins with a musical number as the four actresses put on makeup and sing to the audience, enticing them with their bodies. The monologue belongs to a woman known as the *abeja* (wasp), who tells the public, 'I just want to clarify that I shouldn't be here among the mountain of dead women that you've been hearing about. Not me. I was left out, but I crashed the party anyway'. As she moves about the stage, circling the pink crosses in her red high heels, she reveals her identity: she is a sex worker who was murdered by one of the men who stopped in Juárez as he prepared to cross illegally into the United States. She interacts with the other women as she recounts how she was murdered:

> I didn't even notice when Pinini arrived. He was really high and since he couldn't get it up, he punched me so hard I didn't even feel it when he ripped me open with his trusty dagger. I bled out while the bastard set fire to the hotel room.

This monologue stands in contrast to the other murdered women portrayed in the play – young girls, daughters, factory workers – who speak of their deaths from a position of assumed innocence or purity. This monologue is especially significant, since it signals to the audience that no matter who the women were or what they did for a living, they did not deserve to be murdered. The *abeja* is one of the most brutally honest characters in the play, as well as one of the wisest. She calls out the government and police, even the female officers, for their complicity and involvement in the murders. She reveals:

> Everyone knows police kill more women that anyone else; they grab them in flocks, lock them up, have their orgies, and later that's why a body is found wearing the clothes of another woman. It's them. Why do they play dumb? And worst of all, even the female police officers get into it: they're just as much to blame as the men. I swear it's true.

In the end, she maintains that she, like the other women and girls, is still good. Her final words to the audience confront them with the burden of learning the details of these deaths: 'there's no one more ignorant than the one who doesn't want to understand'.

The final three monologues of the play belong to a *maquiladora* worker, a mother speaking to her dead daughter, and a young girl speaking from her unknown grave in the desert of the Lote Bravo. Together they form the final tragedy of voices that unite the women of the play. The first, Milagros, speaks about her cautious approach to life as a 16-year-old factory worker. She was always vigilant and careful not to place herself into danger. Her monologue recounts the evening she met another worker, from Durango, who danced with her and treated her kindly. As she continues to recall the evening, it is revealed that he murdered her when she would not allow him to come home with her. She is dressed in her factory smock as the other three actresses pantomime working in the factories behind her. She says,

> The daughters of the factory foremen party hard and cut classes and cruise in cars with stereos blaring, their boyfriends putting their hands all over them. But they're decent – we're not – because we work and get off shift at 3 a.m. and the bus leaves us in the middle of the desert and we have to walk for an hour to get home. Could that be why? Because we live like this, that we no longer have the right to dream?

Milagros, denied the privilege of youth because she must work for a living, stands in for the thousands of factory workers whose dreams and ambitions get swallowed up by a system dominated by international trade and commerce.

In the next monologue, a mother speaks to a grave. However, as the audience soon discovers, it is not the grave of her daughter, Elizabeth, but instead the bones of an unknown feminicide victim that were given to her by city officials. She says,

> I told them that it couldn't be you because we had just lost you and these bones were already old ... The investigator shouted at us; that we could do whatever we wanted, that we could accept it or do DNA tests. But how? With what money? The tests are so expensive.

She continues, 'That's why we had a Christian burial for you. Even though it wasn't you. We prefer that the bones be buried'. She narrates the difficulty that she and her family have encountered as they struggled to find justice for their daughter's murder. At the end of the monologue, the other three actresses join her, unwinding a long chain of clothes that are tied together across the expanse of the stage. These jeans, shirts, and blouses represent the remains that are given to the families of the murdered women. The mother says,

> Look! We made this chain with all the clothes they gave us. They say we can surround the International Bridge with it. So that they would notice how many there are, how many are missing from their homes, how many homes are wrecked, and how so many mothers and fathers don't want to know anything anymore.

The clothes belong to different sizes and ages of women. In this moment, they become yet another reminder of the impossibility of representing death on the stage. The scene ends with the four actresses holding their line in visual protest.

The final monologue of the play belongs to Celia, a young indigenous girl who moved north to make money to send home to her family. She is one of the disappeared girls whose body has been buried in the desert of the Lote Bravo and her monologue is staged as a message to her mother. She says, 'How are my brothers and sisters? Did Paco return to grade school yet? Did I send enough money to buy them new shoes? I wake up thinking about it every day'. After a brief description of what it is like to work in the factories, Celia tells her mother, 'I miss you so much, mom. I also miss walking. I can't even do that anymore, now that my legs have dried up in the sun, and my belly too'. She continues to assure her mother that she was a good girl as she describes the details of her death:

> Don't worry yourself mother; I'm only dead. I didn't end up a prostitute, or a careless girl, and I'm not sick either. They just pulled me apart. They tore me apart like sugarcane. They stabbed me. They ripped me apart, completely, made me their property. They tore my breast off and I saw the hole in my chest. I saw my blood flowing out of my body... red. Then, I saw the beast: a being that used to be a man, I watched him tear my nipple off in one bite. None of that hurts me now: not the beatings, not even the piece of rubber hose

> he put inside of me. I left my body, mother; I broke away. Now I'm just here worrying about all of you, and that's the real torture: not being able to relieve you of your doubts so that you can pray for my spirit to find rest.... All of you who still can pray. Because I can't anymore, mother. I've been here seven years, looking up at the sky and I know there's no one up there gathering our prayers, because if there were...

As Celia speaks, she stands centre stage with a spotlight on her. Throughout her monologue the other actresses symbolically tie her up, rip her apart, and wrap her in a black plastic bag. Hers becomes the most visual and detailed description of death in the play. As we toured our production, this was the monologue that always prompted the most tears in the audience. It also prepared the public for the ending of the play.

After Celia's final words, the production reaches its definitive moment. I decided to incorporate some of the voices of the actual mothers of the murdered women of Juárez into the show at this point. It was my way of honouring those who lost loved ones and reminding the audience that this was, in fact, reality. The startling change in the soundscape – women's voices speaking in Spanish and naming their children – helped to introduce the climax of the show. As these voices are heard in the theatre, the four actresses walk behind a cross, each holding a bouquet of red roses. Once in position, four spotlights isolate them and the pink crosses. The actresses begin to recite, one-by-one at first, the names, ages, and causes of death of some of the murdered women of Juárez. Each woman takes a turn sharing the details of one of the deceased as she rips petals off the roses and sprinkles them before her cross. I chose this image because of the symbolism: roses represent a gift of love and an offering at a memorial; the falling red petals can be seen as drops of blood, tears, and sacrificial offerings of sorrow and respect.

In Michaus's original text, the stage directions indicate,

> While a voice reads the names, the forensic examiner pulls out from a large container mortuary masks symbolizing the victims. The container is marked with the symbol: 'Made in Mexico.' The masks are placed across the stage. The task is monstrous, but at times she seems amused.

As Michaus covered the stage with these ghostly masks, the voice would speak the names of 68 women and children, listing their ages, causes of death, and locations where their bodies were found. By the time I staged the play, the number of murdered women had increased significantly and I wanted to incorporate as many of their names as possible into the show. This became problematic in rehearsals because it was obvious that we would never have enough time to incorporate them all. However, I also felt that omitting names would add to the erasure that the victims have already faced through feminicide and impunity. In the end I decided to use audio recordings to achieve the goal: the actresses read and recorded the names of the hundreds of women we collected in our research. We played these over the voices of the actresses as they, too, spoke the names of some of the women in the performance. In the end, our production names 767 women in less than eight minutes time. At points in the climax, the names become nothing but noise; only a few of them are distinguishable throughout the ending of the scene. It becomes clear to the audience, however, that this mixture of sound represents more than just clatter: they are lives lost, women murdered because they were women. In each of our performances, the audience responses during this moment were very pronounced: sobbing, crying, and people holding hands in shock, disbelief, and sorrow. Witnessing this final scene becomes an act of spectator archaeology. Many audience members could only remain frozen.

As the voice recording ends, the women on stage place the bare rose stems at the base of their crosses. Two actresses bring out a Mexican flag and cover two boxes (marked with the 'Made in Mexico' emblem) downstage in a makeshift burial. The four women then walk to the edge of the stage and look directly at the audience. They are no longer characters, but are instead playing themselves: actresses for the cause. All four take turns delivering the final lines of the play:

> In the end, why does it all matter? Soon the play will be over, we'll leave the theatre, and you can all go enjoy a peaceful dinner. Juárez is only an 'experiment of our future' and that of our children. Oh, and please, avoid falling into the stupid trap of always asking: Who is guilty? The Serial Killer – the Collective Killer – is called Impunity… And when you walk up to the sink and look in the mirror, don't be surprised to see an accomplice staring back at you.

These final lines, delivered while looking straight at the audience, are meant to be both an indictment and a call to action. As we remind our audiences in the talkback, it is no coincidence that these crimes escalated when NAFTA went into effect in 1994, calling into question the U.S. and Canada's role in creating an atmosphere where these atrocities take place. Juárez is a city where cheap labour and profit are more important than social welfare and basic human rights. We want our audiences to know that there are consequences to globalization, free market trade, and a desire for cheap goods. It is up to them to decide how they process this information and what they choose to do next.

By the end of the performance, the stage is a mess – it is a chaotic pile of objects that bears witness to the stories of the women of Juárez and represents the memory/trace evidence of the characters that spoke and lived each monologue. The play ends with the pink crosses, isolated in four pools of light, alone on the stage. They are the representation of the missing and dead women of Juárez. When we first began to tour our show, the actresses chose not to have a curtain call, but it became evident as we continued to perform that audiences needed a collective response to what they had just witnessed on the stage. At times, before the actresses would reenter for their bows, the public could hear their muffled sounds as they cried and hugged backstage. The four women would then enter, exposed as young actresses, to receive applause. As Aviva Neff states, 'It feels wrong to get applause or a standing ovation for performing this play. We don't do it for accolades. We don't deserve it. We only want the audience to walk away with a desire to do something positive'.[9] It is in the talkback that the actresses truly open up about their goals and struggles with the show. It is also in the talkback that the early research we conducted becomes integral to our work as artist-activists.

The Tour

As we toured the production, I served as producer and director. All company members – including the actresses, stage manager, and myself – are responsible for every aspect of the show, from design to building, marketing, and touring. Each time we arrive at a new location, we immediately begin to explore the space as a group, talking about how to make the show work in each new locale. Each venue offers different stage dimensions, audience configuration, and technical resources. Some theatres offer us backstage personnel, while others require us to do everything on our own. Each theatre presents new challenges that require new methods (and thus teamwork and trust) for overcoming those obstacles within a limited timeframe. The actresses help to hang and focus lights, construct the set pieces, set up the stage, iron the costumes, purchase and assemble props, and mop and clean the theatre. As director, I redesign the lights, focus on sightlines and spatial relationships, reblock the show to fit the new space, run sound, and work on publicity. The stage manager, when they travel with us, reconfigures the technical elements, as well as runs the show during performances. Janna Haywood says:

> As a collective, we are all trusted and responsible to make each performance work by any means necessary and to know the basic needs and functions of each piece of the puzzle. Any of us can step in and figure something out if necessary.

Stage manager Helen Rooker recalls,

> Many of the duties for making this show happen became interchangeable between members of the cast and crew. If the director or stage manager could not do something that was needed, one of the actresses could immediately step in, and vice-versa.[10]

Summit Starr states,

> As a collective, we are all trusted and responsible to make each performance work by any means necessary and to know the basic needs and functions of each piece of the puzzle. We must work together without complaining and hesitating to make the show. The message is the most important part of the moment.[11]

Sometimes, when we arrive at a new location, we are divided by our hosts: some people stay to work in the theatre while others visit classes and meet with publicity people. Despite all these different circumstances, we know that we are representing the message of the play, Michaus, and the women of Juárez at all times.

As a result of the tour, the show and company are in a permanent process of reinvention. We take challenges as moments of rediscovery and renewal. These unknowns caused nervousness at first, but soon enough the collective gained a sense of confidence and even became excited with the challenges that each new venue offered. As a unit, the members of Teatro Travieso depend on one another for support and clarity in each segment of our tour. Janna Haywood recalls,

> The trust and bond that we developed as we researched and worked on this production allowed us to enter each new space with a confidence that we all had each others' backs. We never felt alone or solely responsible for the show. The unity we felt was because of the mission of the show and we all were on the same page.

Stephanie Castrejón says,

> The thing that made this show possible, and what gave us the strength and power to keep performing it, was that we were a group committed to the play and the message and to each other. Without the strong bond and group support that we developed, we would have never been able to take this show on the road and spread the message the way we did.

The rehearsal approach that prioritized safety and well-being, as well as created a space for reflection, thought, and unpacking continued on the tour. Summit Starr notes, 'We would often gather in our hotel room after a show and deconstruct the events of the night's run and release any remaining tension from the subject matter'. Every show revealed new details of the feminicides and the women were never careless or oblivious to their discoveries and feelings.

As of August 2021, the Teatro Travieso production of *Women of Ciudad Juárez* has been performed 44 times in over 20 locations in seven countries – Mexico, Canada, Colombia, Belgium, India, Greece, and the United States – which is not a small accomplishment. Throughout the years, the production has developed into three different configurations: one with all four actresses; one that employs three actresses; and one with three performers that include a male performer. The latter allowed us to explore the ways in which feminicide affects men in Juárez, including fathers who lost daughters and investigators trying to solve the murders. Even though the members of the company live in different cities and states, we have continued to regroup when necessary to ensure that the show can continue. Despite all our best efforts, however, we have not always been able to accept all invitations to present the show.

In total, we have been on tour together for over 90 days, splitting meals, getting stuck at airports and in traffic, exploring new cities, and meeting new people. We have also shared hotel rooms, gotten sick together for days at a time, and become exhausted by all of the labour created by the tour. Some locations have required us to drive in a van for more than 12 hours at a time or travel halfway around the world, while others have only allowed us up to three or four hours in the space before the show. Some of our audiences have been small (approximately 50 people) while others have been as large as 3,000. Our international performances introduced us to other theatre artists from around the world and helped to forge a better link between us as a company. The group leads talkbacks after almost all our shows and has confronted an array of new questions and emotions each time: in India, for example, the audience discussed the parallels between feminicide and gender violence with their own country; and in Mexico, we witnessed women providing testimony and denouncing their local governments for not doing more to investigate disappearances taking place in Cuernavaca. We have visited classrooms, met with student organizations, lectured at cultural centers, shared meals with fellow artists, and offered workshops on theatre and social justice. At this point in the tour, even all our parents have seen the show and we have met each other's families. We also invited Cristina Michaus twice to Ohio to lecture and watch our performances, and she has joined us as we performed in Belgium and Colombia. Most recently, we joined her in Mexico in July 2021 for a three-city tour of the production to celebrate the 20th anniversary of her first performing the show in Mexico. We presented the play at El Círculo Teatral in Mexico City for three performances, as well as in Cuernavaca and Tequisquiapan. *Women of Ciudad Juárez* has truly bonded us as a group in unimaginable and unforgettable ways.

Conclusions

Teatro Travieso is honoured that we have been able to carry the important message of *Women of Ciudad Juárez* to locations across the globe and we have been humbled by special invitations to perform at such prestigious institutions and venues. What is especially important for us is the fact that these women's stories and names have now been heard in spaces across the United States and world, for what is perhaps the first and only time. We have been deeply moved by our research into this play, and it is our sincerest hope that our production has helped to open up and inspire transnational dialogue about the feminicides of Juárez. As Kathleen Staudt and Zulma Méndez state in their book *Courage, Resistance, and Women in Ciudad Juárez*, 'The only successful campaign to protest and end the feminicides must take place through transnational solidarity campaigns, where groups of individuals group together in an outreach project that touches and influences people in multiple geographic zones, not just Juárez'.[12] We have worked with Cristina Michaus to restage her show in a binational collaboration aimed at spreading the message of Juárez to as many locations as possible. In this way, we hope to help make a difference as a collective and to create a positive and lasting social change.

Early in the tour, the company was surprised to receive an award from the Kennedy Center and the American College Theatre Festival, which recognized the group for 'Making Theatre an Important Catalyst for Sociopolitical Change'. Additionally, reviews of the play have been published by scholars in theatre journals and magazines, as well as in books. It is clear to us that our production has had an impact, though it is difficult for us to measure it.

As Michaus said of our show, 'It is empowering to see a new generation – made up of people from the United States – caring about and fighting for the lives of the women of Juárez'. As we continue to tour, we are happy to know that it has helped to bring attention back to the issues of women's and girl's rights, not just in Juárez, but also in the many places we have performed. It is our sincerest hope that this production moves our audiences to create change that will protect the rights and lives of all women in their communities. For the spectators, watching our play has the potential to become an act of resistance and intervention against national and international forms of gender violence and injustice. And though this play is specifically about one city, it is important to remember that these crimes are part of a widespread crisis that occurs in every culture and country across the globe.

For the members of Teatro Travieso, Michaus is an example of the way we can use our art and passion to make positive change in this world. She inspired us with her work and became a model for the type of global artist-activist that each member of our company aims to become. It is our hope that our production has helped to make some difference. Perhaps one day this play will become a relic of the past –a theatrical record of a horrific episode that was finally resolved through justice for the women of Juárez and their families. The feminicides must end now.

Appendix

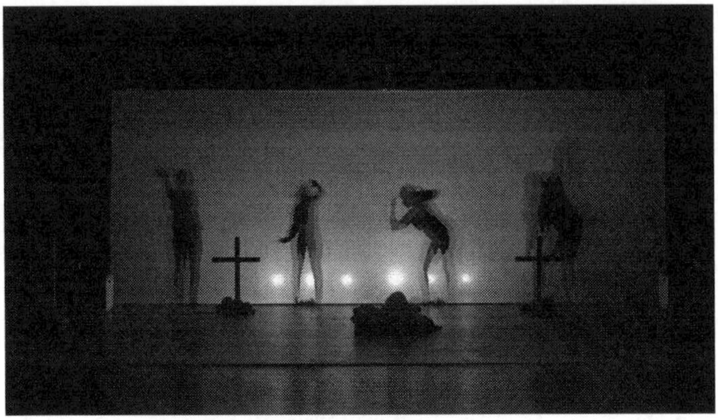

Figure 12.1 The opening image of the play: four figures move behind the plastic backdrop as news clips announce discoveries of women's bodies in the Juárez desert.

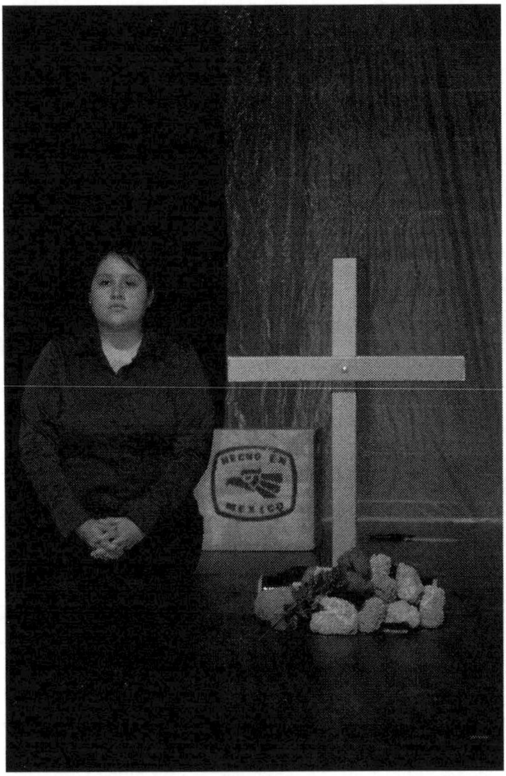

Figure 12.2 Stephanie Castrejón in *Women of Ciudad Juárez.*

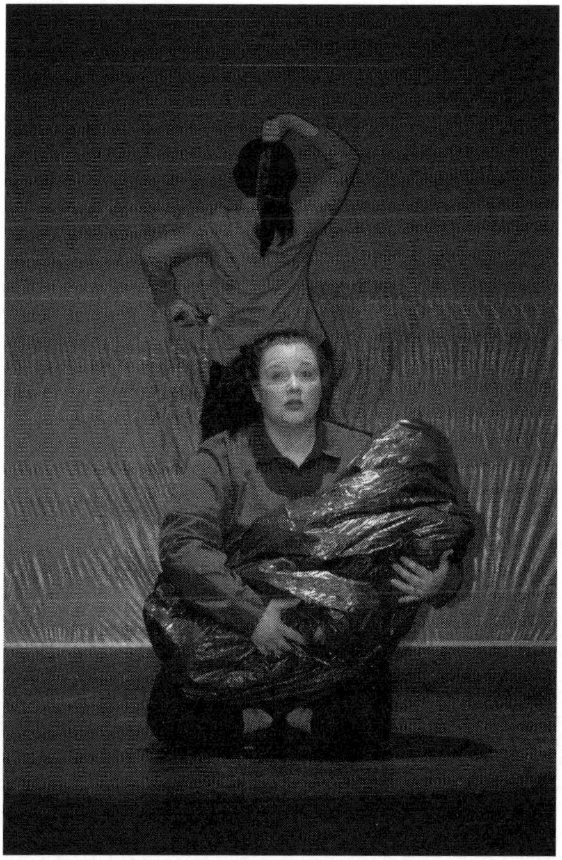

Figure 12.3 The forensic examiner (played by Janna Haywood) holds the body of a young girl found in a deserted lot.

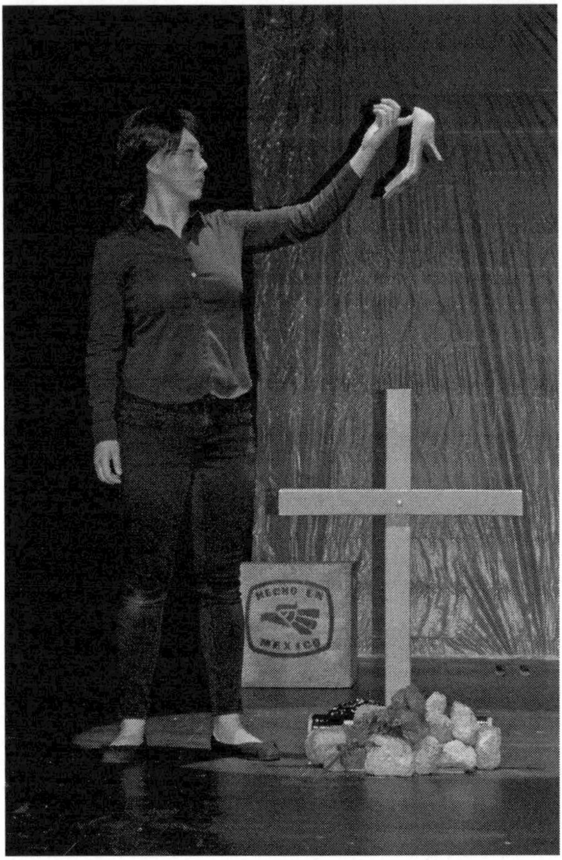

Figure 12.4 Summit J. Starr holds a shoe that was discovered as the only clue to a young woman's disappearance.

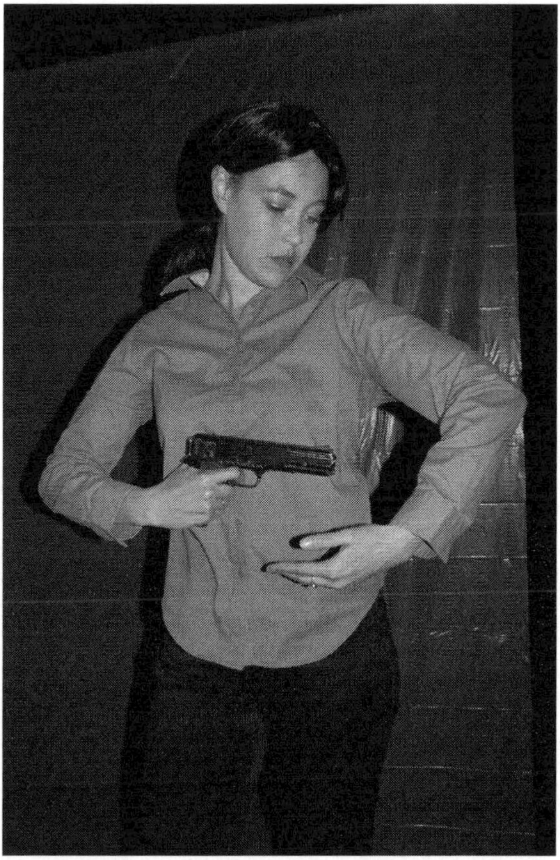

Figure 12.5 Deputy Hortensia (played by Aviva Neff) holds a gun as she describes the murder of a child.

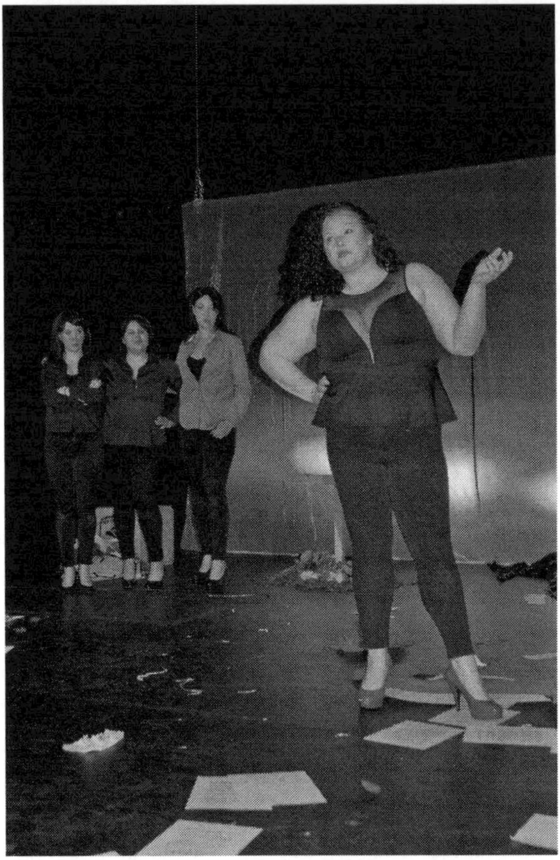

Figure 12.6 The *abeja* (played by Janna Haywood) confronts the audience with the details of her murder.

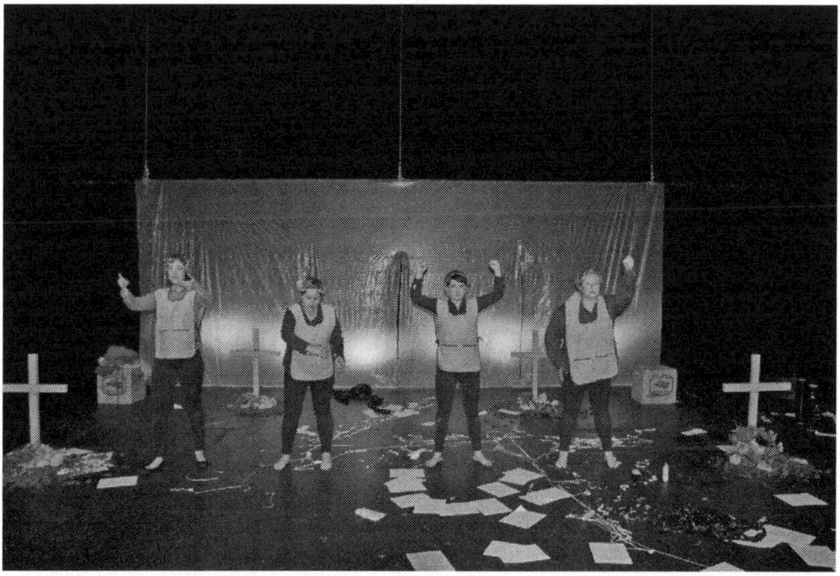

Figure 12.7 The actresses perform the role of factory workers in *Women of Ciudad Juárez.*

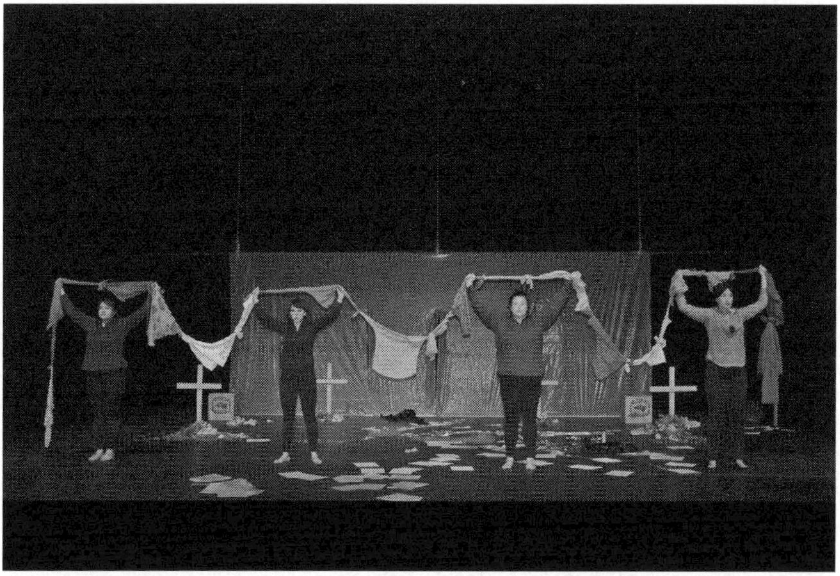

Figure 12.8 The mothers of the disappeared hold a line of clothes in protest of their murdered and disappeared daughters.

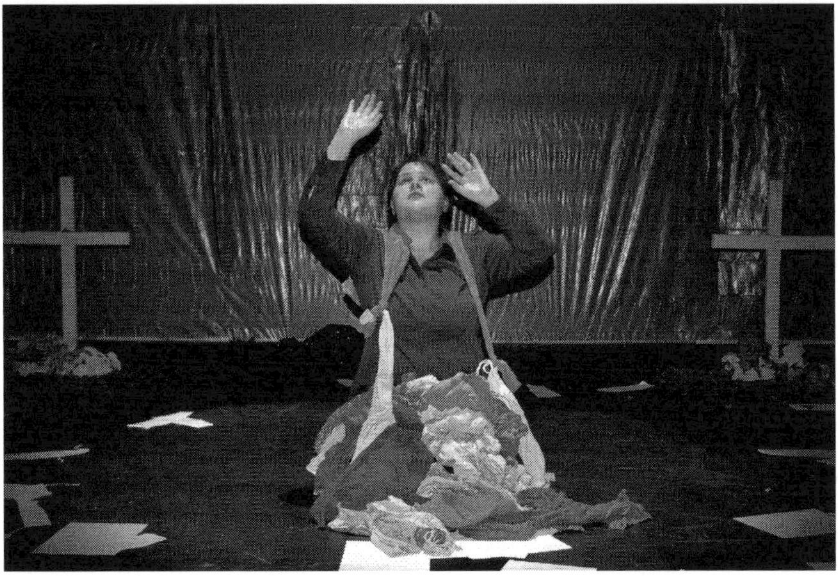

Figure 12.9 Celia (played by Stephanie Castrejón) speaks to her mother from her unmarked grave in the Juárez desert.

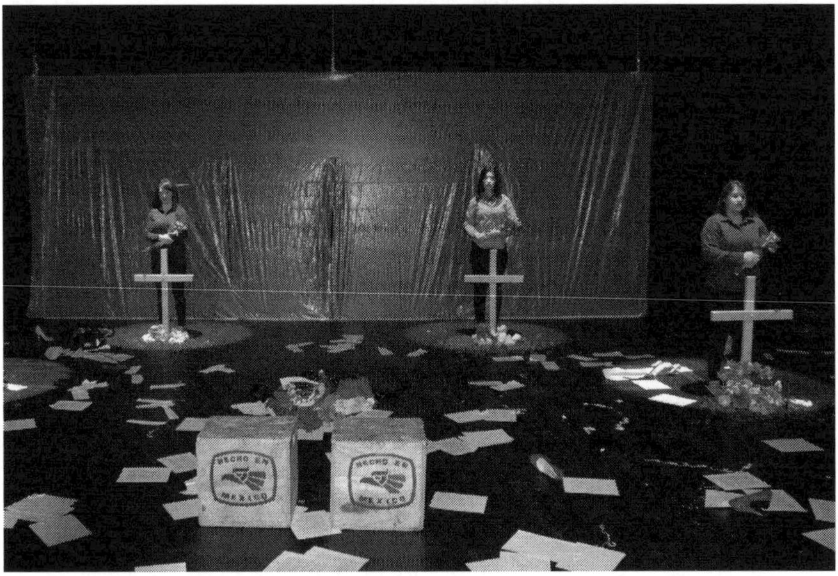

Figure 12.10 The performers speak the names of the murdered women and girls in the climax of *Women of Ciudad Juárez.*

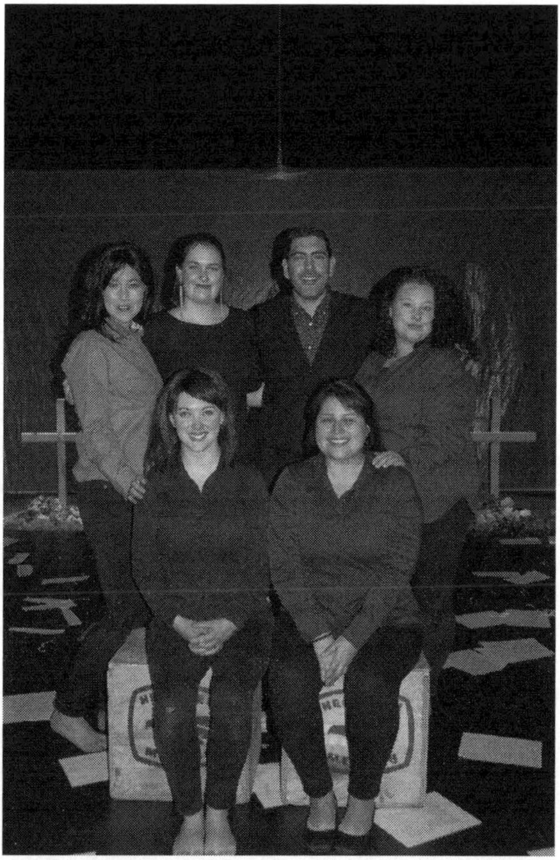

Figure 12.11 Teatro Travieso/Troublemaker Theatre members (from left to right). Back: Aviva Neff, Helen Rooker, Jimmy A. Noriega, and Janna Haywood. Front: Summit J. Starr and Stephanie Castrejón.

Notes

1 Sergio González Rodríguez, *The Feminicide Machine* (Los Angeles: Semiotext(e)), 2012): 7.
2 Cristina Michaus has over 30 years of experience in performing arts, media, film, theatre, radio, television, and activism. She is an actress, playwright, director, teacher, and producer. As a social activist and author of public policy, she has achieved recognition for over 12 years of work in the reporting of Feminicide and Gender Violence. For this, she was named a spokeswoman for UNIFEM (the United Nations Development Fund for Women). As a video artist, her work has been seen in Mexico, Europe, South America, and Asia. She holds a degree in Arts from the Universidad Veracruzana and has taught in various schools and colleges. She has also produced and hosted her own programs on cultural and commercial radio.
3 The group's first production, *Encuentro: Peru!!*, was based on a five-week research trip to Peru and is about being a stranger in a foreign land. It was presented at four different locations in Peru: The Metropolitan Museum of Lima; Casa Teatro Arena y Esteras; La Universidad Científica del Sur; and Teatro Ensamble. In the United States, it was performed in Wooster, OH. The cast of *Encuentro: Peru!!* was also invited to perform as an official U.S. delegation to the UNESCO/ITI World Festival of Theatre, which was held in Romania. *Women of Ciudad Juárez* is the group's second production. The company's third production, *Joto!: Confessions of a Mexican Outcast*, has been presented in: Wooster, OH; San Francisco, CA; and at the International Dublin Gay Theatre Festival in Ireland. Other productions include: *Trouble Down South*, *Walking My Dream*, *Swastika*, *Day of Our Dead*, *A Still Small Voice*, *Baby Food*, *Blood Earth Water*, and *CAGED*.
4 Cristina Michaus, interview with author, 2 November 2018. All subsequent quotes from Michaus are from this interview.
5 Ben Pfister, interview with author, 4 November 2018.
6 Janna Haywood, interview with author, 12 November, 2018. All subsequent quotes from Haywood are from this interview.
7 All quotes from the play *Women of Ciudad Juárez*, including the playwright's notes, are from the unpublished version of the Spanish text that I translated.
8 Stephanie Castrejón, interview with author, 20 November 2018. All subsequent quotes from Castrejón are from this interview.
9 Aviva Neff, interview with author, 21 November 2018.
10 Helen Rooker, interview with author, 14 November 2018.
11 Summit J. Starr, interview with author, 20 November 2018. All subsequent quotes from Starr are from this interview.
12 Kathleen A. Staudt and Zulma Y. Méndez, *Courage, Resistance, and Women in Ciudad Juárez: Challenges to Militarization*. (Austin: University of Texas Press, 2015): 34.

INDEX

Made in the USA
Las Vegas, NV
05 November 2024

1a96194e-1a5f-4c74-8a4c-75203f20f07eR01